Gift of S[illegible]
Rev. Hugh J. Nolan
Immaculata, Pa
Ni4-2201

Gift to Library

THE CHURCH AND
THE NATIONS

THE CHURCH AND THE NATIONS

A study of minority Catholicism in England, India, Norway, America, Lebanon, Australia, Wales, Japan, the Netherlands, Vietnam, Brazil, Egypt, Southern Africa and among the Lele of the Congo.

Edited by

ADRIAN HASTINGS

SHEED AND WARD

LONDON AND NEW YORK

FIRST PUBLISHED 1959 BY
SHEED AND WARD LTD.
33 MAIDEN LANE
LONDON W.C.2.
and
SHEED AND WARD INC.
64 UNIVERSITY PLACE
NEW YORK 3

NIHIL OBSTAT
RADULPHUS RUSSELL, O.S.B., S.T.D.
CENSOR DEPUTATUS

IMPRIMATUR
DATUM KITOVU
15TH SEPTEMBER, 1959

+ J. KIWANUKA
EPISCOPUS MASAKENSIS

This book is printed in 11 on 12 point
Linotype Granjon

PRINTED IN GREAT BRITAIN BY HEADLEY BROTHERS LTD
109 KINGSWAY LONDON WC2 AND ASHFORD KENT

CONTENTS

ACKNOWLEDGEMENT

Ubi Ecclesia, by G. K. Chesterton, is here reproduced by permission of Miss Dorothy Collins and Messrs. Faber & Faber.

PREFATORY NOTE

The Editor thanks all the contributors to this book for their kind and patient collaboration, and also the very many other people who have helped in one way or another to make the book possible.

Each contributor has been free to express his own viewpoint and must not be taken as the official, or even the unofficial, spokesman for the Catholics of his nation.

UBI ECCLESIA

G. K. Chesterton

"You must seek for a Castle East of the sun and West of the Moon."

—*Fairy Tale.*

"For as the lightning cometh out of the east, and shineth even unto the west, so shall also the coming of the Son of Man be."

—St. Matthew, xxiv. 27.

Our Castle is East of the Sun,
And our Castle is West of the Moon,
So wisely hidden from all the wise
In a twist of the air, in a fold of the skies,
They go East, they go West, of the land where it lies
And a Fool finds it soon.

Our Castle is East of the Sun
And abides not the law of the sunlight,
The last long shot of Apollo
Falls spent ere it strike the tower
Far East of the steep, of the strong,
Going up of the golden horses,
Strange suns have governed our going,
Strange dials the day and the hour.
With hearts not fed of Demeter,
With thoughts unappeased of Athene,
We have groped through the earth's dead daylight
To a night that is more, not less;
We have seen his star in the East
That is dark as a cloud from the westward,
To a Roman a reek out of Asia,
To the Greeks, foolishness.

For the Sun is not lord but a servant
Of the secret sun we have seen:
The sun of the crypt and the cavern,
The crown of a secret Queen:
Where things are not what they seem
But what they mean.

But our Castle is West of the Moon,
Nor the Moon hath lordship upon it,
The Horns and the horsemen crying
On their great ungraven God:
And West of the moons of Magic
And the sleep of the moon-faced idols
And the great moon-coloured crystal
Where the Mages mutter and nod:
The black and the purple poppies
That grow in Gautama's garden
Have waved not ever upon us
The smell of their sweet despair:
And the yellow masks of the Ancients
Looking west from their tinkling temples
See Hope on our hill Mountjoy,
And the dawn and the dancers there.

For the Moon is not lord but a servant
Of the smile more bright than the Sun:
And all they desire and despair of
And weary of winning is won
In our Castle of Joyous Garde
Desired and done.

So abides it dim in the midmost
The Bridge called Both-and-Neither,
To the East a wind from the westward,
To the West a light from the East:
But the map is not made of man
That can plot out its place under heaven,
That is counted and lost and left over
The largest thing and the least.

For our Castle is East of the Sun,
And our Castle is West of the Moon,
And the dark labyrinthine charts of the wise
Point East and point West of the land where it lies,
And a Fool walks blind on the highway
And finds it soon.

INTRODUCTION

ADRIAN HASTINGS

This book is an attempt to describe, on a small scale, some of the richness and diversity to be found within the Catholic Church, and to give some idea, too, of the difficulties that Catholics have to face in countries other than our own. It has been written by men and women from a variety of nations and their aim has been to show how far Catholicism is integrated with the national character and national life of their countries and what this integration feels like to them personally. "What," I asked them, "are the proper characteristics and particular 'atmosphere' of the Church, her structure, life and tradition, in your country? Give us a picture of this Church life with its good qualities, but also with its defects and limitations; a very frank statement, at once personal and general. Personal, in that it gives your own approach to the reconciliation of ecclesiastical and national loyalties; general, in that it places this approach within the setting of the actual Church as it exists within your own country."

What does the Church look like in this country or that? Is she really part of its life, of the woof of its social pattern? Can she speak to it with its own voice, Jew with the Jews, Gentile with the Gentiles? And has she at the same time remained authentically Catholic, the high tower, the immovable rock, the witness of a truth and a love which does not alter with frontiers and races?

There was the question of selection. From the beginning the idea was to choose countries where Catholics form a minority. The problem I wanted to examine was how a Catholic can be an integral member of a society predominantly non-Catholic—that is to say, Protestant, Moslem, Buddhist, Hindu, or just religiously indifferent. But only gradually did it become obvious to me that the distinction between non-Catholic countries and those traditionally considered to be Catholic is no longer a fundamental one. What country can be considered Catholic today, except perhaps Ireland? A "Catholic" government does not make a country or society Catholic, nor does a past tradition. The convinced practising Catholic is in a minority in Spain, France or Italy as he is in England or India. Anyway, countries are no longer—if they ever were—separated, "perfect" societies. We all live today in a single human society, and in it Catholics form a small minority. "We are perpetually thrust into minorities", wrote Belloc in *The Path to Rome*. He found it hard, and so it is. But there is no alternative. To imagine a different world is to imagine an unreal one; we can only see ourselves as a majority when we forget what we are and take as our boundary something less than the *orbis terrarum*.

In so far as this book is concerned with how Catholics should behave when placed in a society far more numerous than themselves, it is treating of something which concerns every Catholic without exception.

Nevertheless, it is a sad fact that we often have confined our boundaries, limited Christendom to Europe, and in this way acquired the majority mentality. For this I should make Constantine initially responsible. Have we ever quite got over the colossal consequences of his brilliant improvisation? Until the Constantinian revolution in Church and State there had been no necessary or particular bond between Christianity and the Roman Empire. Some Christians lived within the Empire, others did not. Some people who lived within the Empire were Christians, a greater number were not. The Empire was not the Faith, and the Faith was not the Empire. Constantine's political aggrandizement of Christianity involved an unnoticed, but fearfully important, belittling of Catholicity, and the price paid for political privilege within a particular state was not only a loss of apostolic freedom within that state, but also outside. If the Church's canons were to be decreed by Constantius, her members within the Persian Empire had either to suffer as Roman agents or to sever their communion with the Church. Boundaries of frontier consequently tended to become boundaries of communion, and the Nestorianism which was uprooted by Imperial Rome came to flourish in Persia. If Greek Constantinople was Catholic, then the nationalism of Coptic Egypt would go Monophysite. Once the principle of *cuius regio, eius religio* had appeared, it could not be limited to a single state; and that meant schism.

It meant more than schism; it meant also, for each separate group, a narrowing of the horizon. Very quickly Catholics ceased thinking of themselves as a minority spread throughout the world, and saw themselves instead as a majority within a limited area, politically homogeneous, to be known as Christendom. They acquired a majority position and a majority mentality, but at the price of abandoning the non-Roman world. We have been living ever since within that pseudo-Christendom, based upon the work of a political careerist of genius. We have pretended to be a majority by forgetting the Church's essentially universal mission, for to make of the Church a society containing the people of one continent and one culture is to relinquish her true and far more arduous place in the world at large. That is the high tragedy of the Middle Ages. With all their grandeur they are less than Catholic, and that almost in spite of themselves. The medieval Church is seen at its greatest when it stands struggling to transcend its Latin and European limitations. The Council of Lyons and reunion with the Greeks, the *Contra Gentiles*, the translation of Arabic philosophers, Raymond Lull and the early Dominican and Franciscan missionaries—all these were signs of a moment of tremendous and truly Catholic greatness. John of Monte Corvino, Archbishop of Peking, is an indication of what might have been. Tragically, the mood did not prevail. Catholics fell back on that smaller and less Catholic view—"Europe is the Faith". Christendom was not to be a leaven, a dynamic minority open to the world; it was to remain a closed majority society, extended by the method of crusade and *padroado*.

The method has been a failure, both abroad and at home. Christendom has not grown much, while its very heart has decayed. Even in Europe we can no longer claim to form a majority. This spells liberation, but our present tragedy is that instead of rejoicing in a new-found freedom—our Christian community being no longer coterminous with a political regime—we continue to look back regretfully on the fleshpots of Egypt, the privileged bondage of the past, and to long for some sort of restoration of medieval society, of "the ages of faith". But the truth is that unless the whole world is Catholic we cannot live within a genuinely Catholic society because the only natural social body, adequate for the reception of the soul of Catholicism, is that of the whole human race. We should be sincerely glad that modern secularism, following upon the Reformation, has delivered us from a stultifying situation. Our immediate achievement may be less than the medieval, but the possibilities of achievement are far greater. However, we shall lose them if we do not cease trying to build up walls around every little ghetto of a Christian community which we form, and do not consent with our whole hearts to live as a responsible minority within and among the vast majority of our non-Catholic and non-Christian brethren.

Constantine's legacy lay in the subordination of the Church to statecraft and the tacit reduction of Christendom to the Roman Empire, but also in the use of coercion in place of persuasion. This always provides a tempting short cut for a majority, but it is inimical to the whole character of Catholic Christianity. Ours is a religion of freedom, of love and not of force, of personal conviction, not social convention. The tragedy of the whole Constantinian conception of Christendom, which has always been to some extent among us, has been that of an enforced outward conformity. Coercion is not only utterly different from conversion and persuasion, but it actually kills the spiritual vitality of those who are fully convinced. It is not in a spirit of fear that we have been called, but one of love. I will return to this later on; here I merely point it out as one of the consequences of Constantinianism.

It is a point of simple and indisputable fact that at the present day we have been everywhere forced to abandon the Constantinian and medieval outlook: to assert the rights of the Church precisely against the State, to rely upon the force of persuasion alone, to reassert the truly world character of Catholicism, to live as a minority. What then must be our attitude to the ideologies, cultures, social and religious patterns which we find around us? Should we take our stand upon the Areopagus or retreat into the catacombs? Should we, can we, embrace the cultures about us, or must we cut ourselves off from them? Should we form Catholic political parties, trade unions, universities and the like, or enter those which already exist? These are questions which, in one form or another, face every thinking Catholic in the world today. But they are not necessarily patient of one single consistent answer. Sometimes there is an issue of principle; more often there are problems of expediency, of the art of the possible.

It is strange how apparently contrasting are the Church's chief antagonists in the world today. There is the extreme universalism of Communism, and the extreme particularism of Nationalism. "One class, one society, one state-created uniformity," proclaims the Communist, and of course the Communist's seeming contradictory, the capitalist, aims at just the same, though in different terms. They work together to give the whole world a dull sameness: the same hotels, the same alphabet, the same tinned meat, the same everything. The effects of the new technology are inevitably everywhere uniform, and this makes it a very fitting instrument in the hands both of international capitalism and international Communism.

Perhaps it is the very force of this unifying influence, European in origin though not essentially European in its character, which has provoked the violence of nationalism's reaction. For the nationalist the ultimate criterion of value is that of the "home-made", or at least conformity with the particular national spirit. Asia for the Asians, the superiority of the white man, the purity of the Aryan race, emperor-worship—however it may be formulated, nationalism always presents an inherent, ultimate, particularist and non-rational principle of value, according to which everything else can be either accepted or rejected. But the truth is not national, and in every age the Church has had to fight against the deification of the national or state principle.

There is, then, a false universalism and a false particularism, and the Church rejects them both; both are caricatures of her own nature and mission, and in contrast with them we need to appreciate clearly her dual nature. For the Church is both universal and national, both the Church Catholic and the Church of Philippi, of Rome, of England, of India. *Ecclesia Anglicana* was not in origin a schismatic but a papal formula. The reason for the multitude of creatures, St. Thomas tells us, is, precisely, their limitation. They must be many in order to mirror the many sides of the divine perfection. We see this clearly in the saints. All are saints, and not necessarily greater one than another, yet they are so different. Each possesses something of a fulness which transcends them all. The saints constitute the high points of human and national variety; but every human personality differs from every other one, and each contains some perfectible value not to be found elsewhere. Now, Catholicism does not destroy all this rich variety, but forms and perfects it. The Church possesses a universality which has sometimes been taken, even by Catholics, to mean human and cultural uniformity; but her universality, because it is supernatural, can give unity to the natural order without destroying natural diversity. It fosters personal and national differences, it does not wipe them away. When this has not been the case, it is because Catholics have been less than true to the very Catholicity of their religion, and have identified it with some national or cultural force in which they also believed: the Latin tongue, the Portuguese Empire, French culture, or Irish blood. Such identification, too terribly frequent, is the exact opposite of a true realization of the particularist side of our religion. We must not identify the Church's universal character with the pattern it takes on in this country or that, with the dear local tradition we have known ourselves. Here is the place for tolerance and freedom and for a firm refusal to use the Church to further national or sectional interests of any kind. To impose cultural uniformity in the name of Catholicism, to persecute non-Catholics because a nation is Catholic and its "common good" requires the maintenance of religious orthodoxy, or to extend the power of a state ruled over by Catholics as a means of extending the power of the Church, are all equally wrong. In each case the whole ordering of natural and supernatural has been misunderstood. On the one hand, religious values are far above those of the State, and the natural common good of a country cannot justify interference with the religious life of the human person. Physical compulsion in the religious field is bad for religion and it cannot be held right on the grounds of State necessity. On the other hand, the Church is a spiritual kingdom conquering with the sword of the spirit; the weapons of statecraft are essentially inadequate for such a work. Not only can they do no good, they are bound to do harm, because they identify the Church with a particular political power or cultural group, whose opponents are led inevitably to oppose also the Church herself.

Endless are the evils which have come upon the Church, and do still come, on account of these fatal attempts to bind her to some particular culture, country or political party. The Church blesses everything which is not evil, but she must not be identified with any of the things she thus encourages. No nation has a unique or primary claim to the title of Catholic; the Church is mistress of all the nations, at home in them all, but the servant of none.

Inevitably the problems of a post-Christian society in Europe, or in lands populated with European stock, are very different from those to be met with in countries where Christianity has never been a decisive influence on national life. Both types of situation are well represented in this book. In Europe we are faced with a public opinion moving almost consistently further away from Christian standards. Where will it cease? Here very definite acts of disassociation may be called for: a clear (even seemingly exaggerated) refusal to identify the Christian community with a political and economic bloc whose constitution is entirely unaffected by any real religious motive.

Outside Europe the position is even more complex, and generally less well understood. The problem is often a little glibly described as one of adaptation. Most certainly, it is necessary to steer clear of that fatal identification of the Faith with Europe or with one or another European Power, which until recently was almost taken for granted. And such a mentality still exists: openly with some, beneath the surface with very many. Nevertheless, an attitude of sympathy towards non-Christian cultures will not by itself get us very far, and the attempts to "adapt" the Church's apostolate to them are often superficial and even contemptible in the eyes of non-Christians. One can produce churches, pictures, statues, for instance, in a "Chinese" style which will satisfy missionary demands and be very pleasing to European Catholics of large and apostolic mind but which will seem of abominably poor taste in the eyes of cultured Chinese. In the same way a non-European can often not appreciate the real difference between medieval Gothic and nineteenth-century pseudo-Gothic. The foreigner, in both cases, is satisfied with a rough approximation which is really worse than nothing at all. An obviously European church placed in the middle of a Chinese village is at least attractive because it is different and may give kudos to the humble people worshipping there. Moreover, its obvious otherness symbolizes the otherness of the Christian religion. A church which is a caricature of a Chinese temple will signify nothing at all except the inferiority of the religion which has produced it.

I am afraid that most so-called missionary art, whether it hails from Asia or Africa, falls down completely when considered in this light. Church art must first and foremost be good art, and to be that it must somehow be the expression of a whole living culture and way of life. At present it is not. Adaptation in art must grow out of a deeper adaptation, a thing which hitherto has hardly been attempted. If there is to be complete uniformity at the level of intellectual life and spirituality, identical text-books and courses in Catholic seminaries and colleges throughout the world, then there can be little hope of any genuine variety of Catholic culture at any other level. Whether this can or should be altered is another thing, but it is dangerous to deceive ourselves with a type of missionary adaptation which is really rather hollow.

Perhaps the most fundamental weakness in most missionary work of the last centuries has not been failure to understand the culture of non-European countries, but failure to master the culture of Europe itself. This may sound strange, but deep calls to deep, and the best possible preparation for a missionary who is about to face some non-

Christian Asiatic culture is to have entered profoundly into his own. Only as a man of learning in his own land can he enter the world of learning of his adopted country. Ricci's success in China was founded upon his own Western learning, and the failure of the cultural apostolate in the modern missionary achievement is due, at least in part, to lack of a full European education in mission workers.

The world in which Ricci worked no longer exists, and the problem of missionary adaptation is even harder now than it was then. The reason is that for the Church to adapt herself now to the traditional culture of any non-European country is for her to adapt herself to something which in great part is being rapidly superseded. The "new men", the controlling class in any of the countries which have recently become independent, have been trained in European schools and universities and are introducing, as fast as they can, a Western type of economy, of political system and of ideology. Vast masses of country people may be little influenced by this as yet, but it is the influence of the new men which will almost certainly prevail, and if the Church is to adapt herself to the world as it really is (which in some way she must always do), it is not to the old traditional China or Buganda that she must do it, but to a world which is undergoing extremely rapid transformation under pressure of Western civilization and technology. Consequently, it is easier to believe in adaptation than to know to what the Church should adapt herself.

The central problem, however, lies still deeper. A culture is a whole, and every culture is the coherent expression of a certain ideology, a way of looking at life, a religion. It is no good saying that culture and religion are different things. That is true; nevertheless they are not easily separable. One religion may indeed be able to support a variety of cultures, but no culture can exist without some sort of a religious root; to change the religion of a country is inevitably to cut away the root of its traditional culture. Many elements of it may survive, but as a whole it cannot. The point is not whether it is a good or a bad culture, but simply that it is an organic whole based upon a world view which has now been abandoned and which it cannot survive. I cannot help feeling that there has been a good deal of rather loose talk in recent years among some sections of Catholics about the possibility of Catholicism's simply perfecting the non-Christian cultures of the world. All that is good must survive, and so on.

It is, of course, not my intention to suggest that there is, after all, no other possibility than one of Europeanization. On the contrary: Europe herself has anyway effectively ceased to be Christian, and Catholics in every country have the same problem and the same preoccupation: the formation of something new. We cannot go back to the *ancien régime*, to the *padroado*, or the Middle Ages. We may learn from the past, but we must build afresh. *Emitte Spiritum tuum et creabuntur, et renovabis faciem terrae.* Our work in the Spirit is to renew the world, and the renewal must be as earnest and all-embracing as that effected by the first generations of Christians. It is to them that we should turn for example and inspiration, especially when once we genuinely accept our position as a minority within the national and world communities.

How much they made use of! Jewish, Greek, Persian, Armenian, Roman cultures—all these were at the disposal of Christians as once before the treasure of the Egyptians had been plundered by the departing Israelites. And yet no culture of the ancient world survived under Christian treatment. "Unless the grain of wheat going into the earth die . . ."; society and the values embodied in society had all to be radically transformed; words had to be given, slowly and painfully, a new meaning; art had to come of itself to express a Christian intuition. When did all this happen, and indeed did it ever completely happen at all? There was still a slave-market at Rome in the days of Gregory the Great. Was there ever a really Christian culture in the West?

One thing which stands out with painful clarity from almost all the contributions to this book is the practical intellectual failure of Catholicism. Catholics in general are not doctrinally educated, and Catholicism still makes far too little appeal to the non-Catholic intellectual. This again goes back a very long way. I suppose that the fourth and fifth centuries were the time when Catholicism made its greatest appeal to the civilized non-committed mind. So many of the great Doctors of the Church were brought up in the schools and universities of the ancient world without any decisive Christian loyalty. The Church won them because she was intellectually far more vigorous than her alternatives. Can that be said also of the present day? Since that time we have converted barbarians in and out of Europe, but we have made very little impact on any already civilized people, and at the present day we have also lost the greater part of the civilized world within what has traditionally been

Christendom. It is perfectly true that worldly wisdom, and the conceit it produces, may be a bar of its own to the light of faith, it is true also that it can be a cause of rejoicing that not many of us "are wise, in the world's fashion, not many powerful, not many well born". We are the little ones, not only in numbers but in mind. Nevertheless, we should not hide our light, and we have an obligation "to convince the world". What a tremendous body of philosophy, theology, mysticism and art has grown up out of the Christian revelation, and yet how unsatisfying it seems to most of our contemporaries whether in East or West!

Here again I cannot help feeling that a chief cause of this situation may be found in a tendency to rely rather on compulsion than on persuasion. It is perfectly right to protect the little ones of the flock from insidious propaganda which they are naturally ill-equipped to resist; all the same, the attitude which was responsible for, and also derives from, centuries of the Inquisition, the attitude which may still be manifest in the condemnation rather than the refutation of our opponents, cannot but weaken the intellectual vitality of the Catholic community. What should be considered more is the deep ultimate harm which the silencing of opposition has been able to do to those within the fold. Such silencing has long ceased to be effective; the enemy's voice is everywhere about us; but we unhappily remain enfeebled by the hangover of ancient methods. Intellectually we have nothing to fear so long as we truly face up to our position—a chosen community bearing revealed truth and the seal of the Spirit, but at the same time members of a numerically far greater society which we may hope to convince but not to control. We shall remain weak in so far as we attempt to escape into little intellectual havens of our own to contemplate with snug complacency the so-called Christian synthesis of the ages of faith. Obviously I do not intend to criticize the existence of any separate Catholic college or university, but an attitude of mind which is incapable either of renewing from within the tradition of Christian wisdom, or of satisfying civilized man without (it is incapable of satisfying him because it never really reaches him)—it must be admitted that segregated institutions are at least prone to develop this type of attitude.

The Catholic is both on the left wing and on the right. The Church is the home not of authority alone, or of freedom alone, but of authority and freedom; and she cares for the one as much as for the other. Now, in the harmony of these two contrasted things lies all the problem of human society and human relations. If man is a social and political being, a subordinate part of the State, how can his ultimate personal freedom be sacrosanct? If he is eternal and above society, how can the State have any real value or coercive authority? Our own age is witness of the most terrible of all attempts to make the State the one, supreme value. Only the Church can save human freedom, as she alone can rectify authority. This is her supreme service to human society. I do not say that her representatives have always been faithful to this mission, or that conversion to Catholicism offers a ready-made solution to these problems, but I do say that it is only in God's Church that freedom and authority are reconcilable, and that she alone offers a field in which the rightful and necessary contest between the two can be maintained without the destruction of either. In Newman's words, "It is the vast Catholic body itself, and it only, which affords an arena for both combatants (authority and private judgement) in that awful, never-dying duel. It is necessary for the very life of religion, viewed in its large operations and its history, that the warfare should be incessantly carried on." (*Apologia pro Vita Sua*.) It is necessary also for the very life of society.

So we do not come to our own people emptyhanded. We have what they have; we love what they love. But we have and we love infinitely more, and our gift to them is simple—the good news that the Son of God has become Man to remake the world; and we must proclaim that news though they kill us for it. We know that our message is life for them, but we know too that it means death before it means life; that it is a new spirit intolerant of old spirits, and the old spirits have formed the old societies. They or we must die. They must persecute or be converted. But if they are converted, we can offer them not only heaven but earth as well, the principles whereby their perennial, familiar problems may be resolved, the art, the culture, the *humanitas* which is truly new and yet strangely faithful to their past. We do not, cannot, kill that past. It died, and it lives. They gave it all up, sacrificed it, held it as dung in comparison with faith in Christ, and behold it is all returned a hundredfold.

Yet the new Jerusalem will never be built here below; it would be wrong to look forward to an integrated Christian world society. The kingdom of justice and peace to which we belong has a King whose kingdom is not of this world, and there will always be a "this world" with its society and its culture; never, while the sequence of time continues, can it be fully Christianized. Consequently, the tension between secular society and Christian fellowship must always continue. It is integral to our viatory condition. This world is not evil, and the State can rightly claim our loyalty. Caesar does not die, and we have always to give him his due within a society which he reflects but which we, because of our faith, cannot fully enter into. We are his good subjects, but God's first, and after we have made every effort to fulfil our citizen's duties, to be responsible members of society, to lead our neighbours to the truth, to integrate ourselves with a world to be redeemed, we may at the end have still to take up our cross and witness as castaways to the truth which the world will not heed. The law of the apostolate, it is often said, is the law of the Incarnation—of integration with one's fellow men. But at the heart of the Incarnation is Golgotha, and we must not fear its message of separation. "Jesus, when he would sanctify the people through his blood, suffered beyond the city gate. Let us, too, go out to him away from the camp, bearing the ignominy he bore; we have an everlasting city, but not here; our goal is the city that is one day to be." (Heb. xiii. 12-14.)

As Catholics we enter into human society, its cultural and political life, with an immense zest, because as Catholics we do everything with such zest. We know who made the world, we know who is the Author of all good things, and we can love them as no pagan can, and we do. "It is only Christian men guard even heathen things." Our love for the world's beauty is even greater for our knowledge that it is not our final goal, and that knowledge saves us from despair when things go badly, because the final battle is not lost and cannot be lost. It may save us also from faltering in our methods, from substituting force for persuasion, outward order for free acceptance. The end of the race sets all to rights; that won, nothing is lost, and when the battle is over, when "The line breaks and the guns go under", we shall say with Thomas More, "Son Roper, I thank Our Lord the field is won." The end of our work is no earthly society or culture, no world empire ruled by an even greater Innocent III, it is instead "that holy city, the new Jerusalem, sent down by God from heaven, all clothed in readiness, like a bride adorned for her husband". (Apoc. xxi. 2.)

ENGLAND

John Lynch

Catholicism in England still bears the marks of three centuries' exclusion from the national life. A minority which lived a semi-underground existence, was educated abroad or not educated at all, and was debarred from professional and indeed from all public life, could not be expected to preserve or hand on vigorous cultural traditions. A fresh start had to be made. Of the two new sources from which English Catholicism has been fed since the mid-nineteenth century—English converts and Irish immigrants—it has been the former which has added some intellectual quality to the Church and the latter which has brought the numbers. The modern English State has assured them the conditions in which they can survive and expand. But the climate of opinion in which English Catholicism has developed in the last hundred years has not been exactly one of religious toleration. After Catholic Emancipation in 1829 Catholics experienced only a short period of genuine toleration They passed rapidly from a period of intolerance into one of indifference. By the time Catholics had found their feet they discovered that they were living in a country which was no longer Christian. Rough statistics showing the numerical decline of practising Protestants—though not of Catholics—are available for those who want them, but the evidence is all around us. The majority of Englishmen have lost any meaningful conception of man as a creature with a supernatural destiny. The prevailing attitude to life is a combination of secular humanism and utilitarianism. The working philosophy of the ruled and the ruling classes in England is that of the greatest happiness of the greatest number, a principle which may have been rejected by the moral philosophers but which is still lived by the mass of the people. And human happiness is measured largely in terms of material progress. It is material progress that is preached at the English people by the politicians, the Press and all the agents of mass

---

JOHN LYNCH was born in 1927 and studied at Edinburgh and London Universities. He is now a lecturer in modern history at the University of Liverpool, and has published *Spanish Colonial Administration, 1782-1810*.

communication. These points of view and their preachers are already ensconced: they occupy the platform in all the organs of publicity. Christians are out of it, and whenever they raise their voices they are coming in from the outside in a defensive position. It is the antics of Christians and not their principles that get into the headlines. The Pope's words, usually misrepresented in the secular Press and unintelligibly translated in the Catholic newspapers, are received with indifference or amazement. To most English people Catholics look a bit eccentric: they see only the externals of our beliefs and practices and not the doctrines on which they are based. There are two levels of Catholic thought and practice; the second does not explain itself but can only be explained by reference to something more profound. Therefore it is difficult for most Englishmen to understand why Catholics go on pilgrimages to Lourdes or abstain from meat on Fridays or have distinctive marriage laws, because they do not know the principles on which these practices are based. These barriers are understandable and they will not easily be broken down. There is always an obstacle. It used to be intolerance: now it is ignorance.

On the other hand, conditions in England have had their advantages, and have given to modern English Catholicism some of its most characteristic features. Catholicism in England grew up in the modern world, the world of the secular State, parliamentary democracy, an industrial society, and religious indifference or toleration, whatever we prefer to call it. Unencumbered by any attachment to the old regime of "the altar and the throne" or to economic and social privilege, an attachment which was so damaging to the Church on the Continent and from which she only disengaged herself with difficulty, English Catholicism was in a position to adapt itself to modern conditions and to set an example to other Catholic communities. Many of them needed such an example. Rebuffed by the secular State and endeavouring to escape from the choking embraces of Catholic governments, the Church in Europe began to work more purely as a Church, to follow its essentially spiritual mission, to operate less and less through political institutions and by reliance on temporal power, and instead to concentrate its resources, teaching and sacramental, on the formation of good Catholics so that they in turn could Christianize the new society. But this adaptation was not achieved without crises. In countries like France, for example, where the Church was embarrassed by a Catholic nostalgia for the old regime of absolute monarchy and compromised by its association with an obsolete and unjust social system, the adaptation was agonizing, and by the time the new conditions had been accepted it was found that the industrial proletariat had been lost. English Catholics, on the other hand, took to the modern world naturally, for they knew no other. Far from being tied to an archaic regime, they were themselves the underdogs of nineteenth-century industrialized society, miles below the people at the top and well outside the Establishment. There was no conflict between their religious and their social situation. In religion they were a suspect minority who had just won toleration; socially and economically they were at the bottom of the ladder. But they enjoyed the rights which the State assured all its citizens; they could join their trade unions and vote for their political representatives, and if they did not do so it was only apathy that stopped them. In the slums of Merseyside, Tyneside and other industrial centres of the North and Midlands, large Catholic populations fully shared the conditions and the aspirations of their class, and as they crowded into their ugly churches there was no conflict of allegiance or thought of betrayal.

English Catholics, including those of Irish origin, have learnt that there are conditions in England favourable to Christianity, elements in the national life more potentially Christian than existed in the so-called ages of faith or exist now in the few Catholic countries that survive in the modern world. The relative fairness and moderation of English political life, the justice of the social system, the toleration assured to almost every institution and point of view, these things are valued—indeed taken for granted—by English Catholics and envied by many of their co-religionists elsewhere, above all, perhaps, by those in countries which have a continuous Catholic tradition but where the political system is so often totalitarian or unscrupulous, where wealth is badly distributed and where social justice hardly exists. English Catholics have accepted the Welfare State, enjoy its fruits, and make efforts to improve it: some of them are managing to fill gaps which have been left by the State—in education, in the relief of special kinds of suffering, and in other more anonymous activities.

English Catholicism shares the qualities and the limitations of these national characteristics and reflects the conditions in which it has developed. Compared with the monolithic character of many Catholic countries, English Catholicism displays a healthy variety. To start with, as the circumstances English Catholics have to face in a mixed society are so various, there is a variety of opinion on matters outside of dogma, and even a variety of opinion on the application of Catholic principles. Anyone who has attended a Catholic conference or gathering of any sort or has read the correspondence columns of the Catholic Press will have discovered not so much *a* Catholic point of view as *many* Catholic points of view, and will know that it is very difficult to get agreement. It is not simply that on some of the biggest moral problems of the day—nuclear weapons, for example—there is no obvious and single Catholic line: even on more ecclesiastical matters—like the liturgy—there is much squabbling and disagreement with "official" points of view. These different points of view are represented in different groupings of Catholics. There are the political groupings, with Catholics subscribing to almost every political opinion from extreme Toryism to some point short of Communism. Then there are groupings within the Church around the different religious orders. The English Dominicans, for example, represent a certain opinion and way of approaching problems which attract a particular type of following among lay Catholics, while another kind of Catholic will associate himself with the Jesuits. This variety of English Catholic opinion is not always appreciated by outside observers, who usually imagine Catholics falling into line at the frequent crack of the whip. In England the notion survives that Catholics are more servile than other people, and it is rarely understood that they are subject to no force and that they freely accept their religion and its consequences.

There are also the social groupings of Catholics. In many ways English Catholics display many of the self-conscious attitudes of a minority group and are given to some cliquish tendencies. They will usually find satisfaction in the fact that some well-known figure in the public eye, or some new acquaintance, is a Catholic, and some of them have a bad habit of referring to a newly discovered Catholic as "one of us". This is natural enough. Yet in spite of being a minority English Catholics are not a socially compact group huddling together for mutual protection. They are absorbed by the English class structure, take their social attitudes and behaviour from the class into which they are born or which they enter, and can be just as snobbish and class-conscious as their neighbours. There is a world of difference between the congregations of the churches in the West End of London and the parishes of the East End. In a socially mixed parish there is virtually no communication between middle-class Catholics and those of the working class. After Mass all go their different ways. Few of the former would dream of going to a parish dance or collecting for the parish football pools, while those Catholics who are addicts of the "tele" and frequent the pubs and the football matches hardly ever come into contact with their more cultivated brethren. In a minority that is concerned to preserve its identity this class division is rather surprising. One of the factors behind the problem of "mixed" marriages in England is that Catholics rarely mix their marriages socially.

A second obvious feature of English Catholicism is its resilience. Catholics have shown that they are quite capable of roughing it and surviving in the mixed and largely secular society in which they live. They do not live a ghetto-like existence within Catholic institutions. After an education in Catholic schools—which the Church regards as the minimum requirement—they have to survive in political parties, trade unions and universities that are completely secular and in which a man's religious position will be severely tested.

In politics English Catholics are spared many of the embarrassments which Continental Catholics have to endure. In spite of their ideals Christian Democratic parties can be a scandal as well as a blessing to the Church. In England, however, there is no possibility of a Christian Democratic party, and the Church itself does not usually take political attitudes. The hierarchy regards the faithful as responsible adults and allows them a wide political freedom. At the same time, the moderation and absence of ideology in English politics, where it is the results rather than the doctrine that count, has been a benefit to Catholics. It has enabled them to be Conservatives without subscribing to the reactionary philosophy of Continental conservatism, and Socialists without adhering to Marxism and the class struggle. On the whole left-wing Catholics have taken this situation more for granted than conservative Catholics; the latter often attack the former on the grounds that they are betraying their religious principles and ignoring the incompatibility of Catholicism and Socialism. Yet in fact most English Catholics vote Socialist—at any rate they used to. In working-class areas like the Durham mining constituencies they would automatically vote for a non-Catholic Labour candidate rather than a Catholic Conservative one, even though the latter might promise to do something for the Catholic schools—just as a Conservative Catholic would not normally approve of a trade union leader simply because he was a Catholic. Catholics have been socially integrated in the working-class movement; it has been comparatively easy for them to rise to positions of prominence in the trade unions and in politics, if they have so wished, and in both these fields they have been taken for granted. Catholic Conservatives, on the other hand, are up against a number of obstacles. For one thing, they are a very small minority. Then, Catholics are either cut off from or underrepresented in that milieu—Protestant public school, landed wealth, big business—from which the Conservative Party traditionally recruits its politicians and its ministers. It looks as though Catholics have more chance of rising to positions of responsibility and even to ministerial rank in the Labour Party than they have in the Conservative. Nevertheless they rarely do so, and one of the more obvious features of Catholics in English political life is that they are not producing any leaders or outstanding politicians. Most Catholic Members of Parliament are faithful and quiet followers of the party line. They would not be in Westminster otherwise.

Another secular institution in which Catholics have to find their feet and survive is the University. This problem is a more recent one. As Catholicism in England has been a predominantly working-class religion, it needed the Welfare State and free education to give Catholics the opportunities they so badly needed for higher education. Now they are entering the universities in increasing numbers. There is in England no Catholic university to which they could go if they wished. In a mixed society such an institution would not be desirable, for it would have the effect of cutting off Catholics from the only world in which they have to live, and possibly of lowering their academic standards. Most English Catholic graduates in fact are better equipped to face the modern world, both at a religious and a secular level, than are their counterparts from some Catholic universities one can think of. And in England the "leakage" problem concerns not educated but uneducated Catholics, and is a problem of the Catholic homes and schools and not of the non-Catholic universities. Nevertheless, there is another side to the question. Notoriously one of the great defects of educated English Catholics is that while they progress in secular training and culture, their religious formation and information remain at the Catechism level. This is even true at the universities. Everywhere it means that either Catholics get out of their depth when it comes to explaining or defending their religion, or they will too readily refer genuine inquirers to the Catholic priest or chaplain, to whom such inquirers may never go. It is true that in many cases the new Catholic undergraduates, like many Redbrick students, are not particularly well read; often they are the first ones in their family to read books, and usually the first ones to receive higher education. But this is a start, and with the assistance of some devoted chaplains an attempt is being made to integrate the secular and the religious formation of university Catholics which should bear good fruit for the Church in the future. Moreover, Catholics in academic life are learning how to adapt themselves to a mixed society and to play the game according to the rules. It is my own experience that most of them, both staff and students, earnestly try to steer a *via media* between indifference and apologetics, and almost all of them lean over backwards to be fair, an example which those who do not agree with us might well follow. At the lowest level this adaptation might just mean that Catholics have acquired the technique of using the right jargon effectively, "it can be argued . . . ", "it might be true . . . ", and other formulae of academic caution. But at a deeper level it is a sign that Catholics are trying to integrate themselves, to see and understand all points of view, and, while sticking to their own, to avoid the fanatical and intolerant approach.

Few Catholic graduates enter the academic profession, and those who do have not yet begun to play their full part in the life of the Church in this country. This is not meant as a criticism, though perhaps they can be accused of excessive caution and discretion. Yet they need time. It is not so long since there were no Catholic university teachers in England. Moreover, most Catholics in academic life adopt the view that their proper job and their most useful service to the Church is to be as good as possible in their own fields, to acquire respect and confidence as scholars first, and then as Catholics. Consequently, they publish monographs or articles in their own professional journals, and are unknown to the general public, Catholic and non-Catholic alike. Yet many of them have something to say of general as well as of specialist interest and significance, and if they had the opportunity of saying it they might be worth listening to. The Catholic Press, however, hardly calls on their services; they are rarely asked to represent Catholic opinion on radio or television, and their existence is barely recognized by the Church authorities. The Church in England is not making full use of its available intellectual resources and it is not so rich in this respect that it can afford to waste what it does possess.

This raises the more general problem of the intellectual quality of

English Catholicism. We have our Press, our periodicals and our publishers, but the net result fails to make an impact at a national level. Catholic publishers obviously suffer from a dearth of first-rate material to publish, and some of their best books are translations from foreign works. As for the Press, it is difficult to believe that the Catholic public gets what it wants or deserves. Most English Catholic papers are full of embarrassing headlines, disclosures of "Red" plots, and trivial gossip about prominent and invariably "devout" Catholics. English Catholics are not well informed about the world problems and policies of the Church or about the more creative aspects of Catholicism. One paper makes a commendable effort to provide something more intelligent but is evidently handicapped by lack of intellectual and material resources. The *Tablet*, though often taken to represent informed Catholic opinion, in fact mainly represents the Conservative side of that opinion. It would be a hard thing to say that the Catholic Press is a true reflection of English Catholicism; it might be fairer to argue that existing financial and human resources are not being properly used.

It is true that culturally, English Catholicism is still crippled by three centuries' lack of tradition and continuity. The Irish immigration has added very little intellectually to the Church in England. On the other hand, it would be wrong to underestimate the effect of the few conversions on the life of the Church in this country. Most of our writers and intellectuals who have made any impact on the English public have been converts—G. K. Chesterton, Ronald Knox, Christopher Dawson, Evelyn Waugh and Graham Greene, for example—and from time to time there are still some distinguished conversions. But what does it all add up to? Intellectually, English Catholicism does not stand comparison with French Catholicism. On the other hand, there has been no decline. It is common to find Catholics bemoaning the fact that a vacuum has been left since the good old days of Chesterton and Belloc. But many of us who do not remember them personally wonder whether the old days were in fact so good, whether Distributism, Merrie England, a tendency to disavow modern industrial society and the making of false historical generalizations did any permanent service to the Church in England. It might as well be admitted that Chesterton, in spite of his flashes of insight, now has no influence on the younger generation, in or outside the Church, and little relevance to the problems of the society in which they live. And if we are searching for historical truth we shall certainly not go to Belloc, or to any of the other purveyors of partisan history who masquerade as Catholic historians.

Catholic writers in the English public eye are lightweights, and are admired more for their entertaining novels than for any sustained body of thought. Catholics and non-Catholics alike persist in calling some of them "Catholic novelists", but in fact their works tell us very little about Catholicism and virtually nothing about English Catholicism. No one asks that a novelist should "represent" any body of opinion other than his own, and consequently no one will be surprised that the two Catholic writers whom it is now usual to mention, Graham Greene and Evelyn Waugh, are neither of them representative of English Catholic opinion; and in fact neither of them fits easily into the English Catholic scene. This is not because they are converts, since most English converts are indistinguishable from born Catholics. It is simply that they are laws unto themselves. Both writers, of course, are superb craftsmen, but we are not concerned here with literary criticism. It would be interesting to know to what extent, if any, they reflect the characteristics of the minority to which they belong. Many of us feel that Evelyn Waugh hardly speaks the same language as the majority of his fellow Catholics in England; in fact, he is likely to have more understanding readers outside the Church than in it. How can his romantic conservatism—devotion to landed property, alleged aristocratic virtues and a recusant type of rural Catholicism—have any meaning for the proletarian Catholics of places like Liverpool, or give the English public any indication of what English Catholics are really thinking and doing? This is eccentricity, and English Catholicism has had more than its share of eccentrics. To the younger generation of Catholics Graham Greene has more relevance, for he deals with common human predicaments and his novels have some theological content. He is a novelist who is also a Catholic: he does not use the novel as a vehicle for any point of view, and in fact he has a habit of washing dirty linen in public. At the same time a sort of repository-shop type of Catholicism flits in and out of his novels—there are rosaries and miracles—and it is doubtful whether this makes much sense to the general English public.

Most Catholics find difficulty in communicating with the secular world on religious subjects in intelligible language. In the seminaries and religious communities there are some good theologians, biblical scholars and philosophers, but with one or two exceptions they are not particularly productive and do not make the impact which they ought to. Whether this is because they do not enjoy the right conditions for study and writing it is difficult for the layman to say. Still, the most prominent religious orders are making a good job of educating their own members. On the other hand, the position of the secular clergy is rather different. In England there is no problem of anti-clericalism. Indeed, there is no justification for being anti-clerical: apart from the fact that English Catholics have all the group loyalty of a minority, the Church itself has little public influence, observes the proper boundaries between the spiritual and the temporal, and is served by a clergy which is devoted and accessible. Whether it is intellectually equipped for the conditions of modern society is another matter. It is easy to criticize, and in most gatherings of educated Catholics there is a tendency to indulge in facile criticisms, as though the main function of the clergy was to solve intellectual problems. Secular priests—of whom there are not enough—are so hard worked that they have neither the time nor the energy for sustained reading and most of them probably read very little theology or philosophy once they have left the seminary. Their work is to bring God to the people and the people to God, and this is a full-time mission of celebrating Mass, administering the sacraments and building churches and schools. In coping with the problems of a large urban parish a priest has more important things to do than satisfy the intellectual requirements of the more educated Catholics. Nevertheless, when all this has been said, there remains a disturbing possibility. Most of our priests are educated in diocesan seminaries. While the spiritual formation which they receive there is above reproach, it also seems that academic standards, both in sacred and in secular studies, are lagging behind those of other English academic institutions. Meanwhile, more and more young Catholic laymen and women are receiving higher education in the various universities, an education which is not only of a higher standard than that given in the seminaries, but is completely different in its methods. We shall eventually reach a point when a fair proportion of the Catholic laity in England are better educated than their clergy. This is not a happy prospect for the Church. It is true that the religious orders are much better placed for meeting this situation. The Jesuits and the Dominicans, for example, with a high proportion of graduates in their ranks and their houses of study at the older universities—where some of their members are themselves recognized lecturers—are producing a clerical elite to which many educated Catholics look for leadership and assistance, and each order has its followers and even its fans; their reviews and publications are invaluable for the formation of an educated laity. But this does not solve the problem of general standards in the Church. While it is not unnatural that a few orders, with their specialized functions, should monopolize the position of intellectual leaders of the clergy, a great disparity in standards between them and the secular clergy is not desirable. Many of the latter are handicapped not only by the nature of their work but also by the fact that possibly intellectual eminence does not get its due recognition.

Inevitably, as they are the key figures in the Church's structure, the bishops set the tone and the pace of Catholicism. The English Hierarchy is composed of men of the people who inspire the affection and devotion of their people. They are rarely public figures in any sense that the popular Press would recognize, but at the same time they know how to exist and to direct their flock in a mixed society, quietly ministering to the spiritual and material needs of their dioceses, carefully preserving Catholic belief and practice, yet never disavowing the national life around them and the society in which they live. Catholics in England can be profoundly grateful for many of the qualities of their bishops and for the hierarchical direction which they receive. It is clear that English bishops owe their appointments to no political or mundane pressure, such as prevails in some Catholic countries. Consequently, they are respected because they are independent, give their religious allegiance directly to the Holy See, confine their activities strictly to the spiritual, and are attached to no particular political or social regime. Moreover, English Catholics are spared the embarrassment which Catholics in other countries have to suffer from episcopal attacks on Protestantism and obsession with inches in female modesty. The characteristics of the English Hierarchy are charity and common sense. Is something else now needed? Are English Catholics now ready for a more positive lead and direction? Throughout her history the Church has produced and promoted different types of men to leadership, and has shown herself capable of choosing great scholars, great preachers, great saints, as well as great administrators, for preferment to higher positions. Anyone looking objectively at English Catholicism in the last hundred years will observe that the Church in England has produced mainly administrators, good administrators but with all the limitations of administrators. And this is an essential feature of English Catholicism—a Hierarchy which is sound, capable and discreet, but perhaps over-cautious. Let it be said at once that there are good reasons for this. In the first place, caution is needed and is an asset in a mixed society where it is so easy to tread on toes and to provoke misunderstanding, prejudice and hostility. Secondly, English bishops are administrators because there are a lot of administrative problems to be solved—churches to be founded, schools to be built, and money to be found to pay for them. If to many people ecclesiastical administration in England seems a money-collecting activity—it is a sign of the changing times that the parish pools collectors are now key agents in the Church in this country—it has to be remembered that in England the Church survives on self-help and money has to be collected. But clearly there are other problems too. Christian people need leaders who will stir their minds and their hearts as well as organize their actions and collect their money. It is possible to carry discretion to the point of silence and caution to the point of inactivity.

There is, however, one big lead which the English bishops have tried to give in the last hundred years—they have tried to teach their people and the rest of the nation that there is no incompatibility between being good Catholics and good Englishmen. This leads to the question of how and to what extent Catholicism is integrated with the national life in England. Whatever answer one gives to this question, one thing is clear from the beginning. Granted that Catholics in England are a permanent minority—and that is the only future we can see—then they will never be fully integrated. For the Catholic minority the problem of integration is not simply one of owing two allegiances—a supranational allegiance to their Church and a national allegiance to their own country. This is an old and not an immense difficulty, and since the Church no longer claims or possesses any temporal sovereignty the problem is easier than it used to be. In the ultimate analysis it resolves itself into the perpetual tension between the city of God and the earthly city, and corresponds to that conflict within every man's conscience between the laws of God and human inclinations. The real problem is different. Catholics can never be completely assimilated to modern English society, nor can England itself be fully integrated. And the reason is simple. Our Lord wanted all his followers, indeed all men, to be one. He prayed "that they all may be one, as thou, Father, in me, and I in thee". England is not only a mixed, it is a divided society; there is no agreement about ultimate objectives. The Christian communities are divided among themselves, and an immense distance separates them from the non-Christian majority. In the Catholic view a divided society is in a state of imperfection and all attempted solutions to the problem will share in that imperfection. Consequently, for the Catholic minority in England to imagine that it will ever be fully integrated in the national life is to forget the basic Christian condition for such integration, namely unity of belief.

For this reason, although most English Catholics accept the situation and take it in their stride, the various attitudes they have adopted as working solutions to the problem are not entirely satisfactory. There are roughly two big points of view about integration. The first one says, "Let us show our non-Catholic neighbours that we are just as English as they are." This is an understandable reaction against the association of Catholicism with things Irish or foreign. It is common for English people, including Catholics, to remark on or complain about the predominance of Irish Catholicism in England. But these are mere words. What exactly do they mean? It would be interesting to know what substance could be given to such allegations. In fact, the critics never stop to consider what precisely is the alleged "Irishness" of English Catholicism. If one looks into it the notion begins to evaporate. Names, and even historical memories, do not amount to much. Within two or three generations immigrants have lost their Irish roots—and sometimes their religion too—and have become to all practical purposes completely Anglicized. The ultra-English reaction of some Catholics, therefore, is a reaction against something which does not really exist. But the tendency to be more English than is necessary or desirable has even more objectionable features than this. It leads to some ultra-English attitudes in the Catholic public schools, to a chauvinistic and basically unchristian bellicosity in time of war, and to a display of some inferiority complex. There are many petty, though interesting, symptoms of the predicament. At a West End church in London, after High Mass, the congregation has to stand for a sung version of the National Anthem, even though the more appropriate and infinitely more Christian *Domine salvam fac* has already been rendered; many English Catholics object to using the predicate "Roman"; during the last war the anxiety of some Catholic newspapers to write up the records of Catholic servicemen became quite comical at times. But there are more serious consequences. In the last years of the Second World War there were few significant Catholic voices raised to question either our war aims or our methods, though both of these raised moral implications which were at least debatable. Since then there has been a tendency for English Catholics to join in the post-war British inferiority complex, the attempt to compensate for the reduction in our international power by using the language and advocating the methods associated with the period of our predominance, the adoption of an ultra-patriotic attitude in foreign and colonial issues, the irrelevant concern for national prestige. The opinions of many English Catholics on international and colonial questions which involve moral issues are indistinguishable from the opinions of those of their fellow countrymen whose only criterion is that of British interests. In this case their belonging to a supranational organization does not help them to overcome some of the worst aspects of national pride. Many English Catholics do not make the necessary effort of discrimination or attempt to test British policies against Christian principles. Yet they are in a position to show that true patriotism is the monopoly of no party or group, and that the real English spirit is infinitely more varied and less orthodox than national preachers would have us believe.

At the other extreme there is a temptation to throw in the sponge as far as integration is concerned, to cry that England is pagan and materialist, that we must stand apart and preserve our barriers. Superficially, there is more justification for this view. No good can come from hiding the fact that on many issues—particularly sexual morals and marriage—there is no common ground between English Catholics and the majority of their countrymen. In these matters we no longer speak the same language as our neighbours. Moreover, it is essential for the Church to take a stand on the education of Catholic children and to refuse to participate in the national education on the same terms as satisfy the majority of the English people. These barriers are necessary and have to be preserved. But this is no cause for retreat. An attitude of disavowal has even more insidious implications than its opposite. To reject English life is even worse than accepting it indiscriminately. This is a counsel of despair. Apart from the fact that there are elements of good in English society which we cannot disavow, we have to remember that we are all God's creatures and have some responsibility for our neighbours. We cannot strike our breasts in church like the Pharisee while the publicans remain outside. In Ireland there is a tendency to attribute all the teething-troubles of the new Irish immigrants in England to the pagan English, instead of looking for the source of the malady nearer home. English Catholics, who have learned how to survive, have less temptation to make the same mistake.

Then there is the problem of personal relations with our neighbours. Here it is difficult to generalize: each Catholic has his own approach. In most places a Catholic, unless he is "lapsed", is known for what he is. Many English Catholics, however, tend to keep quiet about their religion and not to let it impinge too much, and they are reluctant to get involved in religious discussions. Or else there is the hearty attitude, to say to one's friends in effect, "Look how easy it is, you see how we behave, nothing narrow-minded about us, we can have a good time and enjoy life with the rest of you—and we are Catholics." In many ways this is a natural approach, but it can lead to confusion. To start with there is the problem of example. This attitude does not usually win converts and it puts a lot of people off. It is not, of course, the job of Catholics to cater for the inhibitions and even hypocrisy of many of their non-religious neighbours. But we still have our obligations. We can argue with people until we are blue in the face, to little effect: English Catholics will exert most influence in the community by their example. This is a difficulty, for most of us are not saints. Where we really differ from our fellow countrymen is that we still call sins by their proper names: we have no euphemisms for adultery or idolatry. But how can Catholics reconcile their own inadequacy with the need to avoid misunderstanding? This is one of the biggest dilemmas faced by a Catholic in a mixed society: he has to represent his religion to an uncomprehending world and to people whose only contact with Catholicism will be their personal acquaintance with individual Catholics.

Intellectual integration is even more difficult. There are two main reasons for this. The first is one of environment. In England there is a common assumption that only Catholics and Communists have points of view, and that everyone else is commendably neutral. In English educated circles there is a distrust of the "engaged" writer. It does not follow, of course, that because writers are not "engaged", therefore they do not have a point of view, but many educated Englishmen fail to draw this conclusion. It is taken for granted that Catholics cannot be trusted to be as intellectually honest as humanists. A university professor of my acquaintance was genuinely surprised to be told that it was the duty of Catholics to tell the truth in all circumstances and that I had been taught by Jesuits to understand that the end did *not* justify the means. Catholics, then, can have little confidence that they will invariably get a fair reception, and this causes them to have some inhibitions about introducing their views in writing or discussion. Yet they themselves hardly improve the situation. Most English Catholics are not equipped to apply their religious principles to the facts of the modern world. What do English Catholics read? It is easier to say what they do not read. Few of them read any theology or philosophy, or indeed any books which would deepen their knowledge of their faith and help them to assimilate secular information and cope with non-religious points of view. At the same time they are subject to all the influences of modern mass communication. Those Catholics who read the "quality" secular Press have no equivalent Catholic publications to turn to. And what of the majority of Catholics who, like the rest of the half-educated English public, are the object of that shameful exploitation by all the organs of modern propaganda and publicity—the popular Press, advertising, television, the "entertainment industry"? By the grace of God their religious belief and practice do survive, but in most cases they are kept in separate compartments of their lives. Those Catholics who do make an effort to integrate their knowledge often follow false approaches. In a mixed society it is essential for Catholics to learn and understand that all truth comes from God, and that there cannot be conflict between scientific truth, philosophical truth, historical truth, and revealed truth—that apparent conflict comes from misunderstanding. Too many Catholics imagine there is such a thing as "Catholic science" and "Catholic history". They take it for granted that a Catholic university lecturer will automatically know and promote the Catholic point of view of his subject. I am often asked "What is the Catholic point of view of such and such a historical problem?", or "Can you recommend a book giving the Catholic point of view?", as though there were only *one* Catholic point of view of historical problems, and as though Catholics inevitably have to tackle historical problems from a point of view, in the narrowest sense of that term. One has to explain that all we are trying to do is to discover the truth and narrate it. It would be very damaging to allow it to be thought that the Catholic "point of view" were different from this.

A Catholic's attitude towards his past history is important. As far as English history is concerned, of course, it is understandable that

Catholics should have difficulty in striking a balanced view of the English past, at any rate of the English past since the sixteenth century. They cannot be expected to share in the optimistic nationalism of so many English historians. In fact, they are fortunate to be immune from the indiscriminate adulation of the "first Elizabethan age" that is now so prevalent, even among professional historians, and they could do a useful service in questioning some of the orthodox interpretations of our national past. They are not helped, however, by the polemical and inaccurate writings of so many authors who pass as "Catholic historians", at any rate in the Catholic Press, and who simply get Catholic historical scholarship a bad name. When a writer of the reputation of Evelyn Waugh can write in a foreword to a recently published diary of an Elizabethan Jesuit priest that it was a national misfortune that England was not conquered by Philip II of Spain, it is a sign that English Catholics are not yet balanced about their national past. And when a Catholic newspaper can publish a discussion about the canonization of James II it is time to throw up one's hands in despair. This sort of "Catholic history" usually simply involves trying to defend indefensible positions. Scandal can work two ways. The polemical approach has done enough damage already and ought not to be encouraged. Fortunately, there are some genuine Catholic historians in the universities and their work will surely bear fruit in the future.

To live as a minority in a mixed society, then, has its frustrations and its difficulties. But it also has its advantages and can bring out some of the best qualities in Catholic life. Self-reliance, absence of political support and pressure, toleration for other groups, the Church pursuing its own mission and no other—most English Catholics find this situation far more congenial than the atmosphere that prevails in some countries where Catholics are in a majority and where close association of Church and State, undue clerical influence in public life, and a tendency to silence opposition by pressure rather than by argument and example, put religious life into a strait-jacket and produce an undesirable anti-clericalism. In many ways, it is true, some English Catholics still have to learn how to conduct themselves according to the rules of a mixed society. Too often they give the impression that they prefer to use pressure-group tactics, to silence an opponent rather than to meet him in argument. But this is a false impression, and is out of harmony with normal Catholic behaviour in England. Moreover it creates unnecessary resentment: if Catholics enjoy the benefits of toleration then they can hardly deny them to others, and anyway they are not in a position to do so. These methods cannot be used in English society and most Catholics do not want to use them. Having experienced intolerance themselves, they are quick to resent its use by Catholics in countries where they happen to be in a majority. And following the lead of their bishops, they have dropped the old-fashioned type of anti-Protestant polemic. This does not mean that English Catholics are compromising their doctrinal position or that they have been affected by the desertion of Christianity that is going on around them, even on the part of many of those who call themselves Christians. On these matters English Catholics, calm in their belief and dispassionate in their piety, give Rome little cause for anxiety. Catholics in England, where the Reformation began with a rejection of papal jurisdiction, have an instinctive loyalty to the Holy See; not for them the indifference of the Spaniards or the suspicion of the French. Papal teaching and direction are accepted by English Catholics without qualification. Moreover, English Catholics recognize that in a divided world they have to be intellectually intolerant, that they have to make it quite clear that "we are right and you are wrong". This is the only honest position and the only one on which we can base the practice of our religion. In maintaining such a position Catholics have a duty to England as well as to the Church, for in the society in which they live they are virtually the last defenders of absolute truth and morality.

English Catholics enjoy another advantage. The fact of being a minority satisfies the dissenting spirit that exists in many of us. If a Catholic in England is radically minded, then to criticize people "at the top" or to dissent from orthodox national attitudes presents no problems. In many ways, to be a Catholic in England is to be a dissenter. In Catholic societies, on the other hand, where there is some sort of integration, however unsatisfactory, between the religious and the secular life of the nation, to dissent is more difficult. One starts by criticizing some secular policy and then finds that this policy is being defended on alleged Catholic principles, that the Church does not like attacking the powers that be, and that one is being branded as heterodox. English Catholics are in a position to test the actions of the State against Christian principles and they need feel no inhibitions about dissenting from some aspects of national policies.

Cardinal Suhard once remarked that the Church has less to fear from Nero than from Constantine. Whether it has less to fear from total indifference and incomprehension is another matter, but most English Catholics would prefer this to intolerance. In England they enjoy the conditions in which they can serve God and contribute something to the national life. Although indifference may be more insidious than intolerance, it does bring one big advantage: Catholics no longer suffer from the hopeless prospect of unemployment to which they were condemned under the penal laws. They are no longer excluded from the universities, the professions and public offices. They have responded to the new opportunities and are to be found everywhere. Indeed, some people think that Catholics are like an epidemic: they imagine that if you let one in the next time you look there will be twenty. From time to time there are alarmist rumours, particularly from the "secular humanists", that out of all proportion to their numbers Catholics have infiltrated some important institution such as the B.B.C. and are operating as a pressure group. They are also supposed to have an insidious influence in the Foreign Office. But these are myths. In the professions and the better jobs Catholics are still too few in number to make any great impact: they have their professional guilds, but these are religious and social organizations and not pressure groups. Catholics are to be found in greatest numbers in the mines, the shipyards and the docks. To say this, however, is no longer to give a complete picture of Catholic life in England. English Catholicism is less working-class than it used to be. As more Catholics receive higher education, so they are entering the professions and securing executive positions in greater numbers. There is a shift taking place: second- or third-generation Irish are moving up, and this creates new problems of adaptation. As long as Catholics were hewers of wood and drawers of water no one worried about them: they occupied the sort of jobs that their critics would not care to compete for. Now, however, as they emerge from obscurity and begin to occupy positions of influence and responsibility, they have to be prepared for some prejudice and resentment. They will find that there is a limit to indifference. It is still too early to say how English Catholics will adapt themselves to this situation. Meanwhile they are endeavouring to show that there is no conflict between Catholicism and the advancement of skill and knowledge.

INDIA

Parmananda C.-A. Divarkar, S.J.

If it is always a hazardous venture to assess the Catholicism of a nation, the task becomes particularly difficult when we come to India. The fact is, there is not one Catholicism in this country; within the unity of faith, there is about as much variety, in rite and liturgical language, in canon law and custom, in origin, religious tradition, social structure and status, as one would imagine possible in the Church Catholic. This makes it difficult not only to present a well-proportioned picture to the outside world, but to form one for ourselves, so conditioned are we by the situation that obtains in our own particular community.

The diversity of Catholicism in India is partly explained by the historical circumstances of the advent of the Faith to our land; Christianity has come to our shores in successive waves of apostolic endeavour, and each wave has left behind more than one pattern on the native soil.

Thus the St. Thomas Christians of Malabar, in South India, who take pride of place in the ecclesiastical history of our nation, are divided into Syro-Malabars, who follow a latinized form of the Chaldean Rite, and the recently reunited Syro-Malankaras, with the Antiochene Rite and a liberal use of the native Malayalam language. The former are again subdivided, racially and socially, into Nordists and Suddists. The Syro-Malankaras have their own hierarchy, but a reunited dissident may opt to be under the jurisdiction of the Suddist Bishop whilst retaining his own rite, the prelate himself having the privilege of biritualism. The picture is further complicated by the presence of "Latinites", with their own ecclesiastical organization, in the same territory. In general the Syrians have followed the social usages of their Hindu milieu and the religious

---

FR. PARMANANDA CORREIA-AFONSO DIVARKAR, S.J., was born in 1922 in Goa. His training in the Society of Jesus took him to various parts of India and Europe, and he has specialized in the problems of Indian Christian culture and the apostolate to the intelligentsia. He is at present Professor of Philosophy in St. Xavier's College, Bombay University, and works also with the University Catholic Federation and other student bodies.

traditions of Mesopotamia, with which they became early connected together with some socio-religious customs of doubtful origin, such as the ceremonial meals connected with funeral obsequies.

The Syrians of Malabar are socially and economically well established and represent the only extant relic of the Christian communities that existed in various parts of the country before the arrival on a large scale of the Europeans in the sixteenth century. The missionary zeal subsequently displayed by the newcomers exercised itself differently (broadly speaking) within the sphere of Portuguese supremacy and outside it: two evangelical approaches may be associated with the names of two saints, Francis Xavier and John de Britto. The latter followed in the footsteps of Robert de Nobili, the Roman Brahmin, who maintained that the acceptance of the Faith did not require the relinquishing of cherished traditions, of cultural inheritance and social conventions. Of this more hereafter; what interests us at present is that the sons of Xavier—and they are many, all along the coast—are not themselves all of one hue; quite literally they are of divers colours, as they belong to different races; but even where they are of the same stock, the flourishing communities of the Konkan Coast in the west and of the Fishery Coast in the south-east, have each a physiognomy of its own; they all belong to the Latin Rite, but this has not prevented them from dressing and eating differently, and in a manner that distinguishes them both among themselves and from their non-Christian neighbours; in many matters of practical moment they think and act very differently one from another.

Today it could be said that the Tamils and Telugus in the south have achieved a measure of homogeneity which is also very much in tune with their environment; in the west too, the Mangaloreans, Goans and so-called East Indians are mixing more freely in the large industrial and commercial cities, but the close contact the various groups maintain with what they ever cherish as their home, still distinguishes them.

Geographical and historical reasons—not to mention social factors—have made the Indian very susceptible to local influence. The first loyalty is to the village community; centuries after the family has left its native place, we still think of ourselves as coming from that remote point of origin; over hundreds and thousands of miles, over seas even, we receive our share of the communal income, if we choose, as many of us do, to claim it. The sense of nationhood has not fully entered the popular consciousness after ten short years of independence. To counteract the universally prevalent insularity, the Christians have had bonds uniting them among themselves and to the wider world without; but they have also had influences bearing upon them that have tended to emphasize their individuality. For instance, for administrative reasons and by disposition of the Holy See, each of the various communities was ministered to by a different body of clergy, and in the last hundred years these have hailed from every quarter of the globe—they represent the last wave of the incoming Faith. There was also—and it is with great relief and gratitude that one speaks of it in the past tense—the unfortunate conflict of ecclesiastical jurisdiction between the dioceses created under Portuguese patronage and the units, originally vicariates apostolic, subject to the Congregation of Propaganda. The difficulties that arose as far back as the seventeenth century from the "double jurisdiction" obtaining in some places, survived the establishment of the Indian Hierarchy in 1886, and the situation, which has only recently been entirely remedied, is feelingly described by a distinguished Indian prelate as "the divisions, the cross-purposes, the mutual recriminations, the check to apostolic endeavour by members of the household, not to speak of the resulting scandal and disedification."

As the State is trying to weld the various, partly heterogeneous, elements in the country into one well-knit body, so too, and very successfully, though gradually, is the Church. The foundation, at the end of the last World War, of the Catholic Bishops' Conference of India, was a landmark in the ecclesiastical history of our land. In 1950, coincidentally almost to a day with the establishment of the Sovereign Democratic Republic, was held the first Plenary Council of India. More significant for the popular mind was the National Marian Congress of 1954, organized and presided over by India's first cardinal. Here, for the first time, Catholic India knew itself, and was thrilled to find itself both Indian and Catholic. Despite its mammoth proportions the Congress was very much of an intimate family feast—a Mother's Day—and left a deep impression on the tens of thousands who took part in it, and on our non-Catholic neighbours. Since then there have been several conventions of a national character, and we have at present more than one nationwide organization, not least being the Catholic Union of India and the All-India Catholic University Federation.

The Catholic communities mentioned so far do little more than skirt peninsular India along a part of the coastline, but they account for about four-fifths of the faithful. Central India and the populous Indo-Gangetic plain, with some two-thirds of the total population claim a bare one-fifth of the Catholic strength—numerically; for if other aspects are taken into account the north fares even worse in the comparison. "It is true," says a recent study of the situation, "a neat network of ecclesiastical divisions, with rather broad meshes, spans Northern India—twenty-five units for the whole territory. It sets up a framework for action, most precious indeed and needed, but not to be misread as a sign that the Church is established in Northern India." After pointing out a multiform numerical weakness, the writer further shows how "that weakness is still more manifest if we reflect that nearly half of the Catholics in the North are of tribal origin or aborigines (not converted from the Hindu or Moslem population), and that another fraction of the remainder are not autochthonous North-Indians but either immigrants from the south, as are the Goans and Mangaloreans, Tamils and Malayalees who have settled in the north (many of them English-speaking), or Anglo-Indians and descendants from Europeans."

The uneven condition of the Church places us in the awkward predicament of having to plead in the same breath that we are of apostolic origin and of long and honoured standing in the land, and that we are not sufficiently developed to cater adequately for our own spiritual needs.

In the matter of development, a remarkable exception in the north is the aboriginal Church of Chota Nagpur, which is not a hundred years old but boasts a metropolitan of its own. I had occasion to visit a small group of aboriginal neophytes in an outlying area. The simplicity of their lives was striking even for one who is well acquainted with conditions in India. They did not eat till the afternoon when, after the morning's work in the fields, we were served with a large plate of boiled rice sparingly sprinkled with some condiments; the spiritual ministrations they receive are few and far between, and inadequate because often enough the priest is not familiar with their language. I offered the Holy Sacrifice with these altogether charming folk and addressed them a few words in Hindi, which they understand, though it is not their mother-tongue. After Mass, the catechist who had accompanied me treated them to a dissertation on the Mystical Body, its theological and juridical aspects and its practical implications. It was the soundest and most lucid, the most satisfying and disarmingly simple exposition of the mystery that I have ever heard, and the neophytes drank it in like mother's milk. Whatever may be said about the material considerations that influence the conversion of the aboriginal and the low-caste, I shall never believe that they do not hunger for the Word of God and the Bread of Life. And they know what hunger means.

To speak of India as mission territory conveys a wrong impression of the position of the Church in the country, but it does correctly indicate that nowhere has the Church attained what might be considered its full stature. In the bewildering variety we have endeavoured to portray, practically the only universal trait of the Catholic minority is that it is a minority. This is true both of the Church as a whole, which does not embrace even two per cent of the population, and of every particular community in its own locality.

And this poses a serious speculative problem: Why should it be so? Why should a Church that claims the ministrations of two of the Lord's Apostles, and of the greatest missionary of modern times, in a land that is proverbially susceptible to religious influence—how could such a Church have made so little progress in so long a span of time? The question may not be pertinent and the answer does not lie wholly within human ken. But an attempt at explanation will give us an insight into the situation of the Catholic community in India today.

Let it be stated here that the Church in this country enjoys a prestige and a position that is far out of proportion to its numerical strength, and that might well be envied by our brethren even in so-called Catholic countries. The Constitution that established the Republic as a secular state, provides the amplest liberty not only for the practice of religion but for the development and material expansion of a full Catholic life. One of the first acts of independent India was to establish diplomatic relations with the Vatican, and the official attitude, expressed by responsible men of state, is that "Indian Christians form a very considerable and important element in the national community."

Difficulties do indeed arise—and where do they not, for the disciples of Christ?—mostly at the local level, due to misunderstanding or to downright prejudice. Isolated incidents, regrettable though they be, often get more publicity than their importance would warrant, precisely because of their extraordinary character. In the matter of education and ecclesiastical property the Church has to be, as everywhere in the world, jealously watchful over her rights. The problem of the entry of foreign personnel is not peculiar to India or restricted to missionaries, and is conditioned by a historical background that must be appreciated before fair judgement can be passed.

Individual Catholics are highly regarded both in public and in private life for their moral integrity and their ability, enhanced by an education that is above the average available. Many hold positions of importance in Government and civil administration, in the forces and the professions. The loyalty of Catholics is unquestionable, but in some quarters their detachment from public affairs and unconcern for matters of common interest is distressing. The past cannot be written off with a stroke of the pen: it suited the British Raj to favour the minorities, and hence the condition and problems of the Christians were not always those of the Hindu majority; culturally too, many Christians found themselves cut off from the great stream of national life and out of sympathy with much that is truly and inalienably Indian. Today there is a strong reaction against what has been dubbed the ghetto mentality; the younger generation shows great promise, and, given the proper guidance and leadership, will surely make amends for the past.

But meanwhile the problem remains of the slow progress of evangelization. Every possible reason has been alleged as an explanation, from the deeply theological to the merely meteorological—the climate has been blamed: it saps one's vitality, and whilst it might meet the requirements of the traditional forest contemplative, it tells heavily against the apostle. But there have been great and very active and successful religious movements and counter-movements in India. Our foremost philosopher and theologian, Sankaracharya, in a brief lifetime of thirty-odd years, covered the whole vast land, preaching his Advaita and establishing *matths*.

The religious temper of the country has been blamed: its achievements have made it self-satisfied and proud, or again, its very receptivity makes it intolerant of a Faith that is not tolerant in the easy fashion in which tolerance is currently understood. The views of the Mahatma are well known and quite representative. In his great heart and broad mind there was no room for the idea of conversion, which he branded the deadliest poison that ever sapped the fountain of truth; after protracted "experiments with truth" he did not feel called upon to reject "any of the essentials of Hinduism", though he was prepared to concede that "Christianity is as good and as true a religion as my own."

At the dawn of independence, our first Minister of Education, a Muslim of the Congress Party, vouchsafed us the paternal advice that "Christ himself emphasized the baptism of the spirit rather than formal baptism by water, and missionaries would be true to the Spirit of Christ if they preached his message of humanity instead of attempting to convert the people to the dogma of a Church. If all missionary societies adopt this enlightened outlook, there is no reason why independent India should in any way hesitate to accept the services which they offer."

The evangelical methods employed in India have been severely castigated both within and without the fold: every venture has had and still has its critics. The European missionaries of earlier days have been blamed for the means they employed and the demands they made on the baptized. These had to adopt foreign names and in many ways to conform to the manner of life of the colonists. In defence of this policy it has been said that it was necessary to lessen the danger of lapse in circumstances where it was not easy to provide adequate spiritual assistance, and that it was an inevitable consequence of the neophytes' being thrown out of their own rigidly exclusive communities. To assimilate them to the European community was Christian charity. Moreover, the extent of this assimilation is grossly over-estimated, and judged almost exclusively on the evidence of an educated minority who, for reasons not necessarily connected with their religious allegiance, went in for a thorough, and in its own way very successful, westernization. In no Catholic community on the Konkan—be it Mangalorean, Goan or East Indian—can the mass of the people be said, by the wildest stretch of the imagination, to be European in its outlook and manner of life, for all that they bear the names of De Souza, Fernandes and D'Mello. In my native village the Church services were exclusively conducted, except for the inevitable Latin, in Konkani, and I owe to them my richest contact with my mother-tongue.

But it must be acknowledged that much that is genuinely Indian and, in the context, irreplaceably human, was allowed to die, or was deliberately killed. The educated few in some places, the most noticeable if not the most notable part of the Christian community, find themselves out of tune with the national culture, and more rarely, with national interests. The sneaking suspicion that Christianity is a denationalizing force draws its vital breath from a policy that is undeniably at variance with the directive issued by the Congregation of Propaganda in 1659 and the repeated pronouncements of the Holy See. But before we judge harshly of our forbears in the ministry we must appreciate the magnitude of the task of a thorough adaptation, which may be gauged from the fact that the Holy See herself, whilst maintaining uncompromisingly the principle involved, has in practice established the Latin Rite and the Latin Canon Law in mission lands. It is difficult to see what else could have been done at the beginning and, once it was done, how far one could go to meet the particular needs of particular peoples by subsequent changes. On the other hand, if the rite and the law have been thus determined, the scope is very limited for local initiative, to show that the Church, as distinct from individual Catholics, "is bounden to no particular culture; she is at home with all who respect the commands of God".

From the history of the Church it would appear that her evangelical efforts have been successful in two situations: the first, when she has approached a people of advanced culture, without being herself cast in a particular cultural mould, as happened in the earliest days; and the second, when after being wedded to particular cultures she has evangelized people with a culture that was not advanced, or already on the decline, as was the case in northern Europe and South America. Even so one may ask—though one may not as lightly answer the question—how far the Reformation and the present-day crisis among the so-called Latin Americans might not be ascribed to the inadequacy of "Latin" Christianity to meet the needs of the peoples concerned. Be that as it may, the Latin Church, it would seem, has had little success before the ancient, advanced and well-established cultures of India and China.

But then, very limited too has been the success in India of the Oriental Church that claims origin from St. Thomas. Pope Pius XII paid public tribute to the Syrian Christians for "their vigorous activity, fruitful in so many good works, and their apostolic spirit, to which Catholic India is indebted for so many ministers of Christ's Kingdom and consecrated virgins". Today the Church of Malabar is the happy hunting ground for missionary vocations, and despite the difficulty arising from difference of rite there are Malayalees labouring diligently and fruitfully in all the missions of India. Many find irksome the restrictions imposed on the Syrian rites, which may not spread to the rest of the country; yet in the thousand years and more when the field was clear, there is no evidence of apostolic effort; at least, nothing has survived. Several reasons have been adduced to explain this phenomenon, the most common being that the Christians too easily accepted the social structure that obtained in India, thus enclosing themselves within the narrow confines of the caste system. So it would appear that the very adjustment to the social and cultural tradition of the country led to the stagnation of the Church.

More generally, too, the caste system has been singled out as the great obstacle to the spread of the Faith, and it might be argued that it is one of those features of the national life that are unacceptable in the light of Christian principles. De Nobili, in his bold resolve to leave untouched, or rather to sanctify "the particular usages and traditional institutions of the people", accepted, with so much else, the caste system. His ideas were bitterly opposed in his day and even at present do not pass unchallenged. A distinguished prelate and great lover of India, in a position to have an intimate knowledge of the country, has called attention to the fact that whereas flourishing Christian communities exist today wherever St. Francis Xavier exercised the ministry, the work of De Nobili has perished, leaving hardly a trace. The obvious conclusion is drawn that where the forthright and uncompromising attitude of Xavier succeeded, the methods of his fellow Jesuit, pandering to the prejudices and pride of the high castes, did not, because on entering the fold these found that they were not in fact more regarded than their lesser brethren. But it must not be forgotten that when the Society of Jesus was suppressed, its missions within Portuguese territory and influence were taken over by other labourers, whilst its bolder and more arduous ventures farther afield were left to perish.

The spirit of De Nobili still lives in his beloved Tamil Nad. There, as we have said, the Latin Catholics of the south are quite integrated with their environment. Their manner of life, at all levels of society, is that of their fellow citizens; they bear long and hauntingly melodious names, fragrant with the scent of the soil and none the less Christian for being thoroughly Indian.

Today the topic of adaptation never fails to arouse a lively controversy, which is also very tedious, because the same old arguments have to be repeated to counter the same old objections, and the same old prejudices and misunderstandings are paraded over and over again. Prejudices proverbially die hard, but the movement towards cultural adaptation is gaining ground, and, though it far antedates the achievement of independence, it has been accelerated in the last ten years. The popular attitude is very understandably marked by an attachment to all one has been accustomed to, be it good (as many a traditional local custom), bad (as the universally prevalent taste in liturgical art), or indifferent (as some of the elements borrowed from the West). The objection, where it exists, is not so much to adaptation as to any change, and this is perhaps the one point in which the younger Church in North India has an advantage over the South: it is free to start from scratch.

It is interesting to notice that whereas the bravest spirits today ask for no more than the retention or adoption of what is indubitably good and acceptable in the national heritage, the directive issued by the Congregation of Propaganda three centuries ago required that nothing should be discarded that was not indubitably bad and unacceptable. In any case, great as is the importance of adaptation—or assimilation, as some prefer to call it—the problem of the Church in India must be expressed in broader terms than those of cultural traditions and liturgical arts.

I submit that, very generally, this problem could be stated thus: We are facing the situation of a young Church with the mind and manner of an old Church. By "young Church" I do not mean one of recent foundation but one which is far from having reached its full stature—a small minority; and in speaking of an old Church I do not suggest that our approach is old-fashioned or outmoded; on the contrary it is ahead of the times and in advance of what our state of development would warrant—our institutions and our outlook are those of a fully established Church. We stagger ineffectually, though perhaps a little complacently, in the magnificent trappings of Saul when a few pebbles from the native stream might have laid low the giant that bars our way.

This is a metaphor, but the thesis could be substantiated by going through the various aspects of Christian life: let two examples suffice, one involving attitude and the other, ecclesiastical discipline.

In a fully established Church it is natural that the terms "Catholic" and "neighbour" should become interchangable for every neighbour is in fact a Catholic and one need spare no thought for any others, at least as far as immediate contacts are concerned. But translated, let us say, from the Southern Europe of earlier days to our own shores, it reads quite odiously: only the Catholic is my neighbour, the others do not count. Such is, in fact, the mentality that has been noticed amongst us, with pain and puzzlement, by many a well-meaning non-Catholic, and it has been variously ascribed to a superiority or to an inferiority complex. In no case does it help the cause of the Gospel.

Again, when we bemoan, as we frequently do, the dearth of sacred ministers, what we really mean, often enough, is that there are not enough priests to do the work of deacons and lesser clerics. Our bishops in the less developed areas are awakening to the anomaly of expecting every aspirant to the clerical militia to undergo the long, laborious and expensive training, and to measure up to the exacting moral and intellectual standards of a full-fledged priest of the post-Tridentine pattern. Celibacy, which, except for the episcopal state, was a gradual (and very desirable) development in the Church, we here presuppose as a fait accompli.

These are serious and delicate matters and we should not lightly express ourselves on them, but there are Indian prelates of long experience and trusted judgement who are reconsidering the situation along these lines; and in a wider field the Holy See herself is in the forefront of a great movement to thaw out the deep-freeze of the post-Reformation and usher in a new spring.

To this spring we look forward with great hope. For there could be no question of putting the clock back in India, or of withdrawing from the progress of Christendom as a whole and thinking ourselves into the sub-apostolic age. We must go forward with our fellows, and we can do so. For the Universal Church is herself a young Church, and will ever remain so, for we never shall know what great task there may yet be to accomplish before the Lord comes. Every hour is an hour of crisis for the Church, and she must ever think out her problems anew. But if there are moments of special import, this is surely one of them; and the Indian Church, we believe, can play a providential role among the resurgent nations of Asia.

But before we presume to occupy the centre of the stage in the changing pattern of history we must learn a simple first lesson from the early Church. We may call it by the currently popular name of the "apostolate of presence", or conveying the Good Tidings simply by living them out in the world. Christianity is not, as many of our countrymen have been led to believe, just a system of doctrines or a code of behaviour, or even an institution or a way of life—it is Life itself, it is a Person, it is Christ. As such it must not only be heard about but met in vital contact. India must not only know about

Christ, as heretofore; she must know Christ, and she can and must meet and know Christ in the Indian Christian.

If the early Christians exercised so fruitful an apostolate of presence, it was because they were both very present in the world and very Christianly present. Not that they were necessarily better Christians than we—the depth of piety and wealth of devotion amongst us is an object of wonder and edification to the visitor—but they appeared more as members of Christ; they had a strong sense of community, built around the altar, and they carried the Church about with them. Yet they were not communal-minded, they did not form a closed social group, and hence they were more present in society. "Christians are not distinguished from the rest of mankind by either country, speech or customs", reads the *Epistle to Diognetus*; "the fact is, they nowhere settle cities of their own; they use no peculiar language; they cultivate no eccentric ways of life . . . Yet while they settle in both Greek and non-Greek cities, as each one's lot is cast, and conform to the customs of the country in dress, diet and mode of life in general, the whole tenor of their way of living stamps it as worthy of admiration and admittedly contrary to expectation."

We, alas, have largely reversed the earlier values; we are communal-minded and not community-conscious; we live in a closed social circle and within it we appear as individuals—good, even admirable individuals perhaps, but at best as members of an efficient organization, not of a Person, not of Christ.

And here we must speak of the Indian intelligentsia, of the relatively small but influential body of educated men and women to whom no effective approach has yet been made. For we must confess that scant as is the success of our evangelization, it shrinks below visibility when we consider the so-called higher classes. Such conversions as there have been are registered almost exclusively among the illiterate and the indigent, the socially underprivileged. We are happy that the Gospel is preached to the poor, and the lesson of Christian charity and social service has not passed unnoticed; but the situation very understandably arouses the suspicion that material, or at any rate natural, considerations predominate in conversion.

It is easy to counter the charge of "forced" or even interested conversions, but very difficult to face with a light heart the tragic fact of a great multitude, not all of whom surely are of ill will, thousands of whom pass through our hands in our various institutions and cherish fond memories of the Fathers and Sisters who have brought them up, and none of whom has entered the fold. If there is a Catholic intelligentsia in India today it is merely because of the educational policy generally followed here by the Church, which has enabled great numbers of our youth, whatever their social or economic status, to have the best formation available in the land.

In this matter we are singularly privileged. Catholic minorities are generally obliged to establish and maintain schools of their own without assistance from the State and for the sake of principle must be content to forego the best. Here it is the Catholic institutions that are the best, and they receive State aid on condition that they are open to non-Catholics. These flock to them in large numbers, attracted by their prestige and by long-standing family traditions; and they are welcome.

Our policy, which is hardly a matter of choice, has been denounced in no uncertain terms by well-meaning critics. Time, money and energy, it is said, are fruitlessly spent in imparting secular education to non-Catholics, for the result shows how little influence we ultimately have on their basic attitudes and outlook; as for the propagation of the Faith in particular, we achieve little more than a mild innoculation of Christianity which effectively prevents the spread of the real thing.

The charge is not altogether unfounded, but inconclusive. For the little we have achieved elsewhere has been in no small measure due to the respect and good will gained among the influential by our schools and university colleges. If prejudice and difficulties militate against the Church today it is particularly in places where we have not entered the field of higher education.

Today, also, our colleges provide an ample and fertile field for contact, where Catholics already maturing to a sense of responsibility can mix freely and deal familiarly with the best type of non-Catholic. There are those who view with alarm such growing intimacy, and doubtless there is cause for apprehension, due in part to the fact that at the moment our young people are not adequately prepared to meet the situation. But we cannot close our eyes to its potentialities. Given the proper formation, our educated youth could exercise a very fruitful apostolate of presence and in a critical hour retrieve our fortunes on this field.

For this is a critical hour. The strategic position of the university student in resurgent Asia is too well known to need stressing. So, too, is his bewilderment: faced with a multiform insecurity peculiar to his own condition and the object of much unwelcome attention, he is also involved in the general crisis, the birth pangs of new nations and the death agony of an old world.

A marked feature of this crisis in India, as elsewhere in the East, is the clash between traditional and modern values, a conflict that is all the more acute in that neither pass unchallenged as values: the claims to achievement of the new technical age are as much questioned as the pretensions of the old, proverbially "mystic", cultures, and to judge between them when the very basic principles of judgement are themselves involved is a task to daunt the bravest.

Attempts at synthesis are not lacking, but the spiritual resources to meet the challenge of the present certainly are. That is to say, whatever we may predict about the reaction of the transcendental outlook traditionally associated with the Orient to the impact of materialism or a more refined humanism, in practice religious and moral principles will go by the board; for they are too intimately linked up with the old society and its group mentality to stand any sort of effective adaptation. Caste and village, the old diehards—not to mention the family—are breaking up under pressure; what will remain is a mass of disorientated individuals with a sentimental attachment to the past and a desperate urge to catch up with the present.

It is a platitude to say that only the Church can meet the situation. But the triteness of the statement should not blind us to its actuality and to the urgent demands it makes on us. For it is not Christian principles as such that will save the day—these India has known long and ineffectually; but a Church that is wholly herself, deeply committed, plunged into the heart of the problem, at grips with the present, and raised above it, naked, on a Cross; a Church, in fine, that is Christ. And a Church that is India, more truly India than India ever was, yet the same old India we have known and loved, united now but never uniform, adorning with variety the Bride of Christ.

NORWAY

Gunnar Höst
Daniel Haakonsen

Much has been said and written of recent years about a growing interest in Catholicism in Norway. Together with anthroposophy and Moral Rearmament, the Catholic Church is believed to have the power of attracting the younger generation. Norway, it seems, has recently become an area of intensive Catholic missionary work. Plenty of people are prepared to regard Catholic priests as men with exceptionally intelligent, highly trained minds. The Press is full of references to a "Catholic peril". We propose here to bring the question into focus, and distinguish, as far as possible, between the measure of truth and the measure of illusion involved in notions of this sort.

It may be useful to begin by glancing at the *Norwegian Journal of Statistics*. Under the heading "Persons Outside the State Church" we find that in 1950 there were 4,753 Norwegian citizens who gave themselves as members of the Roman Catholic Church. Allowing for a variable number of foreigners, it is reasonable to put the number of Catholics in Norway today at about 5,000.[1] As for numerical increase, the diocese of Oslo counted 289 new members in 1954: 123 infant baptisms, 90 immigrations and 76 conversions. On the other hand there were 31 deaths, 31 emigrations, and two persons who had their names removed from the Church's registers.

It is easily seen that so modest a total figure both for Catholics and for conversions should be enough to temper the excitement of anyone who has been imagining a different state of affairs. Numerically speaking, the Catholic Church continues to hold a place amongst

GUNNAR HÖST was born in 1900 and is Reader in French at the University of Oslo. His doctorate thesis was on the work of Jean Giraudoux.

DANIEL HAAKONSEN, born in 1917, is Assistant Professor of Scandinavian Literature at the University of Oslo. His doctorate thesis was on the Norwegian Romantic, Henrik Wergeland.

[1] Norway has a population of nearly 3½ million, of whom by far the majority are members of the official Lutheran State Church, whose clergy are nominated by, and receive their salaries from, the State. The Catholic Church in Norway consists of the diocese of Oslo and the vicariates apostolic of Trondheim and Tromsø.

other "dissident" religious societies of medium size, at about the same level as the Adventists (with 5,500) members. She is greatly surpassed by the Baptists (about 9,000) and Methodists (11,000), and practically eclipsed by the Pentecostal Brotherhood.

This presents us with a first characteristic of Norwegian Catholicism. The Roman Catholic Church is the oldest and most numerous Christian society in the whole world, but in Norway its members form only a tiny minority. Theoretically, in Norway, as elsewhere, Catholicism represents complete universality, the Church *par excellence*; but this does not prevent her from being counted juridically as just one non-official religious society amongst others. Sociologically she is only a small minority, which means that she has to some extent the appearance of a sect and may even be in danger of acquiring a little of the mentality which goes with it.

Obviously, this tension between universality in principle and a minority position in practice creates certain problems. The very smallness of their numbers puts Norwegian Catholics in danger of undergoing what is often the fate of minorities: to have both an inferiority complex and a subtle temptation to exaggerated self-esteem and, in addition, the temptation to disclaim all responsibility: to feel that they are small in numbers, indeed, but that they are the little band of the elect—and so to shrug off all responsibility for what goes wrong in society around them. In our particular case, this means the temptation, in the face of de-christianization, indifference, and the failure of Christianity to make any adequate impact in the intellectual and cultural fields, to put all the blame on the official Church which, with its numbers and its resources, must bear the whole responsibility. But before going further it may be well at this point to make a distinction.

It is true that if we lived our faith to the full in all its richness and plentitude, the problems raised by the minority position of Catholicism would dwindle away, and the tension between the universality of Catholicism in principle and its minority character in practice would represent no more than a slight increase in that fundamental tension which every Catholic has to accept in any case, because he is a citizen of two realms, one on earth and one in heaven. But supposing we do not in fact always remain at the highest pitch of our faith? In that case problems of all kinds raise their heads and may grow to considerable proportions. So it may be well to examine them fairly closely, and this brings us at once to an entirely concrete situation.

We can be sure that there is no Norwegian Catholic who does not feel at Mass that here and here alone is the true place to be, the true word, the true table: who does not feel most strongly that if he were not already a Catholic he would have to become one as soon as possible so as to have his share in all the things which are offered here and nowhere else. No one who has belonged to the Catholic Church could feel it as anything but a frightful mutilation to be cut off, on confessional grounds, from all that has marked the progress of Christianity down the centuries—to belong to a Church which has not built a single cathedral and does not acknowledge a single saint. And how wretched it would be if the Church to which one belonged—unlike others—were not always there, all the week through, a house with hospitable doors ever open to receive one!

But, on the other hand, the little group which has been able, during the Mass, to feel its unity with all the world and the whole of Christendom, has no sooner crossed the threshold of the church than it finds itself face to face with a quite different reality. Dividing and redividing into ever-dwindling groups, its members go back to their islands of family life or their lonely lodgings, where they have to set about keeping their faith alive from day to day in the midst of a national life which is fundamentally alien to Catholicism.

Here is an account which one of them has given of what it feels like to be a Catholic in this officially Protestant Norway:

> Like all my fellow-countrymen, at the end of every January I get down to making out my tax-return. At the end of which I—unlike the others—still have one final rite to perform. This is one of the few moments when I feel the Catholic and the Norwegian in me as two distinct persons. It is the Norwegian citizen who, on the last page of his declaration, writes a sentence drawn up in conformity with the tax law which, for the Catholic, goes much against the grain: "As a member of a recognized dissident religious society, the Roman Catholic Church, I apply for exemption from the Church tax."
>
> There may be others who fill up this form without feeling it as a problem; to me it always seems appalling to have the Church reduced to being a "recognized dissident religious society"—yet that is its official status under the law of our country.
>
> It is not that I attach an exaggerated importance to matters of law, but the fact is that this legal formula is an exact expression of an

opinion deeply rooted in our nation by centuries of tradition. For me, Catholicism is the obvious normal form for the Christian life to take. But for the nation to which I belong it is an anomaly, and a Catholic is often looked upon as something phenomenal.

This is the situation of which my tax-return kindly undertakes to give me an annual reminder. In any case, there are plenty of less official reminders throughout the year.

This morning's paper, for instance. There is a review of a novel with a Catholic theme, or some comment on the "Catholic" (sic) democratic parties in Europe. From a strictly literary or political point of view, the standard of the articles seems to be good. My own convictions in these fields may be practically the same as those of the writer. But he has obviously wanted to give his ideas full scope, so he has launched out into considerations which, if they were to be of any value, would have to be based on a thorough knowledge of Catholicism. It is very seldom that such a writer has this knowledge. So the paper offers its readers, including my own and my wife's families and our neighbours, colleagues and friends —i.e., all the people with whom we should like to have a natural, relaxed relationship—a whole series of more or less imaginary assertions about our faith and our coreligionists in other countries. And since Norwegian newspapers enjoy a high reputation, information of this sort is usually accepted with confidence.

What happens if I try to reply to any particularly unfounded statements? The editor soon grows impatient, and the ordinary reader thinks, "Oh, Catholics—always having to be up in arms about something." Leaving aside the fact that a reply from the writer of the article in question will be bound to supply the readers with a whole new set of grounds for misunderstanding, all of which will need to be corrected in turn. So there are practical difficulties in the way of a reply. For anyone not attracted by a career of professional bickering, the only real possibility is silence.

Hence a Catholic is easily subject to a sense of impotence. This is surely our particular trial. It is not that our situation makes any very terrible demands on us—but there is the ever-present temptation to try to get out of them: it is so much easier to blame our environment and describe it as "impossible" than to face the problems of coexistence with lucidity and courage.

Nowadays we do not, on the whole, meet this attitude in any of its more naïve forms. We are past the stage of thinking that a novel written by a Catholic is *ipso facto* a good novel, that Catholic politicians necessarily govern with wisdom and justice, or that Catholic pickpockets, say, must be better qualified than their Protestant or atheist competitors. But there are plenty of more subtle ways of withdrawing into a ghetto where we can sulk and scowl at the milling throng of humanity outside. We may surely suppose that there is nothing unreal about this temptation.

Perhaps it will be our children who hear it said in the course of tiffs with their friends that their family's faith and customs are not all that they should be. "You're Catholics, you are, you go to St. X's School, yah!" Or in other words: you're different from other people, so you're no good. Faced with discrimination of this sort, children are entirely dependent on their family's moral support. So the temptation may be to give it to them in full measure, by teaching them to be permanently on the defensive against everything said or thought outside their own immediate circle. The result is a really dangerous situation. In the long run, a protectionist attitude of this sort will make it difficult for the children to become strong, independent adults; it will have a retarding and deforming effect both on the parents and on the children in their development as truly Catholic Christians.

If I look at my country with the eyes of faith, what I ought to see before anything else is that Norway and Norwegians bear the same mark upon them as the rest of creation. It is likely that even at Ultima Thule men are made in the image of their Creator. There is no greater God available to St. Teresa of Avila than to any Miss Hansen—and the saint herself would be the first to say so. In the last analysis, the vistas opened up by the errors and generosities of the good people of Svelvik or Toten are no different from those opened up by the interior struggles of the great mystics. For the Catholic in me, Norway should be just one amongst many normal, obvious things: a country inhabited by men. It should surely be the best possible guarantee of the universality of my faith that I should be able to find my own place, wholeheartedly, in the precise environment in which I have in fact been placed. As a Catholic I believe in the structure of the Church and her sacraments as forms which God himself has given to Christian life. But this same faith puts me in contact, too, with everything which is genuinely religious everywhere, so that I can never fail to recognize the spiritual values manifested by other religions or other

Christian confessions. This is why it is my duty to take my place, without any covertly aggressive feelings, amongst my fellow-countrymen, who for their part are not always ready to recognize a Catholic as one of themselves.

In fact, it is not only our integration into our own country which is put in jeopardy by an over-protectionist attitude, but the integrity of our faith itself. We have got to take practical account of our concrete situation in this country: in the popular mind, Norwegians though we are, we arouse the same sort of curiosity as foreigners. It is up to us to be big enough to refuse any kind of easy revenge. It is up to us not to seek to compensate ourselves for our real powerlessness by attributing "power" to ourselves on the spiritual level, and not to put ourselves in the position of the Judge separating the sheep from the goats—groups and individuals who are to be considered "valuable" from those who are to be abandoned to their fate.

Such is one Norwegian Catholic's account of the matter.

Just as it is the duty of each individual Catholic to adapt himself as well as he can to his environment, so it is a matter of the greatest importance for the spiritual balance of the little Catholic community to have plenty of natural contacts with the world of the majority. How are these contacts made nowadays? Here again statistics can be some help.

For instance, out of our five thousand Catholics, a very considerable number—more than five hundred at the present time—are nuns. The great majority of these are devoted to nursing service; they maintain twenty-two hospitals. Throughout the country, from Kristiansand in the south to Hammerfest in the north, we find these little Catholic hospitals with an average of sixty to seventy beds. This means that in one field at least—the care of the sick—Catholicism is making a striking contribution to the life of the country. But it also means that the widest contact that exists between the Catholic world and its Norwegian environment is not a matter of the individual Catholic and his small handful of relationships but of nuns and the care they are giving to tens of thousands of sick people. These Catholic hospitals are a fairly accurate indication of the work of the last hundred and ten years, since the laws excluding Catholics were repealed and they were able, after an absence of three centuries, to obtain access to the country once more. They also show to how great an extent the presence of Catholicism in Norway has been an active but silent presence, far removed from anything rowdy or sensational.

Another element of contact consists in the increasing number of Norwegian Catholic priests. Of the thirty-seven secular and regular priests in the diocese of Oslo, twelve are at present Norwegians. This is a relatively recent phenomenon.

Twelve is certainly not a large figure. Nevertheless, it represents a fact of very great influence. No one wants to deny the international character which is one of the glories of Christianity and especially of the Catholic Church; nor does anyone want to deny the essential and decisive part played by foreign priests in the past and present life of the Catholic Church in Norway. But nobody is going to argue from this that it is a matter of indifference whether the word is preached by a man of the country or by one whose accent is a continual reminder that he is a foreigner. A foreigner always "sticks out" to some extent, and when, over and above this, his faith in any case sticks out from his surroundings, he will quickly be regarded and classified as a being apart and instinctively avoided.

It is another matter when the man representing this foreign faith is himself a fellow-countryman. Thus it will happen that whereas a foreigner priest will never, all his life long, have anyone to hear his sermons except his own tiny parish, a young priest coming back to the country will have a full church—because the whole town is curious to see and hear how he has turned out.

The fact that there are now, and will continue to be, Norwegian priests and religious, has effects on other levels besides the strictly religious one. Besides his actual sacerdotal ministry, a priest, like anyone else who has had an intellectual training, is prepared to take part in meetings and discussions, to give lectures, to write in newspapers and reviews, and to publish books. This is something else to which our country has been unaccustomed: in any discussion group nowadays one is quite likely to be suddenly confronted with a Catholic priest. This is something of a nature likely to purify the atmosphere of religious debate—many of the easy accusations which can be made against the behaviour of Catholics can hardly be thrown at a man who has freely renounced the things which his fellow-countrymen prize above all others: material prosperity, married love, and a home.

So, keeping to the sober language of statistics, what we see is a minority with the problems typical of any minority. The area in which it is in contact with Norwegian life is limited; its ideas penetrate the outside world very little. The fact that it has been possible nevertheless for people to talk about a Catholic offensive suggests that the faint stirrings discernible amongst us are the fringe of great movements at work outside. If we want to understand why Catholic thought has taken on such overtones in our country today, we must consider, on the one hand, certain recent developments in the cultural life of Europe, and on the other the changes which have taken place in the spiritual condition of our generation.

At the end of the war, Europe began to claim our attention to a much greater degree than it had done before, including the Catholic countries, especially France; to a certain degree Italy as well. As is well known, these countries, and England as well, have been having a Catholic literary renaissance during the last few decades, as a result of which works by Catholic authors have passed into the general body of Europe's literary possessions. We need refer only to such names as Claudel, Péguy, Mauriac, Bernanos, Evelyn Waugh and Graham Greene. On a less serious level we may even instance the book and film of Don Camillo, which have helped to make ordinary people familiar with some aspects of everyday Catholic life.

A knowledge of contemporary Catholic writers is not, indeed, anything new in itself. Men like Mauriac and Claudel have long been read and studied in Norway. That great novelist Sigrid Undset, actually one of ourselves, was able to make her contribution to the Catholic literary revival without its appearing, at least at the time, to have any deep effect on the position of Catholicism in our country. Despite the sensation which her conversion caused at the time, and despite the enthusiastic reception accorded to *Kristin Lavransdatter*, it nevertheless appears to be the case that few of her compatriots regarded her Catholicism as a problem to be faced.

But it is surely precisely here that a change has taken place. If we were to see as notable a conversion, now, of a writer of the stature of Sigrid Undset, the effect would be incomparably greater than it was in 1925. This being the case, there must have been a very deep alteration in the current of people's thoughts. This brings us, we think, humanly speaking, to the heart of the problem.

Fifty years ago, the "open-minded" Norwegian was living in the security of a resolutely forward-looking intellectual world. His gaze was confidently and hopefully directed towards the future, which contained the solution of all problems and the resolutions of all difficulties which could still be regarded as worth mentioning. Progress meant science, education and political humanism—liberalism for some, socialism for others. The one great task was to shake off ever more thoroughly the errors of the past. To be old, with roots reaching back into the past, was something suspect in itself—so much so that judgements were normally and unconsciously twisted into the assumption that in any encounter between new and old the issue was inevitably decided in advance in favour of the new. For there was one power which no one could hope to withstand: evolution.

Such an attitude of mind was bound to be wholly without sympathy towards a religion which, besides being doubted in itself, was also intimately involved in all the troubles and abuses of the past, as Christianity is. Appearances were uniformly against it and against Christians. It was considered that Christianity might indeed have produced some good results in the past, but they were all merely accidental, chance effects, which would have been bound to happen in any case because of "evolution". The evils which it had produced, on the other hand, resulted from its essential nature. Many of us can still remember the amazement with which, in certain circles, people would wonder whether it was really possible that so-and-so—a famous scientist, say, and presumably a reasonable man—could be a Christian. And how uncomfortable any circle of young men would feel, thirty or forty years ago, if they learnt that one of their number was ceasing to study science in order to become a pastor!

Inevitably, in such conditions, a special mistrust was reserved for that one of all Christian confessions which seemed most to deny all that the modern man most firmly believed in. The Catholic Church's principle of authority—it used to be referred to as "the Pope's Church"—her dogmas, her faith in saints and miracles, her use of ceremonial, all seemed like so many ghosts from the thickest darkness of the Middle Ages, so many symbols of the abiding power of obscurantism. It was melancholy enough to have a friend going off to become a liberal Protestant theologian, but as for becoming a *Catholic*, certainly no normal Norwegian could really have any valid reason for doing that. And if occasionally it really did happen to someone or other, the explanation was all ready to hand, equally applicable to all converts alike: it was either romantic aestheticism (so delightful to escape from life into twilit churches heavy with incense!) or purely and simply mental fatigue (Poor thing! So out of tune with things that he had to find peace in the bosom of Mother Church!).

Nowadays, this state of mind characteristic of the early part of this century has strikingly changed. The future no longer looks like a clear and radiant horizon. The best we can say of it is that it is once again looking as it is natural for any future to look: uncertain, and with a heavy load of demands and problems.

And it is this which gives people today a chance to reflect and reconsider. Their attention is no longer hypnotically fixed upon a wholly promising future. We are recovering a tragic sense of the basic lot of humanity: alive today, under the sod tomorrow. We have to decide here and now how we wish to use our short life on earth and what meaning we wish it to bear. It may be that past generations have something to tell us on this subject. Then, if we look at past history, what we see is a world in chaos: great and powerful empires which have disappeared; cultures which once expressed the full extent and scope of the mind of man; religions which were once a source of faith and a mainspring of energy for millions of men. We see Christianity, and within Christianity that strange phenomenon, Catholicism. What effect is it going to have today on what we will suppose is an impartial mind?

It is old—but age is no longer counted a shortcoming.

It includes the practice of confession—but in this post-Freudian, post-Oxford Group age of mental hygiene, confession is no longer automatically reckoned as something shameful and degrading.

It demands faith and self-commitment—but no life worthy of the name can do less. The freethinker's dogmas, however unconscious they may be, are not necessarily any less absolute or any better founded than religious dogmas.

The list might well be carried further. But perhaps we have said enough to indicate the general character of the situation, as far as we think we have understood it.

Under the three-fold influence of a changed human situation, of modern philosophical movements, and of the Catholic literary revival, Catholicism in Norway is in process of emerging from the isolation to which it has long been reduced. Official ostracism—except in regard to the Jesuits—came to an end more than a hundred years ago, and even the ban on the Jesuits has recently been lifted. Mental ostracism is gradually dwindling away. One sign of this is that it is not uncommon to hear people saying nowadays, "Supposing some day I had to join a religion, I should become a Catholic." We must not exaggerate the significance of such a statement. But at least it indicates that even in Norway Catholicism is becoming one possibility among others; a possibility which can be taken seriously.

AMERICA

Philip Scharper

No man, remarked Saint Ignatius Loyola, is a good judge of his own case; it is even more true, perhaps, that no man is a good judge of the Church in his own country. He may be too close to some features, too removed from others; too sympathetic toward some movements, too indifferent to others, to give a clear and accurate portrait. The best he can hope for is a montage, an arrangement of images and impressions which may at least suggest to the reader that fuller reality which the author cannot capture.

If one may attempt an initial metaphor descriptive of the Catholic Church in the United States, it could well be that of a young giant, far from slumbering, but as yet only risen to one knee. If we were here concerned with the Church as theology sees her such a metaphor would be, of course, inadmissible, if not intolerable. But we are concerned in these pages with the Church as an historical fact—the Church in a given time and place. In this context, the metaphor of the giant risen to one knee might be helpful both to suggest the present position of the Church—strong but off balance—and to intimate what its future position might well be.

The growth of the Church in the United States has been phenomenal. One hundred years ago there were approximately two million Catholics in a national population of thirty-one million. Today the Catholic population numbers thirty-five million in a national population of approximately one hundred and sixty million. Within this same century the number of priests has increased from 1,700 to 47,000; the number of churches from 2,000 to 20,000; the number of Catholic schools and colleges from 212 to 12,000.

Statistics such as these are informative, but much more important than the mere measurement of growth is an understanding of what caused the Church to grow so numerically strong in so short a time.

PHILIP SCHARPER was born in 1919 and studied at Georgetown and Fordham Universities. He has worked as Associate Editor of *Commonweal* and Assistant Professor of English at Fordham University, and has contributed to many American periodicals; he has also worked in radio and TV. He is now Editor for Sheed and Ward, Inc., New York.

The principal cause of growth was, of course, the tidal waves of immigration which broke over the United States for some seventy years, adding new citizens by the million to the State and making the Church within the single decade from 1847-57 numerically stronger than she could have become in a century of "natural" growth. In successive generations the Irish, the Germans, the Italians, the Poles, came to the new world and brought their old faith; it was the era of America the melting pot, and there were moments when the pot itself seemed about to melt. From the beginning, Nativists were strong in their opposition to "rum, Romanism and rebellion"—all three regarded as the peculiar penchant of the Irish. Convents were burned, priests were occasionally run out of town on a rail, and a former President of the United States, Millard Fillmore, just one hundred years ago, ran again for the same office on a platform of severe restrictions on immigration from Catholic countries and the legal establishment of secondary status for non-Anglo-Saxon, non-Protestant citizens.

This bit of the American Catholic past is important for an understanding of the American Catholic present and for the hint it gives of the American Catholic future.

The Shaping Hand of History

There is a tendency on the part of some American Catholics to feel apologetic for the fact that their ancestors in the Faith came over in cattle-boats and earned their bread in America by hewing wood, drawing water and laying railroad tracks as the young nation spread westward from the Mississippi to the Pacific. But the very fact that the immigrants found themselves resented and their Church suspect forced them to regard the Church as a sociological rallying point as well as a supernatural society. This identification of their cause with the cause of the Church was particularly true of the Irish, the most strategic of the Catholic immigrant blocs in determining the form which American Catholicism has taken. Thus, looking backward, we can note the strenuous efforts of the Irish and other national groups to demonstrate that they could become as "good Americans" as were those whose ancestors came over two centuries before on the *Mayflower* to Massachusetts or on the *Ark* to Maryland. Despite the many obstacles from without and within, the immigrants were rather quickly absorbed into a growing, vibrant America, and, through them, the Church itself was "naturalized", until today it is the dominant single religious body within American life.

Reinforcing the cohesiveness of Catholics as members of an immigrant, minority Church with a dominantly Protestant country was the fact that most of the immigrants had tended to settle in the larger cities. As a consequence, the Church in America has been, from that time onward, closely connected with both urban society and the working class.

This association of relatively dense pockets of Catholicism with the cause of labour has enabled the Church to possess a strength of influence and effectiveness of action far beyond what its numerical strength in the national population would indicate. Thus, Catholicism in America has long had strong support among the labouring class, and the Church itself has been one of the most powerful forces in the development of the now-powerful labour union movement. It is not by sheer coincidence that the last three presidents of the United States have appointed a Catholic to the Cabinet post of Secretary of Labour; further, this close identification of the Church with the cause of American Labour has gained for the Church considerable prestige and support among those who, though not themselves members of the working classes, have nevertheless been concerned with social reforms and expanded economic opportunities for all.

It is likewise significant that, if the Church in America has given leadership to the working classes, it has also received much of its leadership from these same classes in return. Archbishop Cushing of Boston, in addressing the national convention of a large labour union five years ago, said that there was not at that time within the American hierarchy a single bishop, archbishop or cardinal whose father had been either a college graduate or a product of what in America would pass as "the privileged classes". The close ties of the Church in America to the common man could hardly be more complete—a fact which has proved a tremendous asset to the Church, as we have seen above, and has also served to limit its effectiveness, as we shall see later.

The fact, then, that Catholicism in America has been so intimately connected with the legitimate aspirations of both the blue-collar and white-collar worker, has meant that the Church in America has not experienced what Pope Pius XI declared to be "the great tragedy of the nineteenth century—the loss of the labouring classes to the Church".

Again, I would feel that the urban character of the Church in America, centring, until the recent present, upon large city parishes, has made possible a vigorous sacramental life which is, perhaps, the feature of American Catholicism which almost immediately strikes the European observer. While one must be careful not to paint too rosy a picture, one must also point out that most American churches are quite crowded for Sunday Masses, have appreciably large congregations for daily Mass and are filled to overflowing for the distribution of ashes at the beginning of Lent.

There are, however, less fortunate aspects of this coloration of American Catholicism by its immigrant minority status. There is a certain belligerence to be observed even today on the part of many Catholics, in high places and low, whenever it is felt that non-Catholic groups may be in any way infringing upon the rights of Catholics. This belligerence is not an acceptable substitute for Christian charity, and is far less than an exemplification of our Lord's injunction to walk two miles with anyone who forces us to walk one. While neither edifying nor pleasant to behold, this behaviour can be understood, if not justified, when one realizes that it is a relic of the days when American Catholics were made to feel all too often that their Catholicism effectively barred them from high political office, the trust of their fellow citizens, or their acceptance into the social structure of the American society.

As the years pass, however, this all-too-common Catholic stance of the square jaw and clenched fist becomes anachronistic. After all, the peak decade of Catholic immigration was from 1900-10, and it is straining the relation of cause and effect to attribute all our shortcomings to a situation which existed half a century ago. One can only hope, at any rate, that we shall soon see the last, in the pages of Catholic diocesan newspapers, of headlines such as this: "Birth Controllers Tangle With Church—Get Worst of Fight." The image of Holy Mother Church standing sleeves rolled up, athwart a felled opponent is not an image calculated to increase the devotion of the Catholic nor to elicit either the admiration or the attraction of the non-Catholic.

Another unfortunate consequence of what we might call the dominant lower-middle-class mentality of American Catholicism can be observed in the measure of success too often applied by individual Catholics as well as by Catholic institutions. I do not regard America as a materialistic civilization in the authentic sense of that word, but

Americans unquestionably do pay excessive respect to the man who has "made good", and making good is usually associated in this country with making money. American Catholics are, regrettably, too similar to American non-Catholics. Thus there has long been the tendency to build churches, rectories and schools on a scale more elaborate than functional, and the successful parish has often come to be estimated by the rapidity with which it can pay off its mortgage.

Even more serious, the accolades paid by the Catholic Press and the honorary degrees, medals and citations awarded by Catholic colleges and Catholic societies, have too often been bestowed upon the Catholic movie star, sports luminary or egregiously successful (i.e., rich) business man.

Another unfortunate consequence of the minority status of American Catholicism as a whole, and the concomitant fact that it had, as it were, to fight its way upward to general recognition, has been a marked parochialism on the part of most American Catholics, both clerical and lay. Here again the Catholic Press is an accurate reflection of the American Catholic mind. Even within our present shrunken world, wherein the very question of the survival of the race is one that may be answered negatively on the morrow, most diocesan papers and national Catholic magazines read as though they were written thirty years ago. There is comparatively little concern with the pressing problems which confront the modern world: the affront posed to the Christian conscience by the fact that two-fifths of the world population faces hunger as a daily fact, the over-arching possibility of nuclear warfare, the problems of co-existence with an implacable enemy which threatens world conquest yet is beset by internal weaknesses and tensions.

While there are notable exceptions, most of the Catholic Press, judging by the space it gives to news accounts of these problems and its editorial comments upon them, tends to reduce refractory complexity to a manageable simplicity, and to project an inverted sense of values in its pages. One sees all too rarely intelligent comment upon, or even the full text of, important papal statements on the role of the United Nations, the morality of nuclear warfare or the Christian obligation to aid the underdeveloped countries struggling toward a condition of full humanity; more attention is paid to informal papal allocutions to a gathering of Italian motor-cyclists, or the fact that a group of pilgrims from a given diocese has journeyed from Lourdes to Rome to see the Holy Father.

In the absence of informed and responsible comment upon these major international questions as well as upon some of the more nettlesome domestic problems, the average Catholic forms his opinions upon the same sources as does his non-Catholic neighbour: the large-circulation news magazines such as *Time* and *Life*, and his local newspaper. As a consequence, on issue after issue, the attitude of Catholics is frequently un-Catholic, when not secularistic. It is ironic that the immigrant minority background of American Catholicism should have given it both tremendous cohesiveness and effectiveness in the directions which we have seen while, at the same time, it has also contributed to a covert secularization within the Church itself.

Catholic Education

The growth of a completely Catholic educational system from kindergarten to university and professional schools has been one of the great accomplishments of American Catholicism. We have already indicated that the development of the Catholic school system was due, in great part, to the fact that the public schools in the United States were in effect Protestant schools until some thirty years ago, since they were a faithful reflection of the Protestant ethos which dominated the country for over a century.

Catholic immigrants were anxious to have the benefits of education for their children, both because they had frequently been denied education in their homelands and because in America education was usually the key to improved social and economic status. The prelates and pastors of the immigrants early realized that the "Protestant" public schools were a possible danger to the faith of the immigrants; hence, at great financial sacrifice on the part of the laity and through great generosity on the part of teaching priests, sisters and brothers, they developed a Catholic school system which, in its comprehensiveness, is still almost unique.

Two major problems confront that school system today—one the problem of quantity, the other the problem of quality.

The first, the problem of quantity, can be simply stated. The Catholic schools have not in the past accommodated, and cannot in the near future accommodate, the great majority of Catholic students. At the present time, two-thirds of the Catholic children of primary school age and 40 per cent of those of secondary school age are in public schools, even though American Catholics have spent over two billion dollars on school construction in the last ten years.

The inability of the Catholic school, from kindergarten to college, to accommodate the number of students who desire admission, poses a severe problem for Catholic parents, who are faced, on the one hand, with the limited classroom space of the Catholic schools and, on the other, with a public school system which has become increasingly secularistic where the inculcation of moral and spiritual values is concerned.

There is, in addition to a shortage of classrooms, a shortage of teachers to occupy the ones which exist. Since the immigrants could hardly supply teachers from their ranks, most Catholic education, on every level, was conducted by priests and religious. Now, of course, the number of such teachers is utterly inadequate, and lay teachers are assuming more and more of the teaching burden, especially in the secondary schools and colleges.

But traditions are easy to form and hard to break. By and large lay teachers have, as yet, received but grudging acceptance in the primary schools, tolerance in the secondary schools and second-class status in the colleges and universities, wherein the lay faculty frequently out-numbers the religious by a ratio of six or seven to one.

The situation is slowly improving, but Catholic education will never reach its potential effectiveness until the lay teacher is given not only a voice in the classroom but a voice in the formulation of policy and full acceptance as an indispensable part of the Catholic educational mission.

The second problem confronting Catholic education, the problem of quality, is less easy to formulate but is no less significant than the problem of quantity.

The problem, briefly, is this: Has the Catholic Church in America made a cultural and intellectual contribution proportionate to its numbers and its consistent emphasis on education?

To this question, a number of eminent Catholic educators in recent years have given a resounding "No", and have thereby triggered off a debate within Catholic educational circles which is still going on.

I would side with those who, without denying the achievements of Catholic education or without belittling the immense sacrifices which have gone into it, would yet feel that it has failed significantly to affect the cultural and intellectual life of America.

Here again one must keep one eye on the present and one eye on the past. The Irish farmers, the German craftsmen, the Polish and Italian labourers, who were the dominant element in the Church from 1840 to 1910, were largely unlettered. Unlike the New England Puritans, they were not the product of universities and schools. Unlike the Jews from Central Europe, they did not bring the richness of a rabbinic tradition of learning and culture.

As a consequence, the Catholic schools established for them tended to have an educational orientation toward "getting ahead" and a religious orientation toward "keeping the Faith". There was, therefore, comparatively little regard for "knowledge viewed as its own end", in Cardinal Newman's phrase, and a tendency to regard religious instruction as the provision of "the Catholic's ready answer" to attacks upon or queries about one's faith.

It is not surprising, then, that one finds a great measure of anti-intellectualism among American Catholics, even among those who administer and teach in Catholic schools and colleges. It is indicative that in the two decades from 1920 to 1940 Catholic universities were better known for the prowess of their football teams than for their output of scholars or complement of great teachers, even though it usually cost more to maintain "first-class" teams than to maintain a first-class library.

This situation, too, is improving. The very fact that the severest critics of American Catholic education are American Catholic educators is a welcome sign of developing maturity. Much remains to be done, but at least a start is being made in the form of more realistic salaries for lay teachers, greater library appropriations, more professional training for members of religious communities and a developing interest in scholarly research and publication. Developments such as these give one grounds for restrained optimism that in subsequent generations the Church may be able to impart to America some portion of her ancient store of wisdom and knowledge, and to demonstrate again that she considers nothing that touches man to be alien to herself.

The Problem of Authority

The authoritarian structure of the Catholic Church has been a cause of annoyance and alarm to many American non-Catholics. In its political principles, best exemplified in the Declaration of Independence and the Constitution, America has been far more influenced by Protestant thought than by Catholic. The separation of Church and State declared in the First Amendment to the Constitution has been erected, in the thought of most contemporary non-Catholics, into a very high, very thick and unbreachable wall.

It was not, of course, ever thus. Up until the wave of Catholic immigration the Protestant ethos had reigned supreme even in those areas which were, theoretically at least, political and social. As we have seen, American Catholicism strained every effort to erect its own system of schools and colleges precisely because the public schools were, in effect, Protestant schools and Catholics felt, with good reason, that these tax-supported schools could offer a threat to the faith of Catholic pupils.

As Catholicism gained strength in America and as Catholics began to move up the economic and social ladder, American Protestantism made the wall of separation between Church and State higher and wider and attempted to seal off the various passageways which had previously been there. This was done in an effort to keep the Catholic population from receiving any benefits which its voting strength might have won for it in the hurly-burly of elections.

Since we cannot trace the historical development of this long-lived Catholic-Protestant tension, we can only say that at the present time the friction between Catholic and Protestant in the political arena, has become, if not worse, at least not appreciably better than it was one hundred years ago. It was, for example, little more than a century ago that Orestes Brownson declared in a public address that "the most prominent objection brought to the Church at the present moment . . . is that she is incompatible with our republican institution . . ."

That remains, even today, the principal objection of most non-Catholics to the Catholic Church. They fear that the authoritarian structure of the Church does not confine itself to teaching and direction in matters of faith or morals or, at least, tends to extend the realm of morals into the area of social custom or political decision.

Nor is this fear of what is usually called "Roman power" confined to the less educated and least informed of American non-Catholics. It is significant that the distinguished president of one of the oldest Protestant seminaries in America has, for years, publicly questioned whether Catholics should be entrusted with public office when they are by their religious commitments, "obliged to recognize a foreign power [the Vatican] as more binding upon them than their allegiance to the United States". It is equally significant, if considerably more surprising, to find an able young Protestant historian affirming in his current study *Religion and Democracy* that the confessional is the place wherein the Church exerts its political pressure, since it is in the confessional that the priest tells lay Catholics how they should vote!

In fairness to non-Catholic viewpoints such as these it must be pointed out that Catholics who have held rather high political office have frequently been touched by scandal. More importantly, when Catholics have formed the majority of the voting population of a given municipality or state, they have tended to vote less with political maturity than with misplaced religious loyalty. Most important is the absence of any clearly defined principle of the relation of the Church to the State which would fit precisely the rather unusual American political scene. The most knowledgeable non-Catholics are usually aware of the pioneering work of certain Catholic theologians both in America and abroad on the relationship of the Church to the modern State. But the less knowledgeable quite understandably continue to point to some unfortunate statements made by Catholic theologians and prelates several decades ago, which affirm that if Catholics ever did become a majority within the United States, while they would probably continue to extend religious tolerance to their fellow citizens in practice, in theory they could only regard the tolerance of non-Catholics as the toleration of error and heresy.

Perhaps one of the best ways to exemplify the non-Catholic fears regarding the authoritarian nature of the Church spilling over into politics is to consider reaction, past and present, to the possibility of having a Catholic elected to the Presidency. In 1928 Alfred Smith, the son of immigrant Irish parents, was the presidential nominee of the Democratic Party. He had been an honest, able Governor of New York State and was highly respected. During his campaign, however, there was a sudden and frightening upsurge of the old Nativist and naked prejudice against Catholics, pinpointed this time at Governor Smith. The American South has long been a Democratic stronghold, but the opposition to Smith, the Democratic candidate, came principally from the South. The attacks upon him were rooted in prejudice, which was in turn, of course, rooted in ignorance. It is not certain that Governor Smith's Catholicism was the primary factor in his overwhelming defeat at the polls, but it is certain that his Catholicism contributed in an appreciable measure to that defeat.

It is worth noting, too, that much of the support for Smith came from Catholics who, with a touch of pride that one of their own was running for the highest office that the country can give, would, perhaps, have voted for Governor Smith even had he been in the tradition of the scandal-touched Irish American political bosses who had been too much a part of large-city politics.

At the present time, there is much discussion in this country about the possibilities of Senator John F. Kennedy of Massachusetts receiving the Democratic Presidential nomination in 1960. It is interesting to notice the varied reaction to the possibilities of a Catholic again standing for the highest office which the country can offer. When opposition to Kennedy as a potential president is raised, it comes now far less from the relatively ignorant and uneducated. In fact, Senator Kennedy won surprisingly strong support from the South in his unsuccessful efforts to receive the Democratic vice-Presidential nomination in 1956. The major opposition to Kennedy now comes, significantly enough, from the liberal, intellectual non-Catholic. It was the liberal intellectual non-Catholic who in 1928 had thrown his support to Governor Smith; this support was, in some degree, attributable to the fact that Governor Smith was, precisely as a Catholic of immigrant parentage, an underdog, and had a very good record as a supporter of social and economic reform. These factors all served to make him, from the point of view of the educated liberal, an attractive candidate.

The situation now, however, mirrors a certain shift in American attitudes towards Catholicism. It is the liberal, intellectual non-Catholic who reacts to the stereotype pattern of Catholic authoritarianism, whereas earlier it was his southern opposite who reacted to the stereotype of the Irish Catholic as being not only Pope-ridden but also opposed to Prohibition.

An interesting sidelight is the fact that Senator Kennedy can hardly qualify as the type of Catholic candidate whom the non-Catholics profess to fear. How can one trust, they argue, a president whose family training and education have been along the rigidly authoritarian lines which are supposed to be the pattern of Catholic families and Catholic schools? Kennedy actually has no Catholic education in his background, having attended the public schools of an extremely exclusive suburb, Choate Preparatory School, an extremely exclusive and expensive non-denominational institution, and Harvard University, which long seemed to many Catholics around Boston the very hotbed of liberalism, secularism and amoralism.

One must note, too, that the attitude of many Catholics toward a prospective Catholic president has changed from the days of Governor Smith's campaign. While undoubtedly a number of Catholics would vote for Senator Kennedy primarily because he, too, was a Catholic, there is evidence to suggest that a number of other Catholics would actually fear the election of a Catholic president. They believe that anti-Catholic prejudice would enter into the campaign, that the present comparatively harmonious relations between Catholics and non-Catholics might be seriously disturbed, and that Catholicism would be blamed for every mistake which "President" Kennedy might make in the area of international and domestic affairs.

I do not pretend to know what solution can be found which will allay the fears of non-Catholics regarding this and similar contacts of Catholicism with American political realities. Although almost any non-Catholic will admit that there is no such thing as a Catholic vote, either in the general electorate or among the Catholic members of the Senate or the House of Representatives, and will further admit that Catholics have discharged their duties responsibly and well (with no evidence of receiving daily directives from Rome) as mayors of cities, governors of states, members of the Cabinet and justices of the Supreme Court, nevertheless they will still blink and balk at the thought that a Catholic president could discharge his duties without receiving directives, if not from the Pope, at least from his confessor.

Two possible solutions suggest themselves: first, that non-Catholic fears will be allayed only by Catholic performance as more and more Catholics in high office discharge their duties honourably and well, and, secondly, that Catholics should develop a little more political maturity than they show at present. There is, all too often, a failure on the part of American Catholics to realize that politics is the art of the possible, not the pursuit of the ideal. Catholics must also be reminded of the long-standing Catholic distinction between sin and crime, and should not attempt to erect into law every major Catholic moral position. Great acrimony inevitably arises when non-Catholics either feel or know that it is the vote of Catholics which keeps upon the legislative rolls divorce laws which are stricter than the prevailing *mores* of the American community, or which keeps on the books, as in several states, legislation which prohibits the dissemination of birth-control information or devices, even though many major non-Catholic religious denominations have officially stated that birth control is not only morally acceptable, but is, in many cases, the exercise of virtue.

The other major religious groups in America stand in need of such political maturity as much as do the Catholics. Protestant opposition to legalized gambling and Jewish opposition to the laws prohibiting the operation of many businesses on Sunday are counterparts of the Catholic opposition to easier divorce legislation. More would be gained, perhaps, if the religious communities acted in the political arena in a non-political fashion, i.e., without sacrificing their principles and without remaining silent, nevertheless turning their attention to the common good of the political community, of which harmony among differing religions is an indispensable part, and leaving open to persuasion rather than to the polls the possibility of influencing citizens at large to their own moral positions.

American Catholic Culture

In view of the immigrant influences upon the American Catholic Church it is not surprising that the prevailing cultural tone of American Catholicism should be that of the lower middle class. There is hardly a current aspect of American Catholic life which does not show, either explicitly or by implication, the cultural and intellectual inhibitions which have marked the development of the Church in the United States. As we have seen in the case of education, so too in the closely related question of culture, the very factors which have been most influential in forming the American Catholic ethos have at once given to the Church in America a certain strength and passed on a certain weakness.

On the positive side, the fact that American Catholicism has assimilated within itself not only the central Catholic traditions but also the national traditions of the Irish, the Italians, the Germans and the Poles, has meant that American Catholicism has been unable quickly to accomplish that excessive identification of religious belief with the prevailing political, economic and social structure which characterizes so much of American Judaism and Protestantism. The history of the Church in the United States has in effect presented her with a number of square pegs and it has taken some effort to fit these pegs into round holes. Nevertheless, the fitting has partially been done, and just as American Protestantism and American

Judaism possess their own distinguishing marks, so too American Catholicism now bears upon it the impress of the American political and social experiment through which the Church in this country has passed.

Thus, we can note that for generations at least the Church in America has been less concerned with theology, philosophy and speculative thought in general than have been English, German or French Catholics. Again, it would seem that the necessities of proving to America at large that Catholics were truly devoted to the democratic ideals of the country and were capable of taking their places as patriotic and productive citizens has, to a degree, forced Catholics to take their eyes off certain aspects of their Catholic cultural and intellectual traditions.

Abstractly, one might almost have assumed that the pouring of the Catholic intellectual and cultural heritage into the American melting-pot would have served as a catalyst; instead, the Catholic intellectual and cultural heritage tended itself to dissolve partially and to become scarcely distinguishable from the intellectual and cultural mass. No matter how understandable this fact may have been in the days of Catholic immigration, it becomes less understandable and excusable in the present. It is disconcerting, for example, to realize that the scholars in America who are most zealously and fruitfully exploring the Catholic cultural heritage are, for the most part, non-Catholics. Despite the fact that so many American Catholics are first- or second-generation Italians, it is extremely difficult to find Italian taught in Catholic colleges, and therefore practically impossible to find Dante taught in the original. It is extremely difficult, as a matter of fact, to find serious attention paid to Dante on the campuses of Catholic colleges and universities. The people who are busy translating, commenting upon and teaching Dante are for the most part non-Catholics.

Just as an unawareness on the part of American Catholics of the extremely sophisticated tradition of Catholic jurisprudence has frequently sent them into the political arena with the clanking of armour but no weapons, so too, the ignorance of Catholics of their best intellectual and cultural traditions has kept them from contributing the richness of their past to the cultural pluralism of the American present.

An insensitivity to one's past usually means that one will be ignorant of his interests in the future; so, at any rate, it would seem to have worked out to a great degree with American Catholicism. Although Christian missionaries may be almost said to have discovered the Orient, and the Orient is becoming day by day more important in determining what the world of the next two decades and two centuries may be like, one finds that American Catholicism, by and large, scarcely considers the Orient as a subject for serious Catholic study. Secular universities have, for several generations, been conducting institutes in oriental studies, but there have been comparatively few Catholic students found in these studies, even among those religious orders which have been sending missionaries to the East. There is, perhaps, a touch of irony in the fact that American Catholic universities have inaugurated formal studies of the Orient only after a large segment of the East has fallen under Communist influence and has thereby been placed in an extremely precarious relation to the Church.

Similarly, one can find but comparatively few informed Catholics concerned with the problems posed by our increasingly technological society. Historically, Catholicism, more than any other major religious group, has been able to accommodate the advance of theoretic and applied science to its larger perspective, and indeed much of the advance of science has been accomplished by Catholic scientists. It might even be said, so far as the Catholic in America is concerned, that science is in his bones, but not on his brain.

Catholics in America have but lately become aware of the tremendous implications of unlimited technology for evil as well as for good, and cannot but ruefully reflect that if technology has grown with great drive but little direction, this fact must be attributed in great part to the relative absence of Catholics, who were quite content to avail themselves of its products but who remained unaware that they should also examine its premises and principles.

There has been, for example, no single and sustained effort on the part of American Catholic thought to develop a theology of work which would support the individual Catholic in his encounter with an increasingly technological society, nor any measurable effort made to evaluate technological advance with the ancient Catholic concept of the consecration of matter. Catholics have, therefore, tended to stand off in a haze of abstractions and rail against American technological society or to approach it eagerly to accept its benefits with open hands and closed, uncritical minds. It is regrettable to record that the best—almost the only—analyses of the American technological society have come from secular sociologists. No matter how defective Catholics may think these analyses they must at least recognize one fact: they exist, they are there to be read and pondered.

The Catholic Press

It is not, however, only within the area of formal scholarship that one senses the impoverishment brought about by the middle-class mentality of American Catholicism. This impoverishment, and consequent erosion of central Catholic tradition, can also be observed within the pages of the American Catholic Press. We have referred to the Catholic Press before, but it may be helpful to return to it in this new connection. It is a mark of the growing maturity of American Catholics that every criticism I shall raise has already been raised —within the pages of the Catholic Press.

What one notices is that the Catholic Press is slowly emerging from being an almost completely clerical monopoly. As a consequence, there is an ever steady improvement in such technical aspects as layout, typography, management of business details and advertising. As Catholic laymen assume a larger role within the Catholic Press, however, it becomes apparent that many of them are no better equipped than were their clerical predecessors to meet the ultimate demands made upon any Catholic publication: to present the truth in a manner befitting that truth. American Catholic ignorance of both the American and the Catholic past means that very often large segments of the Catholic Press present given political or social positions as either American or Catholic when, in fact, they are neither. There is also a tendency to use truth as a bludgeon with which to reduce one's opponent to silence rather than to view truth as an unmerited gift from God which one offers to others to be shared or at least considered.

There is also observable a tendency, fortunately diminishing but still characteristic of much of the Catholic Press, to demean if not to distort the splendour of the Church by vulgarity of style in content and commercialism of tone in advertising. Both of these qualities are, of course, to be readily observed in American life in general, but it is cause for regret that Catholics, in this area, have not been able to transcend their cultural environment.

The present, however, gives every reason to hope that the future will be immeasurably brighter than the past. The post-war years have seen come into existence a quarterly, *Cross-Currents*, devoted "to exploring the implications of Christianity for our times" by making available relevant articles by front-line thinkers both in the United States and abroad; *The Review of Politics*, two literary journals, *Renascence*, a quarterly, and *The Critic*, a bi-monthly; *Theology Digest*, *Philosophy Today*, *The Natural Law Review*, *Jubilee*, a high-level, heavily pictorial monthly, and a score of other magazines dedicated to some specific need of the American Catholic community.

The editors of these journals would be the first to admit that the level of performance is sometimes less than spectacular, and each commands a readership far smaller than one would hope for in a Catholic population of thirty-five million; nevertheless, the very existence of such magazines would have been impossible twenty years ago, and the fact that they grow stronger and better by the year is evidence of the slow but unmistakable cultural advance which American Catholicism is making.

Towards the Future

There are many other indications, too, that the Church in America is moving toward a greater inwardness and spiritual maturity. The Cana Movement, the Lay Retreat Movement, the Liturgical Movement, the Lay Missionary Movement, the renewed vigour of contemplative communities, the establishment of more and more sodalities for men and women in the professions—are all indicative that the Church is growing in its interior history as well as in its external circumstances.

And it is, of course, precisely this kind of interior growth which will determine the future role of the Church in America.

Defensive attitudes, parochialism and a concentration upon bricks and mortar were among the characteristics of the American Catholic past and were very understandable—in the past. Today they are irrelevant luxuries. America today accepts the Catholic Church for the same reason that Margaret Fuller accepted the universe.

But America, with its tradition of religious pluralism, offers the Church much more than a mere guarantee of legal survival or social acceptance. It offers the chance for the Church in America to be true to her own best traditions, to bring the force of an authentic Catholicism to bear upon the restless movement of American thought and action.

By this I do not mean that America is "ripe for conversion", nor is it likely that, if it were, the present image of the Church in America would be sufficiently compelling to effect that conversion. But the increasing interiority of American Catholicism and the religious leanings of the American people (90 per cent of whom profess to believe in God) give assurance that the Church can continue to grow in strength and that its future will not be unworthy of the burdens and the labours of the past.

LEBANON

Majid Fakhry

Lebanon's association with Christianity is as old as Christianity itself. With the exception of the Holy Land and Egypt, Christ never set foot, during his earthly career, on any other soil save the Lebanese, to which the Evangelist refers obliquely as the "coasts of Tyre and Sidon" (*fines Tyri et Sidonis*), where the Syro-phoenician woman wrested, by dint of sheer faith, Christ's miraculous mercy and compassion. Following our Lord's death, the Apostles, especially Peter and Paul, journeyed regularly through Tyre and Sidon, either on their way northward to Antioch or when, sea-bound, they made for Greece and Rome. Today, centuries after, this close association has not ceased; so that Lebanon continues to bear witness to the graces it was destined to receive. For the Good News which the Apostles preached along these coasts continues to bear fruit, long after it has receded by degrees to the periphery of the Asiatic mainland.

It is not my aim here to recount the story of the rise, growth and gradual eclipse of Christianity in this part of the world. But it is of positive significance that today the only country on this side of the Mediterranean, with a distinct Christian character and a sizeable Christian section of the population, is this tiny little state of Lebanon, whose population does not exceed one million and a half and whose area does not exceed 2,513,000 acres. Apart from a few "islands" of Christianity scattered throughout the length and breadth of the Near East, Lebanon is the only country in almost the whole of Asia, with a comparatively large proportion of Christians. It might help to appreciate the significance of this fact, if we cast a glance at the religious distribution of the population, both Christian and non-Christian, as given in the table overleaf.

MAJID FAKHRY was born in 1923 in a village near Sidon; was educated at the American University of Beirut, and Edinburgh University. From 1949 to 1954 he was Lecturer at the School of Oriental Studies in London, and he is now teaching philosophy at the American University. His publications include *Aristotle* and *Islamic Occasionalism and its Critique by Averroes and Aquinas*. He is married, with two sons.

CHRISTIANS	
Maronites	424,000
Greek Catholics	91,000
Greek Orthodox	149,000
Protestants	14,000
Latins	4,000
Armenian Catholics	15,000
Armenian Orthodox	64,000
Chaldeans	1,000
Syrian Catholics	6,000
Syrian Orthodox	5,000
NON-CHRISTIANS	
Sunni Muslims	286,000
Shii Muslims	250,000
Druze	88,000
Jews	7,000
Others	7,000

From this table, it will appear at once that the country is almost evenly divided into Christians and Muslims and that of these, 540,000 consist of Catholics of various rites; Syriac, Greek, Maronite, Armenian and Latin. This distribution will highlight the complexity of the religious situation in Lebanon and the problems which face Catholicism in this country, which forms a real mosaic of religious creeds.

To begin with, Catholicism in Lebanon faces a unique problem, which has hardly a parallel elsewhere: the fact that, not only must it co-exist with alien faiths which are essentially militant and which draw their main strength from their sense of solidarity with the vast world of Islam without; nor even that it must achieve a *modus vivendi* with schismatic forms of Christianity—a problem which is not without parallel in Europe and America; but rather that it must in addition achieve unity and coherence within. This particular aspect of the problem may be briefly described as the multiple-rite problem.

Now it must be owned that, as some European writers have observed, the spectacle of Eastern-rite Christianity in general and Catholicism in particular is not without its charm. These writers dwell on the picturesque and colourful character of Eastern rites, especially for the Western spectator, accustomed as he is to the more familiar and prosaic spectacle of the one Latin rite. However, this sightseer's standpoint is rather superficial and "armchair"; it does not take into account the concrete issues which this multiplicity of rites raises in this part of the world, which has always stood on the borderline between the Semitic and non-Semitic worlds and has imbibed something from both the Semitic and European cultures. Of the rites mentioned above, three at least are basically oriental, the Maronite, Syriac and Armenian; even the Greek (or Byzantine) should be included in this category. In the case of the first and second rites, the liturgical language is a combination of Arabic and Syriac (a sister language of Arabic and Hebrew); in the case of the third it is Armenian, which is non-Semitic. However, in all three cases, as well as the Greek, the décor, so to speak, as well as the spirit in which devotion is expressed, is essentially oriental: a greater preoccupation with the outward signs of worship, a more concrete sense of the reality of spiritual symbols and attitudes, a greater obliviousness of time and circumstance, with the result that the ordinary as well as the nuptial and funerary services tend to be much lengthier and sometimes more pompous than in Europe.

It should not be inferred from my insistence on the multiplicity of Catholic rites and the cultural diversity underlying them that the unity and purity of the Catholic faith are on that account impaired. The unity of these diverse oriental-rite Churches is safeguarded through their allegiance to the Holy See and their zealous adherence to Catholic doctrine. Most Eastern-rite Catholic Churches, it is true, were originally dissident or heretical, but were reunited to Rome after 1095, the date of the First Crusade. The chief Catholic Church in Lebanon, the Maronite, accused of monothelitism in the past, was never, according to its followers, separated from Rome.

As a result of the process of reunion there arises in Lebanon and the Near East generally the curious phenomenon of an almost equal number of "uniate" as well as "separate" Churches. Thus we have the following list of parallel Churches:

The Chaldean Catholic	Oriental Chaldean (or Nestorian)
The Syrian Catholic	Syrian Orthodox (or Jacobite)
The Coptic Catholic	Coptic Orthodox
The Armenian Catholic	Armenian Orthodox (Gregorian)
The Maronite	No counterpart
The Greek Catholic	Greek Orthodox (or Melchite)
The Latin (or Roman)	No counterpart

Despite the multiplicity of rites, the purity and unity of Catholicism in the Near East is above question. As hinted earlier, this multiplicity reflects the multiplicity of cultural backgrounds. Catholicism is not a cultural phenomenon; and consequently can naturally encompass and assume any cultural manifestations, however diverse. Nevertheless as far as the problem of human relationships is concerned, in a country where religion plays a decisive role in the economic, social and political life of the people, heterogeneity will not make for overall unity. The truth is that every religious minority in Lebanon (i.e., every communion or rite) constitutes an almost closed and self-contained social and political unit. Members of the same communion will elect their own representatives to Parliament, will tend to concentrate on the same trades and professions, avoid exogamous or mixed marriages, etc.

Especially significant in this respect is the principle of religious (or confessional) representation upon which the Lebanese Constitution rests. Both in the election of deputies and the distribution of office at the ministerial and administrative levels, the proportional representation of the various religious minorities (or communions) is complied with. Thus the President of the Republic must by convention be a Maronite, the Speaker of the House of Parliament a Shiite Muslim, and the Prime Minister a Sunnite Muslim. The other Cabinet posts are distributed among the candidates representing the various communions more or less indifferently, except for the portfolios of Foreign Affairs and Education, which usually go to the Maronites also.

Despite the obvious defects of this system, it must be admitted that it has worked reasonably well hitherto, both during the French Mandate (1919-1943) and the period of independence (since 1943). However, the recent events in Lebanon have highlighted the defects inherent in this system, as well as the stress and strain to which the whole fabric of the Lebanese state is on that account subject. For one thing, the pre-eminence of the Maronite section of the population in public life in particular, and the Christian section in general, have been challenged. The Muslims have repeatedly agitated for a census, which has not come off, possibly owing to the Christian minorities' fear that they might be outnumbered, and accordingly lose the position of privilege which they have enjoyed heretofore. For another, the status of Lebanon, as well as its territorial integrity, has been challenged also by Muslims, and various Muslim spokesmen have called for secession.

I do not wish, in this brief survey of Catholicism in Lebanon, to devote to political questions more space than is fitting. But in a country which lies at the periphery of an essentially theocratic area, politics must assume a far greater importance than elsewhere, owing to the gravity of the issues at stake, which are no less than those of survival and self-vindication. Christianity in general, and Catholicism in particular, have secured this rather precarious foothold on this periphery, by dint of zealous adherence to their distinctive beliefs and institutions and the desire to achieve an independent and autonomous status. In this endeavour, Christianity in Lebanon has been assisted by various factors: religious, political, economic. The main religious factor is the existence in this country of other religious minorities (such as the Druzes and the Shiites) who are equally jealous of their autonomy *vis-à-vis* the preponderant majority of Sunnite Muslims. The political factors have been more complex. During Ottoman rule (1517-1919) the Christian subjects of the Sultan, especially towards the end of the last century, began to come to an awareness of themselves and their civil and political rights; and this awareness was sharpened by the memory of centuries of subjection and repression, at the hands of the Ottomans. What is more, the Western Powers, especially France, Britain and Russia, began long before this time to take an active interest in the lot of the Christian subjects of the Sultan, not always out of a disinterested motive.

It will not be amiss to give a brief sketch of the stages through which Western intervention on behalf of the Christian subjects of the Ottoman Sultan passed. The first Christian monarch to treat with the Ottoman Sultan and to secure for his country a privileged position in the Ottoman Empire was Francis I, who concluded a military alliance with Suleiman the Magnificent designed to foil the encirclement of France by Britain, Spain and Holland. The paradox of it is that this alliance dealt the concept of the traditional unity of Christendom a serious blow, but prepared the ground for safeguarding the rights of the Christian subjects of the Sultan. For by the terms of this alliance, France obtained in 1535 certain extra-territorial privileges, known as "Capitulations". And although these privileges were originally restricted to the protection of French nationals and institutions, they were soon extended to Latin Christians, whether foreign or indigenous, and these privileges continued to be enjoyed by France for over three centuries and were embodied in the Treaty of Berlin of 1878.

However, France's patronage of Catholics inside the Ottoman Empire soon roused the jealousy of Russia. By the time of the Treaty of Kutchuk-Kainardji signed in 1774, following Russia's victory in the Russo-Turkish War of 1770-1774, the latter power was recognized as the champion of the Greek Orthodox subjects of the Sultan; and this recognition was destined to usher in a long period of rivalry among the Western Powers over the right of protecting the various Christian communities within the Empire; and in consequence the pretext to meddle in the affairs of the "Sick Man of Europe" whose demise everybody awaited with a mixture of covetousness, apprehension and concern.

Britain's entry into this religio-political arena was less dramatic than either France's or Russia's and was inspired by more mundane considerations: namely, the frustration of the latter two powers' designs on the Ottoman Empire and the prolongation of its existence as much as possible.

The hankering of the Western Powers after a privileged position in the Ottoman Empire reached such proportions in the course of the eighteenth century that it virtually became the key to its subsequent political history, and the decisive factor in determining its destiny. In Lebanon the outbreak of religious troubles, fanned by the Turks, between Druzes and Christians in 1860 gave France and England the opportunity to pit their strength against each other by championing the two rival factions, France championing the cause of the Maronites, Britain that of the Druzes. The end of these religious troubles was marked by the conclusion in 1861 and 1864 of two protocols, which laid the ground for the autonomy of Lebanon, which lasted until 1919, when Lebanon became a French Mandate.

Despite the unfortunate effects of this rivalry of the powers, it must be admitted that their intervention in the affairs of the Ottoman Empire brought the Christians certain advantages. For instance, in 1839 and 1856 two important documents were signed: the Hatti Sherif, which recognized the *civil* equality of Christians and Muslims, and the Hatti Hamayoun, which recognized their *political* equality. Nevertheless, these advantages were outweighed by certain consequences, which are of far-reaching significance for the problem of Christian-Muslim relationships in the Near East, even today. Not unnaturally, the Western protection of the Christian subjects of the Sultan made them appear suspect in the eyes of the overwhelming majority of their Muslim countrymen; and vestiges of this attitude linger to the present day in Muslim-Christian relations. Conversely, the position of "islands" of Christianity throughout the Near East has tended to generate an attitude which one must call a sense of inferiority, on the part of the Christians, in their relations with their Muslim compatriots. This attitude of course varies from country to country, and Lebanon is perhaps the Arab country in which it is least in evidence.

However, the relations of the Christians with the West and their ready acceptance of the Western way of life brought them, as well as their non-Christian compatriots, other advantages which are not of a purely political nature. The Arab Renaissance which started in the course of the last century, and the rise of nationalism which was one of its direct consequences, are without doubt the outcome of the impact of Western ideas on the Arab mind, a process in which the Christians in general, and the Catholics of Lebanon in particular, have played the role of intermediaries or dragomans. Most of the men of letters of the last century who are credited with reviving Arabic literature and the Arabic language, the Yazigis, the Boustanis, the Zaydans, etc., were Christians from Lebanon. Even the early champions of Arab nationalism, like its classical historian (George Antonius), have mostly been Christians.

These of course are individual cases, whose influence in many instances was isolated or incidental. They are, however, reflected on the nation-wide scale in the role that Lebanon has played and continues to play as a bridge between the West and the Arab World. There are in Beirut alone innumerable French, British and American colleges and high-schools, in addition to two foreign universities: L'Université Saint Joseph (founded in 1875) and the American University (founded in 1866). The former is a Jesuit institution, with a Latin curriculum, in which the medium of instruction is French, and whose professional as well as liberal schools are subsidized by the French Government. The latter is an American institution with an entirely secular programme and outlook, which has acted as a melting-pot for ideas and outlooks of the most diverse types and in this way has contributed greatly to the development of a liberal and progressive attitude in the Near East.

It would be idle to dwell on the far-reaching importance of these two institutions, as well as the other remaining missionary schools, in bringing about a real cultural revival not only in Lebanon, but in the Arab Near East as a whole. The French missionary schools have of course been the chief media for the diffusion of Catholic influence throughout the country. Not only Catholics, but many Muslim and Greek Orthodox children have received their education in these institutions. And although they have not achieved what one may call a movement of "mass conversion", they have certainly helped in disseminating the Catholic outlook among non-Catholics and non-Christians. In this way they have rendered Lebanon an invaluable service, by bridging the gap between Christians and Muslims, Catholics and non-Catholics, and have made a *modus vivendi* (which is part of Lebanon's very *raison d'être*) possible. The recent events, although they underline the basic religious tensions at work in that country, have nevertheless demonstrated the existence of a deep-seated spirit of tolerance and moderation, on the part of the various religious groups of the country, and their willingness to continue to live together as partners in a common enterprise.

The Outlook for the Future

We have already alluded to the role Catholics and Catholic institutions have played in the Arab national and cultural revival. It is impossible to grasp the significance of Arab nationalism, one of the most potent political and cultural forces in the Near East today, without reference to this role. However, a line must be drawn between the formative and subsequent stages in the development of this national movement: the stage of preparation or incubation and that of fulfilment. At the former stage, the common national aspirations of Christians and Muslims (i.e., independence from foreign rule) tended to obliterate the religious and cultural differences between them. Today the Arab world is entering upon the second stage, when the basic differences between the two religious groups cannot be concealed or slurred over much longer. In consequence, the position of Christians in general and Catholics in particular is coming up for radical reappraisal. For the very quality which has enabled them to contribute to the Arab cultural and national revival (i.e., their Western outlook and sympathies) is no longer deemed a virtue, but rather a vice, in the present anti-Western climate of opinion in the Near East. Were this anti-Western climate the result of a passing mood or whim the position would cause much less anxiety; but unfortunately it is not. At the root of the anti-Western attitude lies a deep-seated anti-Christian attitude of greater intensity, which will make the normalization of West-Arab relations more than just a political issue. Already some Muslim leaders and pamphleteers are speaking of the turning of the tide in the East-West relations and are looking back nostalgically to Saladin's time, which marked the first serious reversal of the process of crusading penetration into the Near East. The present Russian-Arab *rapprochment* may be partly interpreted as a reaction to the West, which, unlike the East, is at least not avowedly anti-Christian.

In such an atmosphere, Catholicism must take stock of its position in the Near East and its divinely-ordained destiny and vocation. In this respect, it must avoid involving itself in the political conflicts of the times, and, in particular, identifying itself with one camp or one culture (i.e., the Western), however prone it may be to do so. Otherwise it will lose the character of universality which is its most distinctive mark, and will avow itself to be no more than a human movement or institution. Here the Eastern-rite forms of Catholicism have a particularly important role to play, in view of the roots they have taken in Near Eastern soil over the ages. Conversely, it must not stand aloof in the midst of the currents of loyalty and opinion. No matter what its problems and prospects may be, Catholicism has one primary vocation, especially valuable here today: it must dedicate itself to the cause of serving and declaring the truth, without fear or disaffection. In this way, it can render Islam, as well as dissident forms of Christianity, a major service, by rousing them to an awareness of this lofty ideal. It is no accident that some of the greatest scholars, who have made a positive contribution to Islamic and Arabic scholarship, have been and continue to be Catholics: H. Lammens, L. Shaikho, L. Gardet, Massignon, Anawati and others. Catholics in Lebanon and the Near East generally have therefore a clear and inescapable historic vocation: they must stand together as witnesses to the truth in all humility and love, if they are to be worthy of their Church and their forebears. The worst sin to which they can succumb here is intellectual pride or self-complacency.

All this, of course, will call for a great deal of soul-searching and rethinking, on the part of Near-Eastern Catholics. Gone are the times when they could simply turn to the Christian Powers of Europe for protection. For one thing, Christianity plays a decreasing role in determining the policies of Western Powers today; and for another, it is no longer possible for Catholics to ignore the national susceptibilities of their countrymen. Should this mean a relegation of Christians to the background politically and socially, the loss of privilege and even outright persecution at the hands of non-Catholic or non-Christian leaders and mobs, the Christians of the Near East must continually remind themselves of the supreme example of their Lord and the path which the early Church, especially in these parts, had to tread. And if they cannot live up to the challenge they will simply have proved that their faith has been tested and found wanting.

THE LELE OF THE CONGO

Mary Douglas

An anthropologist probably tends to seem unsympathetic to the missions. It is not that he is likely to idealize tribal life, or seriously to believe that it would be better left unchanged. "They are happy. They have no wants!" a traveller remarked complacently to me, as we watched some naked children romping in the sun. But the anthropologist knows as well as anyone the cramped confines of their old life, the suspicions and fears that worried those who lived it, as well as the real hardship of work and want in primitive conditions. He can recognize the sense of freedom, and sudden exhilarating expansion of ideas and needs, which the advent of Europeans has produced.

But his task of understanding how the tribal system works is immensely complicated by the impact of European culture. The adoption of anything so radical as Christianity turns the old institutions upside-down. The anthropologist is, therefore, apt to sound coolly dispassionate, even over-critical, when he writes about Christianity in the tribe he is trying to study.

Furthermore, it is always difficult, and even presumptuous, for an outsider to write of what Christianity means in another community. If the language and ways of thought are foreign to him, he is bound to misunderstand much. For example, the whole process of conversion, an intensely personal experience, must remain a gap in his knowledge. All that he can observe is the effect on the people's behaviour, and the new forms of social life which grow up.

Much of what I say here about Christianity among the Lele has already been reported in other parts of Africa, particularly of the crumbling of old institutions, and the tenacity of beliefs in sorcery. Yet no two cases are exactly alike, and it is not necessary to say that

MARY DOUGLAS was born in 1921, did her training as a social anthropologist at Oxford, and is now a lecturer in the Department of Social Anthropology at University College, London. Her fieldwork was carried out on a research Fellowship of the International African Institute, in the Belgian Congo in 1949-50 and in 1953. She is married and has three children.

what may be true of the Lele may not hold good elsewhere in Africa, or even in other parts of the Congo.

The Change in Scale

The Lele are a small tribe, living about 5 degrees south of the Equator, in the Kasai district of the Belgian Congo. Their favourite occupation and sport is hunting. Because of the dense undergrowth, their best chance of success is by the communal hunt, in which twenty or more men, with dogs, surround a section of the forest and beat the game out into the open. The hunt is a central feature of their culture. With warfare, it was one of the two most glorified male occupations. Many of their religious ideas and rites are based on hunting. Probably more than any other single factor, the communal hunt determines the size of their villages, for a village of about fifty huts can generally produce enough men for a hunting team.

For their subsistence they grow maize in forest clearings, and cultivate raffia palms. The latter yield their alcoholic drink, wood and thatch for housing, staple for woven raffia-cloth; in short, nearly all their daily necessities. Many of the tensions between Christians and pagans arise from competing demands for palm-wine, for labour in hut-building, and for meat.

The Lele came under European influence relatively late, for effective administration was only established in 1935, and it was at the same time that the *Mission des oblats de Marie Immaculée* began to make progress in its work of conversion.

For the Christian, the first great difference from the old life is a radical change of scale. Their whole tribe is less than thirty thousand strong. A little cluster of three or four villages, about eight hundred souls in all, would have been allied together against others, and this would form the largest political unit they knew. Any strangers entering Lele country risked being killed or enslaved. To this day, men of other tribes are chary of walking alone at night near Lele villages, and even Lele men are nervous if they find themselves without protection in unfamiliar Lele territory. Each village was at enmity with others. A man did not walk unarmed to his fields, nor did women and children go unescorted from one village to another. Raids and abductions were part of the regular political relations between villages.

Christianity has not come to them as an isolated influence, but as part of European culture. It has come, together with lorries, bicycles, taxation, wages, tribunals, fines, prison, clothes and cigarettes. Europeanization has also brought in its train an influx of foreign tribesmen, Luba, Mbala, Pende and Chokwe, who work for Europeans, and who travel the length and breadth of the country, exciting the envy of the Lele by their command of novel skills. A sign of the sudden bursting of the old tribal confines is the linguistic effort the younger Lele are willing to make. Very few foreigners learn Lele language. Hence, for those who need outside contacts, the three officially recognized languages must be learnt. They speak ci-Kongo to the missionaries, ci-Luba to the Administration, and li-Ngala to the staff of the oil company, and any one of these in conversing with other tribes. The old narrow Lele community has dissolved away into a vast new horizon, in which Christians feel more at home than pagans. Christians go regularly at Christmas, Easter, August 15th and December 8th, to the Mission, meet each other, renew old contacts, and disperse again with a sense of having participated in European culture much more intimately than their pagan friends can hope to do.

Age-Structure

After the change in scale, the second striking feature of the new Lele Christian community is that nearly everyone in it is young. There are few Christians over thirty-five, and few pagans under twenty-five. This is partly because the mission only became effective twenty years ago, and partly because the policy was to concentrate on the rising generation. One effect of this has been to emancipate the whole younger generation from the control of their seniors, with all the dislocation of authority that can be imagined as likely to follow.

The Lele have always recognized antagonisms between the generations. Old men were jealous of encroachments on their authority. They used to monopolize wives and wealth; they excluded young men from cults; they obliged them to postpone the age of marriage, and the young men resented their disabilities.

The whole society was organized on a basis of rival age-sets. Boys of the same age banded together, built a bachelor hut to share together, pooled the food their mothers sent them, went raiding and hunting together. They even shared a wife in common, generally a girl abducted from another village. They would be recognized as an age-set, given a name, and expected to show solidarity together. One age-set would be open to receive new members for about fifteen years, then it would be closed, and the next group of young boys would take a new name and form a new set with quarters in a different part of the village. There was always rivalry between the age-sets. They quarrelled about women and competed in warlike exploits.

The missionaries set out to abolish the age-set system, mainly because they could not allow Christian men to share one wife between several husbands. Moreover, the common wife of an age-set was frequently the cause of disputes and fighting. If polygamy of the old men, polyandry of the young men, and fighting between villages trying to abduct girls, are all eliminated from Lele society, the age-sets lose their *raison d'être*. This is one major disruption of their old society.

When the first Christians came back from the Mission they were treated as if they had formed a new age-set, dubbed the *Bakrito*. They lived together, and shared their food as age-mates always used to do. Every year newly-baptized men came to increase their ranks. Now there are more than fifteen years between the eldest and youngest Christians, but no new age-set will be formed. They realize that the old system of organization by age has ended.

Marriage

The sphere in which young men are most conscious of a new freedom is marriage. The Lele were polygamists, but as the ratio of the sexes was roughly equal, not every man could simultaneously have more than one wife. The shortage of wives was met by making the girls marry very young, at eleven or twelve, and making the men marry very late, at thirty-five to forty. Young men, who had no prospect of marrying for fifteen years or so, consoled themselves with the common wife of their age-set. Their only hope of gaining a wife of their own, and so of achieving full adult status, was by serving the interests of their seniors.

There were many tasks which needed youth, strength and agility for their performance, and young men had a strong incentive to give the older men the occasional help they needed, notably in repairing huts, and in giving a good share of the meat they killed, or the palm-wine they drew. The whole pattern of residence and co-operation was based on the fact that the young men wanted wives, and the old men had them. For the old men it was a kind of social insurance against old age. When they were past their physical prime, their claim to the services of the young men was based on control of wives.

The Mission, of course, introduced monogamy, and enforced it among their converts. They were also able to give protection to their flock, because their period of active proselytizing started when administration became effective. No longer could one village capture and enslave the members of another, nor vengeance be executed with an arrow or knife. Any baptized young man was allowed to marry any Christian girl whose consent he obtained. The Mission and Administration would protect them both, and ensure that the marriage was recognized by their parents. Inevitably, baptism was seen as a means of early marriage by the men, and by the girls as a means of escape from a polygamous marriage to older men to whom they had been betrothed from infancy. Needless to say, baptism held little appeal for elderly polygamists.

The missionaries sometimes complain of the lack of respect that young Christians show to the aged, and admonish them to honour their elders. Under the old system the old men were not likely to feel neglect or want, and young men had compelling motives for showing formal respect. The distribution of goods was based on a system in which those who were least capable of work had claims to a good share of the produce, because they were served by most women, and also controlled rights to marry. Now, after twenty years of Christianity, few old men have more than one wife, for the girls have been redistributed. The young men are already married, and have become fathers themselves. Old men tend to get nagging and querulous in their requests for help in repairing huts, for meat and palm-wine, but the young men are busy trying to earn money, and have little incentive to heed them. The safeguards for old age which were built into their tribal institutions have gone.

The dislocation of authority resulting from earlier marriage affects particularly the relation of the very young men with the very old. Formerly adjacent age-sets were in rivalry with each other, and alternate age-sets in alliance. That meant that men between twenty and thirty-five would be competing with the under-twenties, and with those between thirty-five and fifty, but they would be friendly with the over-fifties. The latter were the old men who would be helping them to obtain wives, and defending them in village councils. I have shown how the basis of that traditional alliance was removed when the Christians were enabled to marry at an early age. However, the traditional antagonism to the age-set immediately senior to themselves was not mitigated.

The men of thirty-five to fifty are pagans. Often they are the very men whom the young girls had refused to marry when they ran off to be baptized. Furthermore, they are the men most active in village affairs, and who have most to lose by the Christianization of the tribe. They have invested everything in a social system which was due to bring them rewards in middle-age, but now it is being replaced by a new system in which they will have no advantages. They feel too old to go to school to learn writing, or to gain technical skills such as carpentry. As men with responsible posts in the village, they can hardly consider two years' absence for religious instruction at the Mission. They have a stake in trying to make the old system work as long as possible. It is not surprising that for the Christians, in the twenty to thirty-five age-group, nothing of the old antagonism against the thirty-five to fifty age-group has been lessened. The tensions between them show particularly clearly in disputes about hunting.

The Hunt

According to the old beliefs of the Lele, hunting is not only a matter of speed and accuracy, but also of religion. Hunting is the touchstone of most of their metaphysical ideas. A man who has had success in hunting is happy, because it is agreed that he must be standing well with the whole spiritual world. Sorcery has no power over him, spirits in the forest bless him. His game-bag is proof of his spiritual condition. The same ideas are applied to the village as a whole. If the communal hunt is successful, they congratulate themselves on the good omen. It means that the members are united, there is no secret quarrelling, nor sorcery; the spirits and God favour the village.

Most communal hunts are prepared beforehand with special ritual, in which every member of the hunt is obliged to participate. The Christians, being young and active, good marksmen, and often equipped with guns, are expected to join the hunt, and indeed, they ask for nothing better. But they cannot take part in the preparatory rites, since this is regarded as a breach of the second Commandment. Usually, they only join the hunt after the rites, at its meet outside the village. If the hunt is a failure, their absence from the ritual is held responsible by the pagans, and recriminations follow. If it is successful, then the Christians look for a share of the game. But this is often denied to them, for Lele religion dedicates a large part of the kill to initiates of important cult groups. The most irksome of these rules is the one reserving all immature animals, and the breast portion of large animals, to initiates of one cult. Since the other parts of a large animal are always given to particular members of the hunt, or to village officials, very little is left for general distribution. The men who are excluded from cults may well get no meat at the end of a day's hunting.

The qualification for cult membership is marriage and the begetting of children. As most Christians were baptized before marriage, it follows that they are not initiates. They resent bitterly their exclusion from the feast which follows a hunt. In the odd instance of a man who has become a Christian late in life, say, after an illness and a dream, as occasionally happens, he will insist on his rights as an initiate. For the majority of Christians, the problem is insoluble. Some of them abandon the village hunt, and this is a great sacrifice, since hunting single-handed is not a skill at which Lele excel. Others follow the hunt, and quarrel endlessly over their share. The pagan initiates will claim that all the animals killed are young, and therefore to be reserved to the cult feast, and Christians will insist that they are fully grown, and should be divided among all the village. If it is known that they have eaten forbidden meat (and they always will if they get the chance) the pagans are very angry, threaten them with sorcery, or try to chase them out of the village. They are inflexible on this matter, not only because they resent the infringement of their privileges, but because they are afraid that the spirits will punish the village for the violation of sacred laws.

Once, when reproaches and abuse had failed, the pagans tried to crack the Mission whip at the converts, by reporting them falsely to the Mission priest for taking part in pagan cults! Often quarrelling is so bitter that the Christians have to leave the village and seek employment among the Europeans. Indeed, this widening of the social horizon to provide such avenues of escape is a blessing for the Christian in this period of transition.

Having experience, no doubt, of such problems, the Mission at one stage encouraged the Christians to form their own villages near, but distinct from, the pagan villages. This was the more readily adopted because the men of an age-set traditionally built together, and Christianity had come in as the prerogative of an age-group. If the Christian villages were large enough, they could organize their own hunts, and so avoid some bitterness. But in the adjoining pagan village, resentment was exacerbated, since they were deprived of the most active members of the hunting team. And, of course, for the whole younger generation to turn aside from their elders and live apart, would pose problems of conscience as grave for the pagans as for the Christians.

Life Crises

Total segregation of the Christian community is obviously undesirable. Even a policy of partial segregation could do little to buffer the young Christian from hard decisions. If we consider the main crises that can happen in the life of a man, we can see how lonely and painful the Christian life is likely to be. He is lucky if his pagan relatives only think him wrong; quite likely he will be thought a murderer, traitor, and blasphemer by those for whom he has every natural affection. The difficulties of the early Church are probably perennial in the mission field. No doubt St. John had these very situations in mind when he wrote: "Brethren, do not be surprised that the world should hate you." The Lele could take comfort from the Gospel's anticipation of their problems: "And you shall be hated by all men for my name's sake . . . For I came to set a man at variance with his father, and the daughter against her mother, and the daughter-in-law against her mother-in-law. And a man's enemies shall be they of his own household." (Matt. x. 22, 35.)

At marriage, for example, the Christian will automatically be embroiled with the man to whom his wife has been betrothed since her babyhood. The Mission will oblige him to pay some compensation for the gifts which the first betrothed has almost certainly made, but this will not reconcile the two men, or make it possible for them to be on speaking terms again. The girl's parents, pagans, accept him as their son-in-law with some misgiving. As soon as she conceives, they put pressure on him to perform fertility rites to ensure her safe delivery. In the convention of deep respect due to parents-in-law, it is extremely difficult for him to resist.

I knew a fairly typical case. A young man married a girl born in his own village. When she told her mother that she was pregnant, the mother informed the girl's uncles, who, under the clan system, had full authority over her, and responsibility for her wellbeing.

One morning, before dawn, the young husband was woken by three elderly visitors, his in-laws from the next village. They told him that as their niece was pregnant they needed his co-operation to perform the usual fertility rite for her. Respectfully, he refused, saying that he was a Christian, that, when the time came, he would take her to the Mission hospital, where the Sisters would deliver her, and that there was no need for Lele magic. They insisted very strongly, and tried to make co-operation easy for him, by saying that all he had to do was to hand over an iron arrow head, an iron needle, an iron razor, and two raffia cloths, and they would do the rest. As he steadfastly refused, they were very angry. They performed the rite without his help, and went off threatening that if any disaster overtook their niece, they would hold him responsible.

In due course, she went to the hospital, her mother accompanying her, and the Sisters looked after her. The midwifery section of the hospital has earned a particularly brilliant reputation for its work, but in this case, though the child was delivered alive, the mother died. Her own mother begged the Sisters for her baby grandchild, claiming that with Lele medicines she would make milk flow again in her own breasts, and so nurse it to strength. The Sisters, with much successful experience of bottle-feeding, tried to save the baby, but it, too, died. To the husband's personal tragedy of losing his wife and child, was added an accusation of double homicide. His in-laws, consulting their oracles, found his refusal to perform their rites the cause of both the deaths. They claimed compensation for two murders. In the old days, if the claim had been admitted, he would have had to hand over to them rights over two women of his clan, but this way of settling blood-debts is no longer allowed. At that time he had been building a large house for his family. Designed somewhat ostentatiously, its thatched framework overtopped all the houses in the village. He was a powerful wrestler, used to leading the village team, and a successful hunter. In other words, he had felt confident of his position among the young men of the village. Now everything was changed. No longer able to face the silence of his parents-in-law, he abandoned his unfinished house, and left the village to take up employment with the Europeans.

Natural disasters, of course, work either way, for Christians or pagans, according to the context in which they occur. A pagan girl, who has several successive miscarriages, will lose faith in Lele fertility ritual, and decide to run away to the Mission to be married to a Christian. In 1950 a terrible storm broke, in which lightning struck the Mission, and several girls, being catechized there, were hurt; some were killed. For many of those who survived, this reversed their decisions, and they came meekly back to their pagan husbands.

To give birth to twins is one of the greatest trials of faith. Lele religion surrounds twin births with rites, whose neglect is thought to bring disaster to the whole village. For the rest of their lives, twins, and the parents of twins, have to take ritual precautions to avoid endangering other people. Rites have to be performed when they enter any village for the first time. They are supposed to have a close affinity with spiritual beings. If twins are born to Christian parents, it will be hard for them to resist the pressure to submit to the rites. If the twin babies die, they will be thoroughly reviled for their refusal, and other deaths may be attributed to them.

BELIEFS

So much for the effects of Christianity on social life. How far are Christian doctrines compatible with their traditional religion?

The basic concepts of Christianity are much less alien to Lele culture than might at first be thought. They are not incapable of taking an interest in theological problems. I have heard lively discussions about the meaning of the Trinity and about original sin. According to their native religion, they believed in a God, *Njambi*, creator and regulator of the Universe. His name comes to their lips in a very easy, almost offhand way. He is invoked in curses, and oaths. *Njambi Pong*!—"God the Arranger" (regulator)—is the ejaculation of the man who thinks he is being cheated. *Ndi mot Njambi*, I am God's man, one might say to a persecutor, implying that God will look after his own, as an owner looks after his slaves. If one man is less gifted than another, it is because God made him so. None of their native ideas about God seems to be deeply incompatible with Christian teaching.

They also believe in nature spirits, through whom God usually intervenes in man's affairs. Moral faults and breaches of religious observance are thought to be punished by ill-health, barrenness, hunting failure, or any misfortune. Although the idea of punishment here and now may strike us as very different from the idea of punishment in a life to come, in practice the latter does not seem to require any difficult adjustment of ideas.

Their own traditional beliefs about individual existence after death are too ill-defined for there to be any conflict on the score of immortality of the soul. Original sin is not difficult, either, for them to understand. Their traditional culture has much to say about their inherent wickedness, though it is always said in connection with sorcery. They say: "We Lele are bad people. We kill each other off, with spite and envy. Look around you. Do you see many people? Do you see big villages? crowds of children? No! We are few today because we have all been killed off by sorcery." The idea that the rot started with the action of the first woman strikes them as an entirely comprehensible revelation. The doctrines of grace and redemption are therefore intelligible, and welcome, in the existing framework of their ideas about human badness.

In short, on major issues, Christian doctrine would seem to be easily acceptable, a completion, not a reversal of what they already held. Conflict comes only on the subject of sorcery. In their traditional thinking, God accounts for only a small part of human misfortunes. It is true that God, through his spirits, was thought to chastise his people with sickness and failure, but his punishments were always supposed to be mild. No one was likely to die as a result of God's anger. All serious misfortunes, and nearly all deaths, were attributed to sorcery. If it were not for sorcery, people would live out their full span of years.

The relation of God's power to sorcery was not difficult to define. Sorcery existed with God's permission. He allowed sorcery to be effective, and if he chose not to allow it in a particular case, it would not work. The spirits who mediate God to man can reveal secret techniques for combating sorcery, detecting it, preventing it, defeating it. Most of Lele ritual is taken up with anti-sorcery techniques, for fear of sorcery, and accusations of sorcery loom as large in everyday life as ideas about God and the spirits.

The Lele cults, in which esoteric knowledge is passed on, are based on initiation, with heavy payments of entrance fees, and special privileges reserved to members. Consistently with the other trends we have seen, three out of four cult groups exclude unmarried men, and the age of marriage used to be late. Most of the Christians are not cult members. They therefore have little difficulty in believing that the whole tangle of beliefs and behaviour concerning sorcery is an abysmal error. They laugh secretly at divinatory practices, and talk cynically about the political aspects of initiation, fee-paying and privilege. When they discuss the institutions of anti-sorcery, they seem to be thoroughly emancipated, and glad to be rid of a dead-weight of mumbo-jumbo.

You would often get a different impression if you asked a young Christian why someone died, or why his wife is barren. He might well reply by blaming sorcery. It is possible for him to slip from one attitude to the other, without perceiving the change, because their language is full of circumlocutions for sorcery, phrases which are so conventional and well-worn that they glide off the tongue, and do not in themselves seem to contradict the new attitude learnt at the Mission.

However, if you press the matter further, it soon appears that the Christian, in the context of personal affliction, has not completely rejected the notion of sorcery. He will often confide that old Lele men have powers which the Europeans underestimate, that Lele occult powers are very potent and dangerous, and that it is impossible not to believe in them. Incidentally, something of their strong faith seems to infect Europeans, for I have heard impressive accounts of the African's alleged magical powers from settlers and business men.

Their belief in sorcery is further supported by a linguistic confusion. They have a word, *nengu*, which has no exact translation for us, but to which I shall here refer as "magic". "Magic" is a rite, revealed by spirits, validated by God, which is efficacious in counteracting sorcery. Acts of sorcery are also "magic". Good "magic" is expected to have therapeutic effects. It generally includes a potion to be drunk, or injected, or a morsel to be eaten, as well as formulae to be recited. It only works if it is administered by a qualified person, that is, one who has received the power to use it, as well as the recipe, from another similarly empowered to hand it on. Each transfer of "magic" power must be accompanied by a payment, or it will not be efficacious.

There are no other healing remedies recognized in Lele language, except for *bilumbele*, which are merely some little-esteemed herbs used for minor ailments.

When the Europeans set up their clinic, and hospital, the effectiveness of their treatment became famous. The only Lele word which could at all adequately be used to refer to the novel powers of healing possessed by quinine, castor-oil, vermifuges and antibiotics, was "magic". The same word is applied to the petrol which feeds combustion engines, paraffin which fills pressure lamps, yeast which raises bread dough, D.D.T., lightning conductors, and so on. They are all classed as types of European "magic".

Now, since it is natural for the Christians to think of Europeans as possessing good "magic", it is consistent to think also of Lele possessing bad "magic". Hence, while they do reject part of their cultural tradition concerning sorcery, especially anti-sorcery ritual, the belief in the power of sorcery is still strong among Christians. In a sense, sorcery has become desacralized. It has been lifted out of its old context of religious belief and ritual. It is now classed as a power analagous to European powers, no whit less mysterious than the radio, telephone, photography, obstetrics, plastic surgery and the rest.

Belief in sorcery is erroneous, but, as it is now held by Christians, it does not seem to be a specifically pagan error. It is a case of mistaken reasoning about the causes of misfortune. It resembles the mistaken belief that sitting in draughts causes the common cold. It is even more like psychopathic delusions of persecution, or like anti-Semitic convictions, or the conviction that coloured peoples are inherently inferior. Since, like the two last-named beliefs, it provokes uncharitable thoughts, it is presumably un-Christian, though not specifically anti-Christian, to believe in sorcery in this way. Some Christians, believing in sorcery, and believing themselves to be victims of sorcery, regard it as one of the trials and crosses which, as Christians, they expect to face in life.

Sorcery beliefs certainly make for unhappiness. They tend to make adjustments between Christians and pagans more difficult. Every conflict, grudge, annoyance, is magnified by the fear of sorcery. To all the good reasons a man may already have for fearing and disliking his neighbour, there is the added fear of his occult powers. Pagans frequently threaten sorcery, though in the old days they would have been inhibited by the fear of being convicted as sorcerers, and dying under the poison ordeal. As all ordeals are punishable offences, and as accusations of sorcery cannot be made before tribunals, threats of sorcery are nowadays more freely made than before.

The adoption of "magic" for the marvels of European science was one of those spontaneous linguistic movements which no deliberate action can prevent. The survival of sorcery beliefs, after generations of Christianity in other parts of Africa, suggests that in the Lele case the linguistic point is only a minor factor in perpetuating these beliefs. Experience in Europe has shown that it is not full acceptance of Christianity which finally eradicates beliefs in witches, goblins, evil eye, black magic and the rest, but more complete scientific understanding. Teaching about the principles of transmission of disease, on the one hand, and about principles underlying European technical knowledge on the other, will eventually do much to help Lele to control belief in sorcery. These tasks are already well in hand at the Mission secondary school. But, until popular science has filtered down into the villages, to replace popular "magic", confused thinking on such a complex subject is inevitable.

Anti-sorcery rites are forbidden to the Christian, not, of course, on the grounds that the sacraments are more efficient than Lele ritual for dealing with this evil, but on the grounds that it is a non-existent evil. Lele keenly watch for occasions to convince Europeans of the reality of sorcery.

One village succeeded in getting its alleged sorcerer committed to prison in Luebo for homicide. A young European doctor had chanced to arrive on the scene soon after the death, found the victim indubitably dead, found the villagers all bearing witness that he had been poisoned, found the contents of a phial (which the accused admitted having administered) to be highly noxious. He reported the matter as a case of poisoning. However, "poisoning" is the usual Lele term for referring to a lethal act of sorcery. The rejoicing in the village when the sorcerer was convicted at the Tribunal was not only because a public menace had been removed, but because Lele beliefs were vindicated.

The missionaries perhaps do not fully realize how intently their own behaviour is watched for clues to resolve this conflict of beliefs. In fun, they sometimes claim to possess "magic" powers. I myself have had "magical" control of the weather attributed to me, and so I know the temptation not to disabuse the credulous. One priest told me that, for the sake of privacy while eating his dinner, he used to announce that he was one of those "who eat alone". Knowing that powerful sorcerers are supposed always to eat alone, and perhaps not knowing that their diet is thought to be human flesh, he laughed to see the onlookers scatter out of his sight in fright.

Christians have found that the priest, though he will not listen to accusations of sorcery against the living, is more sympathetic to accusations against the dead. Lele believe that a dead man can use sorcery against his enemies. A man may make it known that he has obtained "magic" which will infallibly kill anyone who kills him. When a death occurs soon after the burial of such a man, it is universally supposed to be his posthumous revenge on his own slayer. However, these dead sorcerers are sometimes thought to be too powerful, and if many deaths are laid to their door, the whole village may have to be moved to a new site, with ritual to sever them from the ghost. In one such case, the Christians explained their predicament to the priest, and he consented to say a Mass on the haunted site. The results were agreed by pagans and Christians alike to have been entirely effective, for the hauntings ceased. The Christians had the additional satisfaction of implicit acceptance by the priest of some of their own views on sorcery.

The Christian Community

I have said much about the disruption of social life that followed on Christianization, and something now should be said of the emerging Christian community. Naturally, this is centred on the Mission. Its native leaders are the mission-employed teachers, men who have built their huts and raised their families near the Mission. They have considerable prestige, partly because they have the ear of the priests, and therefore participate a little in white man's power, and partly because they enjoy a regular salary.

At the time of my visit, the Mission station was situated at Brabanta, in the far north of the region. Every boy undergoes two years' instruction at the Mission before baptism, but eventually they all go back to their own villages. The idea of the Christian community must, therefore, be concerned with local, relatively autonomous, units. In each village there is a catechist, appointed by the Mission. It was the practice not to appoint a local boy, because the conflict of loyalties was likely to be great, if he was exercising his duties among his own kin. Of necessity, he could be paid very little for his work, and he was expected to earn money by using the labour of the school children in his village, either for cultivating cash-crops for sale, or for doing jobs in the village for wages.

In any village, whatever his personality, the catechist seemed always to be in the centre of a field of tension. He was expected to represent the Mission, and to report un-Christian behaviour when the priest made his quarterly visit. An easy-going catechist might be popular in his village, but not highly esteemed by his employers. A stern catechist attracted innumerable complaints about his behaviour, accusations of adultery, theft, and even sorcery. Some, not surprisingly, found the situation of power too tempting, and exploited it by a kind of blackmail, making informal levies of palm-wine, or money, or even demanding sexual privileges as the price of a good report when the missionary arrived. Probably these difficulties are bound to occur so long as the person who has the allotted role of leader in a community is not himself a member of it.

I have said that the Christians' first impression was of entry into a wider community than ever before imagined. But on the tribal and inter-tribal scale, the sense of community is extremely diluted. Nothing of the tight solidarity, nor of the animosity, of the traditional Lele village, can be carried over to the new intertribal Christian communities, for these have been developed out of long association in narrow confines.

Even between Lele villages the sense of community is not noticeably strong among Christians, except in the case of men who had been together for their two years as catechumens. These years at the Mission are, inevitably, and always, a time of hardship. The boys are away from their families, on short rations, often hungry, in strange surroundings. Between those who have shared their food and slept together, a close friendship grows, on the model of the traditional Lele friendship between age-mates. However, as these friendships are generally between boys from the same village, they do little to break down social barriers.

It must be rare in Africa for contact with Christianity to be experienced without simultaneous contact with commercial culture. In the case of the Lele, commerce and conversion came together. The missions have actively encouraged them to adopt new attitudes, to work, to save for the future, to keep shops, take paid employment, and so on. They see economic progress and the commercialization of native life as a part of their civilizing mission. The priests are anxious for the Lele to be sufficiently advanced to be able to take over from the foreign tribesmen who are the mechanics, lorry drivers, carpenters and traders of the district. They would also like to shelter the Lele from contacts with these Christians of other tribes, since some of them, middle-aged, disillusioned, hostile to Europeans, are regarded as subversive elements. At present these foreigners are indispensable to the new Euro-African economy. Their presence poses several problems, of which the most serious is whether, in the next generation, Lele themselves can be expected to produce a Christian society which is different.

The wide scale of the new society, in itself, makes the development of community life more difficult. The possibility of evasion, of escape from one formless society into another, equally formless one, is always present. Formlessness is another way of writing chaos, and chaos tends to make for disappointment and unrest in any society.

It is inevitable that the old forms should go. Age organization was related to war between villages, wife-sharing and polygamy. Kinship organization was largely stimulated by the wish to take common action against sorcery. The village held together partly because it was at war with other villages, partly because its members co-operated in cult groups, now dwindling. What new forms are emerging?

At present, catechists and Mission teachers depend for their status on the support of European missionaries. Authority is not usually accorded spontaneously to outsiders. When the economy has been fully commercialized, the catechist may well find himself in rivalry with leaders whose influence derives from wealth, and whose authority in the local community is more firmly based than his own. This process has already begun. When it is complete, the Lele Christian community can be expected to show many features in common with its modern European counterpart. Whether the Missions should be pleased or disappointed with such a result of their work is hard to judge.

One thing emerges from this study. There can be no question of grafting the spirit of Christianity on to an old society, and expecting that, apart from the excision of a few incompatible institutions, the old culture will survive the operation. Lele culture, Christianized, would be quite unrecognizable, changed from top to bottom and in its most intimate recesses. Lele Christians have more in common with Luba, Pende and Chokwe Christians than with their own immediate forbears.

AUSTRALIA

Denys Jackson

The "Pilgrim Fathers" who founded the first British Colony in Australia were not refugees from religious persecution, like those of North America, but condemned felons who were, to a large extent, victims of a social order which was just entering into the industrial age. In Great Britain, the oligarchy of the wealthy—the great landlords and merchants—was firmly entrenched, in the last half of the eighteenth century, while the poor, both in town and country, were ground beneath the wheels of a system to which the concept of social and economic justice was completely alien. The subordination of politics and the law to property interests was taken for granted: the severity of the laws protecting ownership kept the gaols filled to overflowing—more than ever after the revolt of the American colonies had deprived Britain of the outlet afforded by the demand for forced labour on the southern plantations. The discovery of New South Wales, therefore, was seized upon as providing the opportunity of disposing of these undesirables in a cheap way. Not only poachers, petty thieves and other troublemakers, but "Village Hampdens" who made themselves a nuisance to the squires, could be sent to Botany Bay with every hope of never hearing of them again.

The first Catholics who arrived in the country were mingled with the general mass of outcasts. Transportation from Ireland began as early as 1791, but the first large flood came after the desperate revolt of 1798, provoked by the new hope of getting rid of the English and Protestant Ascendancy which the French Revolution had aroused. The Irish exiles were of a different type from the ordinary convicts: few were "criminals" in any but the political sense—all were in ardent revolt against an authority which stood for a tradition of hostile oppression against their race and religion. At the turn of the century, Irish Catholics formed about a third of the convict

---

DENYS JACKSON was born in 1899 and was educated at Westminster Abbey School and the Liverpool Institute. He served in the war of 1914-18 and was received into the Church in 1917; edited the *Tribune* (Melbourne, 1935) and worked on the staff of the *Advocate* (1934), and is a broadcaster and lecturer. He is married, with two sons and one daughter.

population, but their spiritual destitution was truly lamentable. The few priests among them—themselves convicts—were forbidden to exercise their ministry: they were forced to attend Protestant religious services under pain of savage punishment. As may be imagined, they were the most unrestful and rebellious of all the servile population, forever engaged in conspiracies, revolts and attempts to escape—their offences being answered by the sort of brutal reprisals we are accustomed to associate with the Soviet penal system of our own time.

The dawn of change came under the governorship of Colonel Lachlan MacQuarie (1810-26), the ablest of the early autocratic rulers of New South Wales. A prefect apostolic to "Botannibe" was appointed at Rome in the person of Father Jeremiah O'Flynn, and succeeded in landing at Sydney—but the Governor refused to allow him to say Mass publicly, and despite a joint petition of Catholics and Protestants, his deportation was ordered and carried out after a six-months' period of underground apostolate. He left the Blessed Sacrament behind, however, and his adventures aroused interest in England and Ireland, producing a newspaper campaign on the plight of the Catholics and convicts generally.

In the Bigge enquiry which ended MacQuarie's rule the Catholic question was considered and later Father John Therry arrived in Australia with an official appointment as Chaplain. In his attempts to provide for the spiritual needs of his people he soon found himself engaged in an uphill fight against a system of Protestant privilege which cribbed, cabined and confined all his activities. He was refused access to Catholic sick and orphans; his religious instruction manuals were submitted by the Governor to the Anglican authorities for their approval—and, of course, rejected. He succeeded, however, in preventing the State endowment of the Church of England—though at the cost of his dismissal as a Government chaplain, brought about as a result of Anglican complaints. The struggle of Father Therry is worth noticing, as the first phase of a fight which has continued in various forms, throughout the history of Australian Catholicism, against concepts which assume a special status in public life either for Anglicanism or Protestantism in general. The principle of State *secularity* has always been insisted upon by the Catholic minority as a guarantee against all forms of Protestant ascendancy.

Father Therry also struck another note which was to be a continuing one in Australian history—that of radical Catholic social action.

His apostolate had made him the champion of the rights of his convicts, and he was engaged constantly in battle against the abuses and brutalities of the penal system and the "assignment system" associated with it. He is a pioneer, too, in the struggle for freedom of education of these "forgotten people" and their children. Long before he died in Melbourne in 1864 the age of convictism was ended and the Australian Church had her own hierarchy and full freedom of worship, Bourke's "Church Act" having ended the question of Protestant privilege by placing Government support for each religious denomination on the basis of numbers.

The founder of the Australian Hierarchy, Bishop John Polding of Sydney, was no Irishman but an English Benedictine. He was, however, a mighty missioner who enjoyed the deep love and confidence of his Irish emancipist flock and their "Currency lads and lasses", and nobly supported his vicar-general—another great Englishman, Dr. Ullathorne—in the successful campaign which he waged to put an end to convictism once and for all. The Australian story of Ullathorne is far too little known—it is one of the great heroic episodes in the history of nineteenth-century Catholicism. This brave pioneer penetrated into the very depths of horror in Norfolk Island and Van Dieman's Land in order to rescue desperate and dehumanized men and women—and he did not mince his language in telling the world what he saw there, and in naming and denouncing the "Tory landholders" whose greed had created this hell on earth. If a true "Catholic national culture" ever emerges in Australia, Polding, Ullathorne and Bishop Willson of Hobart Town will surely be numbered among its heroes—and, perhaps, its patron saints. Incidentally, Dr. Willson's evidence, given to the Home Office and a House of Lords Committee, and the report furnished by him to the British Government, were decisive in their results, leading to the final abandonment of the penal establishment in Tasmania—whose very name was changed in order to expunge the dreadful associations of the past.

It will be seen that the Catholic radical tradition, which has been so strongly marked a feature of the history of the Faith in Australia, stems not only from the Irish revolt against Protestant-British ascendancy, but also from the social experiences of the immigrants in their new country. They were more powerful in numbers, proportionately, in the early nineteenth century than they are today: but, with a few notable exceptions like Attorney-General Roger Therry, they were numbered in the ranks of the poorest and most under-privileged, and were obliged to fight stoutly for their rights every step of the way, under the leadership of their clergy, against the organized power of wealth and sectarian privilege. The zeal for social action which is the mark of this Church arose from no abstract Christian humanitarianism, but from the presence of horrors and abuses backed by powerful authorities, and from the constant arising of new problems and emergencies, which had to be solved by gigantic personal efforts. The Catholic Press, like the other activities of the community, was begun by a group of laymen who started the bi-weekly *Australian Chronicle* in 1839, for the specific purpose of answering the ridicule and vituperation constantly poured upon Catholic things and persons in the existing Sydney newspapers.

The mark of these "men of might" of the last century, and of the valiant woman, Caroline Chisholm, who was in some ways greater than any of them, was that their reforming crusades were launched and carried on for a "common cause" transcending all distinctions of creed. Mrs. Chisholm dedicated herself to the rescue of the immigrant girl from destitution and worse evils, in the same spirit of universal love as had inspired the labours of Dr. Ullathorne and Dr. Willson for the convicts—it was their opponents, in both cases, who invoked sectarianism and the fear of "Popish" designs as a diversion to cover their defence of evil practices against reform.

Catholics, in fact, were among the most notable pioneers of the social planning and social welfare policies, which are the peculiar mark of modern Australian social life, translating their Christianity into the Australian philosophy of the "fair go". In particular, the remarkable Mrs. Chisholm worked out a complete theory of colonization on the basis of her own experience and vigorous Christian common sense. She urged the creation of a society of small-holders by family settlement. "Children," she said " . . . ought to take precedence over sheep." It was not a comfortable doctrine to the wealthy squatters, and the lady's ruthless interference in the question of the food and accommodation of individuals and families on shipboard during the long journey to the Antipodes was no less unwelcome to the shipowners. But her vision of an agrarian Australia has been revived in our own century by Catholic rural groups: and her place in the country's history is unique, as our first scientific social worker, and most constructive feminist. At a cost of less than £2,000, between 1850 and 1852, she sent to Australia a thousand families of the most stalwart pioneering stock—an achievement which the planners of our own day seem unlikely to match!

The famine era in Ireland and the discovery of gold in Australia brought a new tide of Catholic migration, in which the Irish element was again overwhelmingly predominant, displaying its same radical tendencies, fervent religious loyalty and reverence for priestly leadership. They were the natural allies of the "Chartists", the pioneers of the new democracy, and the ideas of this school of thought are reflected in the Catholic journals of the mid-century. The newcomers, however, were not condemned men driven to despair by an organized system of brutality but decent peasants and workers, leavened by men of the middle and professional classes, and by an influential handful of political exiles. It was men of this kind who headed the miners' fight for justice on the goldfields which culminuted in the Eureka revolt. The details of this conflict, which has become the basis of a Labour legend, do not concern us here. It is sufficient to notice that the attempt of the Communists to "interpret" the incident in terms of their own class struggle theories—initiated by Karl Marx himself—produces a grotesque caricature of the truth. Its leader, Patrick Lalor, was a Trinity College graduate belonging to a family which had formerly favoured O'Connell's fight for Repeal in Ireland: his own views were far from radical—he repudiated Chartism as well as Communism and Republicanism, and later played a decorous part as a politician in Victoria, dying as speaker of the State Assembly there. His expressed opposition to "a tyrannical press, a tyrannical people, or a tyrannical Government" is an utterance which might have been written by a modern Tory individualist denouncing mass-totalitarianism! It was, in fact, typical of the radical-conservatism of the Irish Australians, which had no touch of the Jacobin revolutionary spirit, but was strongly "democratic", in the sense of opposing social stratification on English lines. They insisted that popular institutions must be made an instrument for promoting social equality and economic justice, while their attitude to "British institutions" was marked neither by hatred nor by love—but by cool, objective criticism based on long experience of life on the under side of them.

In the fight of the 'sixties and 'seventies to "unlock the land", Catholics, naturally enough, were aligned on the side of those who fought against the squatters' privilege to secure a "place in the sun" for the ex-digger and the new immigrant. They played a leading part in forming the Land Reform League in the latter part of the gold decade—in particular, Wilson Gray and Charles Gavan Duffy, both of whom had played a part in Irish politics before their migration. The Chartist political programme was blended with the new programme of opposition to the great landholders, and some success was gained, though the pastoral interests remained predominant. It was in this period that most of the Catholic rural families of Victoria were established on the land. But the bulk of the new migration was absorbed by the cities and new industries, and this led to the rapid growth of trade unionism, whose development followed the pattern of that in Britain. The transport workers, clothing workers and engineers were unionized between 1860 and 1890: the miners also organized, while the sheepshearers, a unique "nomad tribe", formed the powerful Australian Workers' Union. On the other side, employers and pastoralists began to move together in order to defend their interests, so that a regular pattern of capitalist-labour "class-war" began to emerge.

The Catholic people, who had taken a leading part in the fight for the land, gravitated naturally enough into the rank and file of the new labour union movement. Its earliest leaders however, were English radicals with a Chartist background, who had experience of proletarian conditions in the home country. It was only by degrees that the Irish Catholic element began to rise to influence in councils, committees and federal conferences, and it was not until after the split of the First World War that Catholic Labour leaders became prominent at the highest level.

The one great controversy of the nineteenth century in which Catholics found themselves opposed to the democratic "spirit of the age" was that concerning education. In opposing Protestant privilege, they had upheld the principle of secularity as essential for securing the equality and freedom of the Catholic minority, but in the 'sixties and 'seventies they found themselves faced with a "secularism" which was something very different from the doctrine of a fair field and no favour which they had supported. A small but energetic group wished to "get rid of the sects in dealing with education", because they regarded the influence of organized religion in modern life as reactionary, and opposed to liberal enlightenment. Others saw in denominational education a nursery of sectarian divisions and conflicts, while others still regarded full State control of education as necessary to efficiency, and accepted secularism as inseparable from this new design. Since the State must stand apart from all religious creeds, the few who hoped to make secularized education a means of dechristianization found allies in many Protestants who saw in it a weapon against "Romanism", and who hoped to retain a "simple Bible teaching" which, in combination with Sunday School instruction, they believed would serve their own purposes sufficiently well.

The educational battle took place in Australia, it must be remembered, at a time when the causes of infidelity and liberalism were closely united in Europe, and were identified with the nationalist cause in Italy, Austria and Germany against the "old order" of political reaction. Only in Ireland and Poland was Catholicism allied with the upsurge of democracy against the established order, as it had been throughout Australian history.

Archbishop Vaughan of Sydney, the leader of the Catholic Hierarchy, was an Englishman of the ruling class who saw the local struggle in terms of its European background and denounced the secularist design as a scheme of practical paganism, whose promoters would find that they had undermined the faith and morals of the community in their desire to strike a blow at Catholicism. He appealed for a truly "National" system of education which would respect essential differences of creed and legislate for them: but, though the Catholics gained substantial Anglican support—Bishop Moorhouse of Melbourne throwing his influence strongly on their side—they were not able to prevail. All the forces of anti-Catholic sectarianism were enlisted in the cause of the secularists, and many Protestants who desired some kind of Christian teaching in the schools were still unwilling to identify themselves with a strong Catholic lead in favour of denominationalism. For the rest, the issue as between a "God-centred" and "man-centred" philosophy of life was still unperceived for the most part, except by the clearer foresight of the Catholic leaders.

The great defeat of the 'seventies has never been reversed: but it failed to "rend the Catholics asunder" as their enemies had hoped. On the contrary, it has drawn them together more closely under their Bishops' leadership. By the mightiest sustained effort in their whole history of struggle in Australia, the Catholic community created a complete denominational school structure of their own without a pennyworth of public aid. The "fight for the schools" has gone on ever since, the Australian Catholics being obliged to contribute to the education of their fellow-citizens in schools they cannot use, as well as to provide the full cost of training their own children in Christian institutions. Their claims for justice have been, in general, ignored—it seems that the secular-minded Australian of today is incapable of grasping the Catholic attitude or the Catholic grievance at all: while as the cost of education has risen the economic obstacle to ending the system of secular privilege has become more forbidding and, however good rational arguments may be concerning the equal title of schools of various types to public aid as a public service, they have not prevailed against the hostile emotion aroused by the suggestion of a grant whose benefit would mainly fall to "Roman Catholics". The best that Catholics can hope for, it appears, in the foreseeable future, is that their secondary education may possibly benefit from a system of public aid designed to prevent the collapse of the private secondary schools under the burden of increased costs: since it is not possible to assist the non-Catholic private schools without helping the Catholic ones also. In the primary field the matter is different, since the benefit would accrue almost entirely to the Catholic parish schools.

The hostility of left-wing secularists, however, to all private schools, remains unrelenting. They are denounced as "segregating" Australian children into class or sectarian groups. The argument that the artificial unification of the educational structure under the State is based on a totalitarian concept of nationalism and that a completely state-controlled system can easily be made an instrument of ideological despotism is as little considered as were the former arguments concerning the danger of dechristianization. Finally, the deep prejudices against Catholic cultural influence derived from the past retain their force, even though they are not so openly expressed as in the days when Protestantism was a more lively religious influence. The Catholic Church is suspect as standing for an alien way of thought and life: her adherents are largely of Irish or foreign descent and their "British loyalty" is open to doubt. Nor has the long history of Catholic radicalism in Australia removed the belief that Catholicism is undemocratic and reactionary: even her social protests against oppression are often attributed to sinister motives of domination rather than any genuine zeal for justice.

In the Labour Party, the growth of Marxist influence in the present century has created a hard core of radical secularism: but even earlier, the radical nationalism of such men as Lane and Lawson was frequently associated—as in Europe—with revolt against Christian orthodoxy as part of the "old order", and with secularist assertions inconsistent with Catholic thinking. The unresolved tension has continued in the ranks of Labour until our own time, when it has been a main cause for the latest split, which has reduced the whole Labour movement to a state of chaos and demoralization.

The conflict in fundamental philosophies which has run through the story of Catholic activity within the Labour movement did not, however, prevent the general Catholic body from playing its part in the fight against what the Sydney *Bulletin* once called "the clothing of the ass's body of social conditions and feudal law traditions in the lion's hide of pseudo-democratic institutions". The end of the century saw the Irish-Australian still, comparatively, an "underdog" in the new land, and therefore prone to combine domestic radicalism with anti-Imperialism, identifying his own fight for a more democratic Australia with that of his brethren in the "Old Land" for Irish liberation, and with that of the African Boers for republican independence against the British Empire. Moreover, Catholic social radicalism found a Church leader in this period very different from the English gentleman who had presided so strangely, though energetically, over the fight for the Christian schools. Patrick Moran, who became Archbishop of Sydney in 1884 and Cardinal in the following year, was a militant Irishman whose background of thought predisposed him to sympathy with the "revolt of the masses". Like Cardinal Manning in England, he threw himself wholeheartedly on to the side of the workers in the social struggles which were in progress at the time of his coming to Australia. He declared in favour of trade unionism, despite the "socialistic" associations which dismayed many of the more conservative clergy. He spoke out openly for the strikers in the great dock dispute of the 'nineties. The great encyclical *Rerum Novarum*, which aroused so much bitterness in powerful circles of Catholic Europe, was hailed joyfully by the Australian Cardinal: not only did he reject "liberal capitalism" with its myth of free contract, but he declared for revolution, if necessary, in order to redress "manifest injustice". Nor was he satisfied to stress the advantages of workers' unions: he held the view that they should have a share in the capital which was the fruit of their toil. He was an ardent advocate of the system of arbitration and conciliation in which Australia was a social pioneer; and he insisted that there was room for a considerable amount of "socialization", of the kind favoured by the Labour movement, without falling into the kind of "socialism" which the Church had condemned as incompatible with Catholic principles.

The Australian tradition of vigorous, radical-minded social leadership of the Catholic Hierarchy was established by Cardinal Moran, who took a leading part in the movement for Australian Federation. He saw prophetically far ahead of his time, to an age in which the Commonwealth would become a fully independent Pacific nation: and he stood for a patriotism which was completely devoid of sectarianism. But while "men of goodwill" of every creed paid tribute to his splendid patriotic leadership, he suffered inevitably from the jealousy of petty minds, and the obsessions of the sectarians on the subject of "Popish intrigue" were effective in preventing his election to the Convention which drew up the Constitution for the new Commonwealth.

In the first years of Federation, the Catholic body was on the crest of the tide of the new social legislation, which was in the spirit of its own tradition as well as that of the Encyclical of Leo XIII. The Hierarchy refused to be alarmed by the Conservative outcry against "socialism", but carefully distinguished between the moderate reform movements described under that heading and the total socialism of the Marxists in their 1905 pastoral; while the cardinal himself debated against the Protestant, George Reid, who had tried to exploit the papal letter against his political opponents. At his death, the Labour leader Holman hailed him as a "great statesman", as well as a great churchman—and his welcome given to the support accorded by His Eminence to Labour "from outside our own ranks" contrasts strikingly with the denunciation by Dr. Evatt, in our own time, of the "alien influence" of the Catholic bishops and lay social movement.

The First World War brought heroic fame to the Australian soldiers who fought in Anzac and in the Near East, as well as in France and Flanders, but it checked the development of Australian nationalism by the emotional fusing of the Australian and British ideas, which had tended to become distinct from one another.

Australia was involved in the struggle as a member of the British Empire rather than on her own account, for the matter of German New Guinea was quickly settled, and in the height of the war a struggle at the other end of the world placed Catholics in violent conflict with a large section of Australian opinion, at a time when that opinion was most worked up in its loyal devotion to Great Britain. The Catholics were as responsive to Irish emotional loyalties as the rest of the nation was to "British sentiment", and they were intensely moved by the controversy on Irish conscription, which was the prelude to the Easter Rebellion of 1916. The abhorrence of conscription in Ireland certainly had its effect in determining Catholic feeling towards the same proposal in Australia, and to this was added a traditional repugnance associated with the military autocracy of earlier Australia, and a sense—more strongly developed in the Catholic community than elsewhere—of Australia as a distinct Pacific entity, with especial interests by no means identical with those of Britain as regards a war in Europe and the Eastern Mediterranean.

The supreme symbol of this tragic war-time contradiction came to be a dynamic Irish prelate upon whom the mantle of Cardinal Moran had fallen—Archbishop Daniel Mannix of Melbourne. Claiming the same right as the cardinal to speak as a leading citizen of his adopted country, he flung himself whole-heartedly, in the name of Australian nationalism, into the fight against conscription. His insistence that national interest should be the first consideration rather than "Empire loyalty", and his note of scepticism about the moral meaning of the war itself, were calculated to exasperate his opponents to the highest degree—and, as might be expected, they were ascribed to Irish hatred of Britain rather than to genuine Australian patriotism.

But whatever might be said of the great archbishop's tact, his condemnation of conscription in general was in line with Catholic social principles. The Papacy had named the practice as one of the "incitements to war" in the modern world, only to be justified in the utmost emergency—and it was questionable whether such an emergency existed *for Australia* in 1914-18. In taking a strong line on this major social political issue, Dr. Mannix was only following the lead of Cardinal Moran, and, indeed, the tradition of Australian Church leaders from the days of convictism. Finally, like the cardinal, he was ahead of his time in his view of Australia as a "thing in itself" and his rejection of the primacy of "Empire loyalty". In our own day, we have seen the Empire transformed into a tenuous "Commonwealth" association which has not even the Crown as a common symbol, and even the Conservative Federal Government now in office has, in effect, accepted the view for which the archbishop stood—that Australia is the central object of the Australian's loyalty, and that the Commonwealth must have a distinct pattern of policy based on her Pacific interests. Australian national defence, foreign policies and economic policies have been redesigned—under pressure of reality—on the lines towards which Catholic opinion has tended for a long time, and the doctrine that the British viewpoint must be the determining factor in forming our own is less and less accepted.

Naturally enough, it was easier for Catholics of Irish origin to see the Australian situation in this light, because their vision was not obscured by hereditary emotional attachments to "home"; while the tradition of British authority was identified with conservative privilege in Australia and alien ascendency in Ireland. Hence, they have tended to march ahead of the rest of Australia in four-square nationalism—and to be condemned as "disloyal" for doing so. But now that the Monarchy itself has been presented officially as an *Australian* Monarchy, and not as a British Monarchy extended over a dependent Dominion, this particular charge has become a meaningless atavism from the age of colonialism.

Whatever the view of Australian patriotism the majority of Catholics may have held, it has never prevented Catholics from answering their country's call to arms. They provided more than their proportion of fighting soldiers in both world wars, and no one anywhere has questioned their valour or loyalty to the cause for which they offered their lives.

In the breach in the Labour movement which resulted from the conscription issue, Catholic politicians and left-wingers found themselves joined together in opposition to the handful of leaders under Hughes and Holman, who were united with the Conservatives on this question. In the inter-war era, many of them emerged into leadership both in the State and Federal sphere as well as in the trade unions. Their influence checked the trend to revolutionary Marxism, which was strengthened in social-democratic labour movements all over the world by the Bolshevik Revolution of 1917 in Russia. These Catholic Labour men, however, were far from being well-informed concerning the development of Christian thought on the social situation, and they had too little sense of the dangers of increased "nationalization" to the fundamental liberties of the individual and family. They tended to accept the pattern of "socialization" uncritically, to favour a dangerous increase of State control in every field, and to reflect Marxist thought on the relations between labour and capital, despite the warnings of papal encyclicals and of leading

Catholic thinkers. Their attitude to immigration and the "White Australia" policy was also formed on nationalist principles of expediency without much reference to any sense of responsibility to humanity to be expressed in public policy as well as private conduct. For the rest, party politics and union politics are a corrupting game which engenders un-Christian passions and appetites: and it is to be feared that the Catholics engaged in it were not, in general, better than their non-Catholic fellows—even if they were not worse. Too many were absorbed in the struggle for power and "jobs for the boys", and concerned little enough with promoting policies based on Christian principles. They were able to work in every harmony with radical secularists because their own outlook had become secularized: and it is significant that, even in those States where Catholics exercised the most notable political influence, no attempt was made to challenge the secularist privilege in the field of education, which imposed so heavy and unjust a burden on the Church.

For the rest, despite the advance of Catholics in the sphere of party politics and industrial influence, little had been done in Australia to bridge the spiritual gap which separated them from their fellow-countrymen, whether Protestant or pagan. The name "Mick", which is currently used to describe Catholics among the plain folk of Australia, is eloquent of the way in which they were regarded—as an Irish-born minority committed to their Irish religion, just as the Jewish community were committed to *their* hereditary cult. With the drying up of the Irish immigration, and the replacement of Irish clergy and bishops by products of Australian seminary training at Manly or Werribee or elsewhere, what we may call the element of Irish "colonialism"—corresponding to the British "colonialism" of the other Australians—became more and more tenuous, and after the success of the Irish struggle for liberation, the events in the "Old Land" ceased to arouse any great concern among the Catholics of Australia generally. Attempts to arouse their interest in the campaign to end Partition have not produced any great public response; and activities to promote an interest in Irish culture, language and history, have only affected a very small minority. But the association of Catholicism with Irish symbols and with the celebration of St. Patrick's day has survived the ebbing away of genuine Irish feeling, and the habit of thought of many non-Catholics has not yet adjusted itself to the actualities of the new situation.

Australia has never had anything resembling the Oxford Movement in England, which brought a tide of convert intellectuals into the Church, and revolutionized the Catholic position by the new leadership it introduced in the thought and life of the community. The High Anglican movement has, of course, had its colonial reflection, and there has been a trickle of converts from Anglican and non-Anglican Christianity, as well as from infidelity. But none of these has attained eminence as a Catholic leader or writer, so as to be able to command attention over a wide field and translate the two worlds to one another. The contribution of Catholicism to the modest stream of national culture has been inconsiderable; its influence on University life outside the Catholic hostels and colleges has been small, and the power exercised by Catholics on the left side in politics and in the labour unions has probably contributed to its isolation by the distrust it has engendered.

In the course of time, a fairly large body of middle-class and well-to-do Catholics has come into existence, which has tended to gravitate towards the Conservative side in politics, but the historic pattern of Australian development has made it difficult for them to gain any foothold in Conservative organizations.

The link between Catholicism and the Irish radicalism has created an ingrained prejudice and distrust, while the Whig-Protestant British tradition is here at its strongest, and Masonic influence is added to this prejudice, so as to create an impalpable obstacle to the advance of the Catholic who seeks to make a career, or to exercise influence on the right wing of politics. There is nothing so crude as an open or absolute embargo, and it is always possible to point to eminent figures who have surmounted the handicap of their Faith because of exceptional qualities of tact or good fortune. The political barriers are most formidable, at the present time, at the lowest level of the Liberal party—the men at the top recognize the value of Catholic collaboration with the Conservative forces in the moulding of national thought and policies. But the fact that the Conservative Prime Minister of the 'thirties—Joseph Lyons, who broke away from Labour—was a devout Catholic and that the Country Party leader of that day—afterwards the Speaker of the House—was a convert, does not alter the truth that Catholic influence has remained negligible, in general, on the right wing of Australian political life.

Again, while Catholic names are prominent in law and medicine—the traditional professions towards which those of their faith have gravitated—they have contributed comparatively little to creative activity and management in big business and industrial enterprise: and the pattern of privilege to which we have already referred still makes it more difficult for them to rise to the top in the world of business and finance than for others. The fault, however, does not lie entirely with hostile prejudice, either in these fields or in those of science and engineering, where so many doors of new opportunity have opened in the new age of large-scale planned projects and active organized research. The truth is that the young Catholic—coming up from a working-class background with a traditional dread of insecurity—is inclined to "play safe" by settling into a job in one of the Civil Services, where he is secured against unemployment, and the method of promotion is designed so as to give him a certain protection against the hidden operation of prejudice. One paradoxical consequence of this is the large number of Catholic teachers to be found in the State Education Departments, teaching in the very schools which the Hierarchy condemn as undesirable for Catholic pupils on account of their purely secular character.

It is not only in regard to his own "design for living" that the Catholic Australian tends to be unadventurous—his attitude to the Faith is also essentially a defensive one. He keeps the Faith, he supports the Catholic Church and school with model generosity, so that the treasure may be passed on to his inheritors. He responds valiantly to calls to make public demonstration of his belief, and is proud of the size and impressive splendour of the great ceremonies in which the Church appears splendidly arrayed, and he is warmed by the sense of belonging to a mighty universal family, and uplifted by the inspiration of shared faith and loyalties. There is no "anti-clericalism"—the bishop is his father in God, the priest his good friend, in whom he confides without fear or inhibitions. But he is, in general, inactive as regards the personal propagation of the Faith, and is content to live in the midst of his non-Catholic neighbours without attempting to make any impact on their minds. The powerful influence of converts has given English Catholics generally a lively concern with the question of spreading the Faith in their country, and making it better known, but in Australia, clergy and people alike have been content to extend their plant and build their defences as strongly as possible, while asserting their claims to a "place in the sun" socially and politically. Hence, while they have exercised a powerful influence at times, in the social and political field, it has too often been a disturbing influence which has aroused distrust as "alien", rather than a leavening influence which has affected the tone of Australian thinking. More often than not, Catholic leaders have seen further than the rest of the community—for instance, in regard to the effects of secularized education, the development of Australian nationalism, the gravity of the Communist menace and the need of large-scale European migration. But their warnings and advice have not been understood or trusted, and nothing of importance has been done to remedy this state of affairs. Catholics have become more and more universalist and "mission-minded" during the present century, in regard to the world of Oceania—but the organized lay apostolate directed towards the Australian non-Catholic has not made the same progress and the study of the technique of "winning friends and influencing people" in his own parish and place of employment is a closed book to the ordinary Catholic of our time.

The most recent period of Catholic history begins with the era immediately after the first War. At this time, the Labour party had been weakened by the split over conscription, and the large body of Catholics who supported it found themselves regarded with increased ill-will by their fellow-citizens in the Conservative camp, on account of their strong sympathy with the fight for Irish freedom, which came to its bloody culmination in the early 'twenties—a sympathy which was voiced eloquently by the Archbishop, Dr. Mannix, with a sound which went round the world. Meanwhile, the nation had entered into a period of capitalist prosperity which did not prevent the continued fall of the birthrate (41 per cent between 1912 and 1933). In the Labour movement, despite growing Catholic influence, Marxist tendencies had been strengthened by the Russian Revolution, and it is at this point that the modern crisis between Right and Left really begins, though its development was only to come after the great Depression. The "socialization objective" expressed in Marxian terms, was accepted by a conference at Brisbane, and became a centre of controversy in years to come, though an "interpretation" acceptable to Catholics was ultimately ruled to be allowable.

The Conservative rule came to an end on the eve of the Depression, the Bruce-Page Government seeking to impose new regulating discipline on the unions, and ultimately appealing to the people on the issue of Commonwealth Arbitration, which it proposed to abolish.

This brought Labour into power under the leadership of the Catholic, James Scullin. It had the overwhelming support of the Catholic body, who were little troubled by the "socialization objective".

The Depression fell heavily on Australia, and produced effects far more permanent and grave than those of the First World War itself. The working class suffered terribly: wages fell to the level of 1907, and the unemployment figures were enormous. The memory of these years is still vividly alive among the older Labour men of today—including the Catholics. The disillusionment following the bright hopes of a "new democracy" of social welfare which Labour had hoped to build drove many to Communism—and among them were a few apostate Catholics who rose high in the service of the Party, especially as trade union leaders. These embittered men responded to the attraction of Communism, perhaps because it was the extreme opposite to their former faith, and satisfied their need for a clear-cut way of thought and life, and for a "sacred cause" to whose service they could dedicate themselves. Moreover, Communism gained ground because of the prevailing ignorance of its nature, which led many to swallow uncritically the current propaganda about the "great experiment".

The Catholic Church in Australia, however, was successful in holding the great body of its working-class adherents—partly because its tradition was radical, and it could not be identified with the cause of the conservatives, whose harsh policies eventually led to a recovery of financial stability—though the restoration of workers' living standards was a slower process. It was another split—that of the Lang faction in New South Wales—which had once again sent Labour into the wilderness, there to remain—so far as the Federal Government was concerned—until the Second World War.

The 'thirties were a flowering time for the Left Wing and for Communist propaganda both in the unions and among the "intelligentsia". The Catholic Church—which had the guidance of the social encyclicals—was in advance of the rest of the community in understanding the full implications of this development, as it had been in the case of the secularization issue of the 'seventies. A Catholic group for self-education, the Campion Society, founded in 1931 by seven young men—lawyers, students and schoolteachers—marked the beginning of a native Catholic Action movement to meet the challenge of the new era. The number of Campion groups expanded—the men in them built up a knowledge of Catholic history and of Christian social thinking in Europe, which had hitherto had little impact on Australians. In particular, they were affected by the doctrines of Hilaire Belloc and the English Distributists, whose agrarianism and dread of the "Servile State" were reflected in their new designs for Australian living. Their first organ, the *Catholic Worker*, favoured a pattern of Christian vocational society, as well as the decentralization of industries and Government, and social reforms based on strengthening the economic foundations of family life. They stood apart from the "socialism without doctrines" of the Catholic Labour men, and were for the most part indifferent to the Irish tradition. When a full-scale Catholic Action movement was brought into existence by the Hierarchy, these men naturally played a leading part in the work, since they were an organized group, and were not involved in party politics. But the fact that a number of them were critical of Australian and British political institutions and interested in the social experiments in Europe, was naturally used as a basis for Communist attacks upon them as Fascist.

Once again, Catholics were to suffer alienation from their fellows through seeing a danger ahead—Communism—which the community had not, for the most part, begun to take seriously. However, this obsessed them, so that they were less concerned than others with the one which was the immediate object of fear at this time—"the menace of Fascism". Fear that a democratic crusade against "Fascism" would produce a situation favourable to the more dangerous Communist offensive determined their attitude to the sanctions campaign against Italy: while in the case of Spain, their opposition to the prevailing trend was very marked indeed, in view of the savage anti-Christian persecution of the Republicans, and their open alliance with Communism. At one point, the Spanish issue threatened to cause a Catholic crisis within the Labour Party, but the split was averted by the dexterity of its leaders in evading the left-wing attempts to commit the party to the "loyalist" cause.

On the other hand, there was no serious disagreement between Catholics and other Australians on the subject of Hitler—though a far greater awareness among Catholics that war with Germany was likely to give the Communists their greatest opportunity. As yet, European affairs bulked more largely in the minds of Australian leaders of thought than those of Asia: the Sino-Japanese struggle aroused little interest, and only a few were awake to the dangers of the "trade diversion policy" of the Lyons Government, which created a new bitterness between Japan and Australia.

In the Second World War, unlike the first, there was almost complete unanimity between the Catholics and the rest of the nation—more especially after the Japanese attack of 1941, which made the war a national fight for survival. There was no return of the conscription controversy—the Labour Party, which came into power under John Curtin, was almost unanimously supported in the adoption of compulsory military service for the Territories. The large body of Catholics, whose nationalist Australianism was still tinged with rather more distrust of British policy than that of their neighbours, gave full support to Curtin in his insistence, against the desire of Churchill, upon the return of Australian troops from the Middle East in order to defend our own northern approach.

The alignment of Russia with the Allies, however, and the lifting of the ban imposed on Communism after the Nazi-Soviet pact in 1940, brought the Communist power in the trade unions to its height. Throughout the country there was deep sympathy with the Russians in their valiant fight against the common enemy: and Communist influence was used to support the war effort; while it was widely believed that the alliance would lead to a new and friendly understanding between "East European Social Democracy" and the democracies of the West. Hence, the Communist penetration and capture of key unions met with little resistance except from small groups of Catholics, who were not deluded by the Communist collaboration. It was to represent the views of these, and publicize the truth about the Communist conspiracy in the unions, that the new paper *Freedom*—later to become *News Weekly*—was begun, not as an avowedly Catholic organ, but as one expressing the views of Australian Christian "militants" who regarded Communism as the chief internal enemy of freedom in their country, and of true industrial democracy. For the time being, the Labour Government was content to "put off the evil day" and the administration itself—as later revelations showed—was deeply penetrated by Communist and "Red-appeasing" elements: while large numbers were caught up into "front" organizations like the Eureka Youth League.

The leaders of Catholic Social Action had become more sophisticated and "down to earth" in their application of their principles to the actualities of Australian life since the 'thirties. The social activity of Catholics, meanwhile, had continued to develop during the war period. In 1939 the Catholic Rural Movement was founded—and it soon had members among the country folk of every State, and formed a federation with its own organ *Rural Life*, drawing on American and Canadian rather than European experience, for a new philosophy of the land, and advocating practical schemes for mixed farming, co-operatives and rural debt reform. Moreover, the bishops—whose activity in the leadership of Catholic social reform was a national tradition—adopted the policy of regularizing their advice to the Catholic body, and, indeed, to the whole nation, by establishing the observance of Social Justice Sunday, each year, when annual statements were issued under their authority.

The first was a general "Statement of Social Principles" in which they urged the reorganization of society on occupational lines. Thereafter, the principles of the social encyclicals were applied to some aspect of Australian conditions in a simple fashion in pamphlets addressed to the laity and distributed in the churches, which could also be used for the instruction of Catholic study groups, and in schools. They dealt with the land, the meaning of liberty, the question of living standards, the birthrate, full employment, the growth of cities, migration, Pacific relations and so forth—the idea being to create a well-informed Catholic lay opinion capable of seeing the Christian implications of these issues, and of giving a Christian tone to Australian nationalism.

In answer to a request by the Government for the views of various bodies on post-war reconstruction, a summary of the views of the Catholic Social Movement among the laity was presented to the authorities in 1942; this was *Pattern for Peace*. It contains not merely a long-range plan for the building of an organic society, but practical proposals for agriculture and for industrial self-government. The emphasis is on the need for population growth and rural development—the trend towards greater industrialization and urban centralization had become alarmingly intensified in war-time Australia. The attraction of country people rather than city-dwellers to Australia was urged, and planned land settlement on a large scale. Other matters are dealt with, e.g., the family wage, a plan for graduated endowment being favoured to replace the fixed "basic wage" based on the three-child family. Measures are recommended for the protection of the small independent owner, and checks on the growth of large-scale industry and monopoly, as well as public control of the credit mechanism.

As in England, so in Australia, it seemed for a moment during the war that a "common front" of Catholics and other Christians might be established to promote a new pattern of Christian social reform, breaking the long isolation of the Catholics: and the fading away of the "Irish question" and other controversial issues gave added ground for hope. A joint manifesto was issued by the Catholic and Anglican Archbishops of Sydney, expressing their common views on the social question: in Victoria, a Christian Association for Social Justice was formed including Catholics, Anglicans and members of the Free Churches, and a twenty-point programme was agreed upon—calling, among other things, for national education on a Christian basis.

In Adelaide, the Catholic Archbishop, the Anglican Archbishop and the Head of the Council of Churches made a joint recommendation on substantially the same lines. In a "Religion and Life Week" held at Newcastle in 1942, a Catholic lay representative took a prominent part in the lectures and discussions, and other Catholics, lay and clerical, took part in similar gatherings in subsequent years. At one time a Catholic layman was even invited to address the Anglican Synod at Ballarat on the subject of Christianizing the Social Order. Local Christian movements flowered here and there in the countryside, whose aim was to draw Catholics and Protestants into collaboration on the basis of the truths and values shared by both.

Unfortunately, with the return of peace, old divisions and prejudices have prevailed, and—for the time being at least—the "united front of Christians" seems farther away than ever. In particular, Protestants have hitherto been unwilling to stand firmly with Catholics on the matter of their education claims—though some of them have urged the need of aid for secondary education, where the burden of cost is a problem to their own private schools.

Finally, the Communists and "fellow-travellers" have made considerable progress, of late, in the "infiltration" of clerical circles; and many of the Protestant clergy have thrown themselves wholeheartedly on the left-wing side in regard to recent trade union struggles and controversies concerning external policy in the Pacific.

One of the most important developments of Australian life since the war has been the great European immigration into the Commonwealth, under a plan for which a Catholic Labour Minister, Mr. A. A. Calwell, was mainly responsible during the Chifley Government's term of office. This has meant the influx of a huge number of Polish, German, Dutch, Jugoslav, Ukrainian, Lithuanian and Italian Catholics, whose traditions and outlook differ much from those of the native Irish-descended breed. Their spiritual care, the training of their children and the absorption of the "new Australians" into the older Catholic community has posed immense new problems, while it has created a "schools crisis" of very grave proportions. Not only must accommodation be suddenly found for great numbers, but the flow of vocations to the teaching orders has become a mere trickle—a phenomenon which is not peculiar to Australia, and which seems to arise from the ultra-secular atmosphere of the time, the break-up of family traditions and pieties, and the "industrialization" of young women as well as young men, both being paid high wages and leading lives of varied enjoyment unknown to their ancestors. It remains to be seen whether the denominational system can surmount this latest crisis, in which even the State structure finds itself under heavy pressure, and also what effect the new Australians will have on the development of Catholic nationalism in the country. One thing is clear—that refugees from Germany and East Europe will prove a strong accession to the anti-Communist forces, once they are drawn into the activities of the Labour organizations. A sense of this is already reflected in the hostility of the Left to the existing migration policy, which has been very marked in the last few years. For the rest, the entry of a large number of new people without either Irish or British sentimental attachments, may be expected to hasten the development of a purely Australian-Antipodean Catholic culture, emancipated from the last remains of colonialism.

It remains to describe the growth of a new conflict within the Labour movement since the war, which has now brought about grave divisions in the Catholic community, of which one section finds itself in a state of isolation between the Right and Left in politics, while the social influence of the whole Catholic body has been dangerously enfeebled by internal strife and confusion of loyalties, so that a renewed wave of Communist power in the unions, and Communist social sabotage, threatens the nation.

In the period immediately after the war, the Labour Government began to reap the fruits of its "appeasement" policy in the unions, as the "cold war" era began, and Communist power advanced in the Far East, through China into South-East Asia, and Indonesia, where the collapse of Dutch power—aided by the Australian

Labour Government's policy—had produced a native republic threatening to dissolve into chaos. In the circumstances, the Labour leaders were glad to welcome the support of a Catholic movement formed to add ideological stiffening to the "Labour Industrial Groups" of Catholics and non-Catholics established to combat the "militant" Communist minority in the unions. The planned strategy of this "movement" was kept under cover, and its discipline and devotion did much to carry the Labour groups to victory in successful counterattacks, aided by legislation passed by the Chifley Government and the Menzies Government, which followed it, in order to secure democratic union elections under proper control.

The militant Catholics in the unions and Labour branches and the "Groupers" who stood with them, however, were not content to fight Communism: nor could they accept a purely negative role. As they gained ground, it was necessary to select trained and trustworthy men to carry on work in unions and Labour branches, and make policy decisions affecting the Labour Party generally. The "Groupers" began to exercise an influence upon the thinking of the party which was unwelcome, not only to the Leftists, but also to certain old-time Labour politicians who disliked the new kind of thought, and resented the challenge of new men to their influence—sometimes exercised in corrupt and undemocratic ways. It was no longer a question of whether the Labour Party should offer a political career to Catholics, but whether its ideas were to be transformed by the thought of men who applied their Christian social principles in order to modify Labour policy.

The struggle between the new creative Christian-minded Labour men on one scale and the hidebound traditionalists of Socialism and left-wing doctrinaire Marxists on the other, had become a serious matter even before Mr. Chifley died. When he was succeeded by Dr. Evatt, whose sympathies were strongly Leftist, the crisis followed very soon. The new leader was resolved to commit the Labour Party to a strong socialist policy in line with that of British Labour in external affairs, involving closer relations with the "neutralists" and the recognition of Red China, and the virtual abandonment of the defensive association with U.S.A. In domestic policy he wished to abandon the fight against the Communists in the unions and work in concert with them as far as possible. He showed his colours first by coming out strongly against the Menzies Government in the referendum to ban the Communist party—in which he gained a success, despite the scarcely-veiled hostility of the "Group" Labour men generally, largely through a brilliant propaganda campaign on the theme of "threatened liberties", which won many Catholics, and a solid body of Liberals, over to his side.

The ending of the Korean war led to a revival of the agitation for a "new understanding" with the Communist world of the Far East, and, while the "Groups" continued to enjoy official countenance, and to win victory after victory, it soon became clear that opposition was hardening against them. The crisis finally came when Dr. Evatt revolted against the discipline of his own party, and provoked a crisis by his action in intervening in the Petrov case on behalf of certain accused *protégés*. The story of the violent and unconstitutional campaign launched in Victoria in order to create a "New Executive" under Leftist control, and the subsequent "gerrymandering" of the Hobart Conference so as to bring a new Federal Labour policy into existence, would be too long to tell here. It is sufficient to say that a split was accomplished in Victoria, where the majority of Labour branches and a number of the unions refused to recognize the authority of the new Executive; and a minority of Labour men in the State and Federal Parliament were isolated and forced to organize a new "anti-Communist" Labour Party, committed to the principles of the Industrial Groups.

The emergence of the "splinter group", with little hope of acceptance by the general body of Labour electors, has caused a severe internal crisis among Catholics, and controversies have developed in their ranks over a joint pastoral of the bishops declaring strongly in favour of the Industrial Groups for their work in fighting Communism, and urging Catholics and men of goodwill to give them full support. A wave of sectarian hostility has been whipped up by certain of the Protestant clergy in alliance with Leftist politicians, and a general nervousness about "political Romanism" has been aroused in wide circles. Labour is torn asunder in Victoria and Queensland, beset by bitter divisions everywhere: and the Communist power in the unions has profited as a result of the debacle, which has enabled them to regain ground with the support of those Labour men who have swung against the "Groups", now banned by their party.

It remains to be seen whether the setback to Catholic influence in the social-political field will be permanent, or whether they can re-establish it by coming to terms with Labour, which seems unlikely to regain power while it lacks a solid block of the former Catholic Labour vote. But if Australia is to be preserved as a nation of Western culture under genuine democratic government, it would appear that it must accept many of the things for which the Catholic radicals have fought in public life. The "middle way" they stand for is a way based on a clear-sighted perception of the things that belong to their country's peace and safety. Australia must populate, decentralize, design policies in which defence of her Western culture and Christian heritage is combined with a sane and realistic policy of friendship and understanding with Eastern neighbours, from Japan to Indonesia, and her people must develop a lively sense of Pacific-minded nationalism, and cast off the mental shackles of "colonialism". The leaders of Catholics are deeply aware of these truths, and of the *urgency* of the kind of social policies they call for: they are, far more than the rest of the people, obsessed by the sense of a coming hour of crisis, whose issue will decide the question whether the Australia they love is to survive at all. They dread the short view of the party politician, the industrialist who follows the line of immediate profit and advantage, the worker and union organizer who see no further than the next step in the struggle for shorter hours, higher wages and margins, and better amenities. The chaos of meaningless conflict and unordered development which this kind of thinking can produce—the habit of acting as though Australia were still alone in a world of security and had only to consider patterns of convenience in her social policy—this sort of thing can mean, not merely loss of freedom, or social deterioration, but actual death by violence for a nation situated as we are.

The "activized" Catholics know that they see these things with unique vividness while others are largely blind to them—and they feel the burden of a great responsibility, and of a great fear. They know the difficulty of awakening the rank and file of their own folk—excellent people who wear the badge of their faith valiantly, but wear it on a garment of thoughts and prejudices and traditional loyalties which often act as an impediment to the wider vision of Christian nationalism. They realize too, the difficulty of overcoming the barrier of hereditary distrust and mutual ignorance between Catholic and non-Catholic, which prevents their message from being received by many men of goodwill, and seems, at times, to confine them in a sort of hopeless isolation while the world flows around them, unseeing and unhearing.

All this they know: but they are heartened by the knowledge that their leaven has affected the mass to some extent, so that there is a body of Catholic opinion upon whose support they can rely, and a smaller group of intelligent non-Catholics who are beginning to pay some heed to what Catholics have to say. They have been uplifted by the sight of simple men who have dedicated themselves with heroism to the fight to save Australia from the enemy within, and to build her future as a free nation on the foundations of Christian principles and Christian social sanity. The spirit of fighting Christian radicalism which informed the founding fathers of Catholicism in Australia is not, they believe, dead—and they look to it to renew the face of Australian earth, so that our people may live and become a centre of new life, in the Pacific world of tomorrow.

WALES

Catherine Daniel

Neither is there at this time prince, or leader, or prophet, or holocaust or sacrifice or oblation, or incense, or place of first fruits before thee that we may find thy mercy: nevertheless in a contrite heart and humble spirit let us be accepted. (Dan. iii. 38-9.)

The position of the Catholic Church in Wales today cannot be appreciated without some understanding of the historical relation of Wales to the Catholic faith. From that vantage point we are enabled to scan the complex pattern of Welsh religious life and to assess, as far as is humanly possible, the future probabilities.

The population of Wales today numbers about 2,750,000. About one-third of this total is an indigeneous Welsh-speaking society. Its pursuits are rural and agricultural. Its culture acquired its definitive forms in the period of transition from Roman rule to the status of Welsh nationhood. Its language contains a rich stream of Latin derivations absorbed during the Roman occupation of Britain, and it is a unique example of a living link with the Imperial Rome of the early Christian era. By the end of the Roman occupation in the early fifth century, the Welsh language had fully emerged as a precise instrument of literary expression. Welsh epic poetry of that period indicates the discipline of a literary tradition nurtured in the aristocratic setting of the Romano-British ruling class. Literary Welsh has deviated very little from the forms which it assumed between the fifth and sixth centuries and the poetry of that period can be understood today after a minimum of initiation.

Later, however, Teutonic tribes arriving in Britain called the inhabitants of Wales *Wealas*—Welsh. This was the term by which

---

CATHERINE DANIEL is a convert from Welsh Nonconformity, and an honours graduate in Welsh literature and language. She is the author of many pamphlets and articles in Welsh and English and of a short history of Bardsey Island, and also broadcasts and lectures; she acts as Chairman of the Northern Regional Committee of Y Cylch Catholig. She is married, with six children.

they designated all races who had formed part of the Roman Empire. All such races had been granted Roman citizenship by the Emperor Caracalla between A.D. 211 and 217. The Welsh were therefore Roman also. The early history of Wales is part of the history of Imperial Rome, and the Welsh have deep in their consciousness this knowledge of their Roman origins.

Rome departed on the eve of the era of Celtic monachism. This was the age of the saints who were to weld the emergent nation into the religious unity of Catholicism. What the Roman occupation had effected on the political and civic level the saints perfected on the religious level. In the Welsh mind the emergence of Wales is so intimately connected with her Roman and Catholic origins that even today, four centuries after the Protestant reform, Welshmen regard the era of Celtic monachism with nostalgia. March 1st, the feast of the national patron, Saint David (d. *circa* 588) is observed by the entire nation, by all the Protestant denominations and the numerous cultural societies in Wales. Wales remained explicitly Catholic and devotedly Roman until the accession to the English throne of the Welsh Tudor dynasty.

In 1535 Henry VIII decreed the political amalgamation of Wales with England. The native Welsh dynasty had come to an end in 1282 with the death of Llywellyn the Last Prince. Tragic as this was, it had not caused the social structure in Wales to disintegrate; this had retained its stability under the patronage of the wealthy *pendefigion*, the landed gentry, hundreds of whom traced their genealogy back to the sub-Roman period. They were the patrons of the arts, sheltering and supporting the bards, the professional curators of family trees. They were European as well as Welsh. They journeyed frequently to the Continent. At their tables fine foods and wines of France were served. On their hearths were debated obscure points of philosophy. The debates of the Aristotelians against the Platonists are echoed in the Welsh classical poetry of the period. The Universities of Oxford and Cambridge were their points of contact with the life of the Continental universities, especially that of Paris.

In this stratum of society ancient prophecies were current, and one romantic theme in particular which recurs in the prophecies had in it the compulsive attraction of a national mythus. This was a prophecy commonly attributed to Merlin of the Arthurian epoch—that a Welsh king would some day reoccupy the ancient throne of

Britain in London. We cannot say that this alone accounted for the wholesale departure of the Welsh aristocracy to the Tudor Court, but quite certainly a deep urge to reclaim a former privileged position did play a large part in their minds. They took up what they regarded as their rightful prerogative, their position as courtiers in a Welsh Court, thus depriving Welsh society at one blow of its natural leaders and lords.

In 1536 Henry decreed the dissolution of the monasteries. By the earlier decree Wales had been deprived of the possibility of a future system of native legislature and official representation at Rome. One need only compare the failure of Giraldus Cambrensis with that of Morris Clynnog and Gruffydd Robert to realize the extent of the impact which the changed political status had wrought even in her religious fortunes.

By the second decree she lost her spiritual mentors, the monks and friars of every religious order in Christendom, but notably the Cistercians, prime patrons of the arts, tillers of the soil, educators of the poor and confidants of souls. There is little doubt, however, that at that time the Welsh monasteries were functioning at a low spiritual pressure. They frequently had more affinity with an eighteenth-century Oxford college, suffering from decayed revenues and a scanty membership, than with the great Cistercian houses of the twelfth century. Nevertheless, as an integral part of the social landscape, and above all as patrons of the bards, and in many cases as pilgrimage centres, they still played a most important part. And when they went, they left a gap which nothing could fill. Within Henry's lifetime the entire structure of Welsh society was pulverized. Wales entered upon a grim century of religious persecution. Her people held to the Faith with a tenacity which is admitted with respect by every Welsh historian today. From 1537 to 1680 Wales yielded over seventy martyrdoms of priests and laymen for the Faith. In this connection it is pleasing to realize that three of these—Bl. John Roberts, O.S.B., Bl. Richard Gwyn and Bl. David Lewis, S.J.—traced their descent from royal Welsh lineages. In these three martyrs the blood of Welsh princes was assumed to rule from Christ's Cross, whereas their compatriots, following material gain, have passed into oblivion in service to a kingship of a very different order.

Wales now found her spiritual fortunes governed by an alien and unsmiling stepmother—the State Church. The verdict of the people, except for that of a new class of civil servants with a vested interest in the regime, was unanimous. The State Church, even when it gained a precarious footing, was rejected by the Welsh in their essential being. Its clergy were apathetic and its ministrations amounted often to formalisms which had long lost their interior content. For two hundred years no other form of worship was tolerated in Wales. The hunted priests came and went and ministered secretly to the people. The very special case of Wales had no official interpreter in Rome. But among the numerous Welsh Catholic exiles on the Continent were those who planned for the return of the Faith to England, by political strategy, exploiting the Catholic loyalties of the Welsh to secure a safe conduct for troops from the Continent via Wales to England. Such naïve plans bore no fruit.

By the middle of the eighteenth century Continental Protestantism was stimulating Welsh hopes. Nonconformity in Wales grew out of a vital urge for a real and personal approach to Christ, and was a direct consequence of the rejection of the formalisms of the State Church, which had never become integrated into Welsh life. Nonconformist piety, whether Calvinist, Wesleyan or Independent, emerged as a vindication of a truly personal approach to religion. In no context could the following words of Louis Bouyer be so well justified as this one: "All teaching, the whole point of the spiritual exhortations of spiritual men and saints, are in this; to persuade us anew without ceasing that neither cleaving to the Faith of the Church, nor the frequenting of her rites and sacraments avails anything without that effort which nothing else can achieve for us, the efforts to place the Faith in our lives."[1] It was an intuitive recognition of this need of a personal response to grace that provided the motive force of Welsh Protestantism, and the consequences for Wales were dramatic. A nation which had been spiritually starved came alive, demanding food for its soul. They could not have enough of it. Vocations to preach God's word came in hundreds. This preaching was no ephemeral oratory. It dealt with the mighty themes of God made Man, of sin, the necessity for Redemption, its achievement through Christ; the death on the cross; the end of man. In contemplation of these fundamentals of Catholic doctrine multitudes were moved. All the Celtic eloquence and dramatic talent of the preachers were absorbed in this task of depicting the themes of salvation. Often three hours went by as huge congregations overflowing from chapels

[1] Louis Bouyer, *Spirit and Forms of Protestantism*, London, Harvill Press.

into fields and hillsides listened entranced to the words of life. And its one linguistic medium was Welsh.

On the crest of this resurgence came the poets—the hymn writers. The study of Welsh hymnology is in itself a major task. The hymn performs for the Nonconformist in the psychological realm the function which liturgical prayer performs for the Catholic. (They are not, of course, the same thing.) Releasing the believer from the tendency to egoistic inwardness and subjectivity, the hymn became a paean of praise and a restatement of doctrine. Many of the hymn writers attained to sublime heights of knowledge of Christ's Person, a perfectly valid knowledge granted to the intuitive powers of the soul. The conjunction of these inspired hymns with the gift of song and harmony, which is a natural Welsh endowment, very often threw whole congregations into a state of exaltation bordering on ecstasy. An experience of this intensity, commonly shared, bound the nation together in a religious unity which, combining spiritual and sensuous factors, created a solidarity as real to the Welsh as it is inexplicable to the outsider who sees only the external manifestation of ugly chapels.

It is tempting to see in this expression of the subjective content of truth divorced from its authentic outer form a resurgence of a Catholic piety long buried in the Welsh unconscious, but we cannot force this point, for inasmuch as they were explicit about their historical position the Nonconformist Fathers in Wales certainly regarded themselves as protagonists of Protestantism and spoke of Rome in the terminology of some of the Continental reforms as "the Scarlet Woman", "Whore of Babylon", etc. The all-important fact that the Welsh had not, as a people, rejected Catholicism and had never been guilty of national apostasy, seems to have been obscured. It is to this psychological ambiguity that we owe so many of the conflicting trends in Welsh Nonconformity. By its own confession it is separatist and Protestant. But deeply spiritual and life-giving elements within it prove that at a deeper level it is orientated towards the true Church, and by its administration of the Sacrament of Baptism it has in numberless cases conferred at least an embryonic membership of that Church on its adherents. Nonconformity has been for all of two centuries the characteristic expression of the Welsh religious mind. If fifteen centuries of Catholicism in Wales created that national ethos which David Jones, Welsh artist and poet, has dubbed *Romanitas*, Nonconformity also has formed a national ethos at once non-authoritarian, non-hierarchic. This ethos has been fashioned by mass responses to a succession of religious revivals and by a religious experience of unique intensity mediated entirely in the vernacular. From this time dates the indissoluble bond between religion and the Welsh language. In the Latin exactness of Welsh, the great preachers (many of them preternaturally endowed with telepathic and clairvoyant gifts) found a perfect medium in which to convey definitions and principles of theology. Throughout this period the Catholic Church, except for a few isolated and marginal strongholds, was physically not present in Wales.

The State Church in Wales was finally disestablished in 1921 after a century's intermittent agitation. While the material loss of revenues and endowments greatly impoverished the Church,[1] her psychological advantage has been greatly increased, for she is now enabled to present herself to the Welsh as the primitive Celtic Church purged of the Roman and English dependence. Her appeal is varied. She appeals to Welsh Nonconformists who are impatient of the nebulous and undogmatic trends in Nonconformity. To them she offers a degree of doctrinal certainty and of ritualistic observance. But she is strongest of all in her appropriation of the national mythus. We have seen how Welsh nationhood was ethnologically a Romano-British amalgam which received its final stamp from the discipline of the Celtic monastic saints. The popular cults of these saints, among whom David is pre-eminent, were very much alive in Wales, some of them until well into the last century. Parish churches throughout Wales bear their dedications and are identified in the popular mind with the golden era of Welsh Christianity. As this era has a special significance for the Welsh consciousness of nationhood, the advantages of the Church's identification with these saints are obvious.

Under the leadership of certain able, scholarly men, both clerical and lay, a determined attempt is being made to present the Church in Wales to the nation as her spiritual *alma mater*. The increasing use of the Welsh language in her services and the renewal of much traditional Catholic usage—pilgrimages, the saying of Mass and the hearing of confessions, help to promote the identification with the "original" Catholic Church in Wales. These efforts are quite obviously made in all sincerity, and it would be a rash protagonist

[1] i.e. what had been the State Church, hereafter referred to simply as "the Church", in the Welsh sense of distinction from "the Chapel".

who blamed the Church in Wales for a presentation of the nation's religious history which contains pitfalls even for the most scholarly. Nevertheless, any serious Catholic treatment of the Welsh question *must* elucidate this historical tangle on the scholarly level.

Ironically, however, the Church in Wales has recently suffered a blow in the very field wherein it had staked its particular claim to represent modern Welsh aspirations, i.e., that of a Welsh and Welsh-speaking hierarchy. In 1957, contrary to the recommendations of its governing body, two appointments were made to the hierarchy, one a non-Welsh-speaking Archbishop of Wales and the other a non-Welsh-speaking bishop. These appointments provoked bitter public denunciations which drew grave warnings from two bishops of the risk that the Church runs of being split into factions—the Welsh faction against the traditional enemy, basically a political power which is the ultimate and secret arbiter in Welsh Church affairs: the power of the English State Church. In a bitter denunciation in the Welsh vernacular press a contemporary Welsh poet[1] describes his own disillusion. He who had sought refuge and a spiritual home in this Church which he believed could best deal with Wales' present religious impasse has left her in disgust. With eloquence he denounces this "traitress" who, he says, for all her fair promises, has once more appeared in her true guise of a political institution which has always run counter to all that the Welsh need. Significantly he turns his attention to the Catholic Church, saying that many, like himself, are now wondering whether it is not there at last that the true mother of Wales is to be found. The one religious issue to be decided in the near future of Wales, he says, is this: is it the Church in Wales, or the Catholic Church, that represents the authentic religious tradition of Wales? No other issue will rival this in importance for the religious destiny of Wales. He recalls the gesture of the present Archbishop of Cardiff, who, although an Irishman, had, as previous Bishop of Menevia, learnt Welsh and had regularly issued Welsh pastoral letters to non-Catholic leaders of Welsh thought and culture. Was not this an essentially Catholic act, he asks, showing forth the Roman Catholic Church as a true Mother of Nations?

It will be deduced from this line of argument that contemporary Wales is deeply involved in the crucial issue of survival on all fronts.

[1] Gwenallt, Senior Lecturer in Welsh Literature, University College of Wales, Aberystwyth.

In this respect Wales participates in the same struggle as so many other national minorities. The threat to Welsh survival from our industrialized and dehumanized Western civilization is a real one, and whether Welsh claims are articulate on the cultural, economic or political level, they form part of the Welshman's instinctive defence of his patrimony. Thus it is that on the religious level the Welshman insists that his conversion must imply also his conversion as a social being, that is, as a Welshman.

Against such a background we must now consider how the Welsh convert to Catholicism fares. To appreciate his position we must indicate what circumstances characterize the return of the Catholic Church to Wales. There are today about 110,000 Catholics in Wales. Of this total 87,000 live in industrialized South Wales. These form a substantial minority in a land of so many religious divisions. For the most part these Catholics came in the wake of the Industrial Revolution. The mid nineteenth century, the years of the Irish famine, saw a great influx of Irish into South Wales and today's Catholic bourgeoisie and working-class communities are their descendants. For generations the pastoral activity of the Catholic Church in Wales has been almost entirely concerned with improvization to meet the needs of immigrants. Not until our own generation has there been a breathing space in which ecclesiastical leaders could lift up their eyes and scan the native horizon and appreciate the complexity of the situation at their doors.

The immigrants were regarded with hostility by the Welsh, who feared in them a source of cheap and plentiful labour and a consequent threat to their own economic security. Since those troubled days, Welshmen generally have regarded the Catholic Church in Wales as an intruder, alien in appearance and representing in her hierarchic and authoritative aspects the complete negation of the values which, for them, have been born of valid religious experience.

Yet, by a providential irony, nearly all the Welsh converts to the Catholic Church come from Nonconformist bodies. Most of them come in consequence of their marriage to a Catholic. A minority has come as the result of a personal conversion which makes it imperative to take the step, cost what it may. But by whatever divinely ordained means they find their way to the Church, their position in relation to the society which has bred them undergoes the same profound change. They become strangers upon their own hearths; suspect and misunderstood by those to whom they matter most. Nor is their human loss in any way recompensed by a tantamount human gain in their new milieu. As we have seen, the Catholic Church in Wales is not an indigenous nor a homogeneous body. In her ranks are to be found members of every nationality; the flotsam and jetsam of our industrial era, owing no allegiance to Wales and under no obligation to her save that of making a living within her territory. Between the Welsh convert and his new-found brethren in Christ there is no social affinity whatever. There is but a common obligation, that of worshipping God in spirit and in truth. Naturally, converts in the bigger Welsh towns fare best. There, in a more highly differentiated society, the individual convert is more likely to discover a milieu wherein his Catholic life can expand. But seven-eighths of Wales is a rural area, and the inhabitants of rural Wales are largely engaged in farming and kindred occupations. Catholic churches, schools and Mass centres are few and far between. To compare a map of sixth- to seventh-century Catholic settlements in Wales with a contemporary map of the Diocese of Menevia is to realize at once how entirely of foreign origin is the Catholic Church today. Gone are the innumerable sites of local and native piety which studded the map of Wales.[1] Our modern centres of worship crowd along the seaboards of Wales in the wake of the summer visitors and immigrants.

In rural and Welsh Wales, in villages and market towns alike, the focal point of local society is the life of the Welsh chapels, and to a lesser degree that of the Church in Wales. The medium of communication is Welsh which, in all probability, owes its survival to Nonconformity. Such religious values as still permeate Welsh culture are certainly to be attributed to the influence of Protestant preaching and teaching.

Today these religious values are under direct assault by many forces, and the Welsh language in particular is suffering the full impact of an alien culture through radio and television. Welsh parents and educators in areas where the national culture is rapidly being impoverished have been energetic in founding and obtaining public support for primary schools whose medium of instruction is Welsh. This movement received a strong impetus after World War II and now caters for nearly 10,000 children. Their educational achievements are impressive, and this, together with an added

[1] See E. G. Bowen, *Settlements of the Celtic Saints in Wales*, Aberystwyth, University of Wales Press Board.

respect for the Welsh language, has given the Welsh child in non-Welsh areas of Wales a new prestige. The next step was the opening of Welsh secondary schools to accommodate the 11-18 years age group, and inevitably plans are now afoot to establish an all-Welsh constituent college of the University of Wales. Welsh text-books on a wide variety of subjects are being produced, and in areas where Welsh is already predominant, all teaching in State primary schools to 11+ level is given in Welsh.

This is all as it should be, of course. Judged by Catholic standards, the Welsh determination to defend cultural and human values in an age which derides them is a moral act of deep significance. Pope Pius XII spoke more often on this theme than on any other. In his Christmas Message of 1954 (*Catholic Documents*, XVII, p. 40), speaking of true and false nationalism, he says: "National life, the right and prized possession of a people, may and should be promoted: nationalistic politics, as a germ infinitely harmful, will never be sufficiently repelled. National life is in itself that operative composite of all the values of civilization which are proper and characteristic of a particular group, for whose spiritual unity they constitute, as it were, the bond. At the same time it enriches as its own contribution the culture of all humanity. In its essence, therefore, national life is not political; and this is confirmed by the fact that as history and practice demonstrate, it can develop alongside of others within the same state, just as it can also extend itself beyond the political frontiers of the same state."

And again: "In a sense it can be said that the popular culture of a country is the summary of its character. Centuries have contributed to it; the institutions, the language and its customs are at the same time both its fruit and the instruments by which it is produced, because they reflect the spirit of the age in which they began and then contribute towards maintaining it. It suffices to pass from one country to another to perceive the sometimes noteworthy differences which mark even neighbouring peoples. Behind the differences of individuals we find a common treasure of culture and a patrimony of art, literature and folklore in which all share in greater or less degree." (Discourse of Pope Pius XII to Adult Educationists in Italy. 19th March 1953, *Catholic Documents*, XI, p. 30.)

We have previously observed the close connection between the Welsh language and Protestant Christianity. We must not therefore be surprised that Nonconformity has hailed the initiation of a Welsh educational system with relief and that already, dependent as it is upon the comprehension of the spoken word, it is benefiting by the emergence of a resurgent Welsh language.

But the Welsh Catholic convert also participates in this consciousness of nationhood renewed. He will regard himself and his children as having a particular apostolate to fulfil towards his fellow Welshmen. In the process of conversion to the Church he will have found not only the God-given means of his own salvation but also the *alma mater* of his total Welsh heritage. He will have discovered this heritage as something ineffably enriched and deepened, and his love of his country will have taken on that additional *pietas* which derives from a religious regard for her. But while the convert regards with loving recognition the lineaments of his true mother's face, he will have to realize that each feature is one which will set him apart from his own kith and kin and from his Welsh neighbours, who will not regard sympathetically a conversion to Catholicism at a time when Wales is fighting a prolonged action for the very values of which our Catholic congregations are apparently either independent or ignorant. As Catholic educational policy in Wales bears no relation at all to Welsh cultural needs and values it is, moreover, a contentious topic between the Catholic authorities and educational bodies. And in view of historical circumstances it is difficult to see how things could be otherwise at this stage where only a fractional minority of Catholics are to be found in the reaches of Welsh higher education.

Thus it is that the convert in Welsh Wales fares hardest. So lacking is Welsh life in institutions other than those which derive from religious contexts that the convert feels that an abyss has opened between him and his fellow countrymen, for they no longer use a common vocabulary in reference to Wales. All conscious communication between them ceases. The convert, of course, knows that the living dialogue is carried on on a level deeper than that of speech. But this, if anything, only makes the apparent lack of contact more poignant.

But, it will be objected, all this is amply recompensed by the joys the convert has in his new-found security. On the deepest level this is most true. But the convert must also accept the discipline of suffering through his own children. They are Welsh-speaking, and by every Catholic standard of morality and justice they must remain so. The Welsh Catholic parent will face a cruel dilemma. His choice lies between adopting English as the language of the home, thus cutting the child off from his historical roots in order to adapt it to its non-Welsh Catholic milieu, or sending him to the local Welsh state school and bearing himself the responsibility of instructing him in his religion in Welsh at home.

It is pre-eminently in the field of education that the Church could and should create a rapprochement with modern Wales. The Welshman has a regard which sometimes verges on the superstitious for learning. And in his mind there has never been any dissociation between religion and learning. Catholics should spare no efforts to be involved in educational procedure in Wales. In the few cases where this has happened the results have been fantastically in excess of the efforts made. University chaplaincies should be a prime consideration; tutorship in the innumerable further education schemes which are typical of the Welsh countryside is another. There is in Welsh Wales a growing appreciation of that Catholic past which modern Welsh scholarship in literature, history and archaeology is revealing. Probably the worst enemy of Catholicism in Wales today is the culturally denuded aspect of Catholicism, its discarnate appearance. Yet some protagonists of the Catholic *status quo* would elevate this grave deficiency to the level of a spurious supernaturalism, identifying the ethos of our *déraciné* industrial proletariat with a kind of angelic superiority over the trivialities of language, historical situations and customs; in effect, over all those characteristics which keep man from becoming less than man. Nothing is more likely to estrange the Welshman, who is the product of a culture of unique religious intensity, which incorporates all these features in a high degree.

It will readily be conceded that religious issues in the modern world are decided in very different contexts from those which characterized the ages of faith. Ours is not the age of the Crusades, nor the age of great doctrinal heresies. What, then, lies behind the Welshman's insistence that the Church should accept him not only as an individual but as a human and social being? What is the real issue at stake? It is man's instinctive defence of the natural and social order into which he has been born. It is his insistence on a primary truth of the psychology of religious conversion: that it is nature which grace must sanctify and nothing else. The entire order of nature in our universe today is suffering a massive assault from dehumanizing powers, and the disruption of the family of nations is but one aspect of this disregard of God's moral laws.

All that relates to and defines our human condition comes within the providence of almighty God who has himself condescended to assume it. All that our heredity has made us, together with our own relation to others by, with and in whom we have a certain mode of existence, is bound up in that mysterious organization which is a Welshman, and equally with a Saxon or a Gael. And perhaps it is not until we recognize ourselves in some far past aspect of our human condition, at some long past point of history, that we realize who and what we are in relation to a grace which we may, in that moment of self-recognition, be enabled to receive. So it is that mighty moments of our past may become forever that climax which we yearn to attain again before we fully acquit ourselves in God's sight. There are such moments in the history of every nation and their potency is hidden in the soul of each of its members. Is it too much to discern in the present nostalgic interest in Wales' Catholic past an intuition of this kind which is a fruitful foundation for grace? And is not this a totally different aspect of history from that which is valued by the simple *laudator temporis acti*?

De Lubac, in his book *Catholicism*, writes: "All races, all cultures have something to contribute to the proper use of the divine treasure which she [the Church] holds in trust . . . She believes in fresh providential harmonies for her expansion." Undoubtedly today the most formidable attack on the human spirit comes in the guise of a spurious universalism whose progress is made rapid and superficially successful by the technological achievements of our time. These in turn bolster up a false standard of living and of progress, and the old and venerated pieties which nations had garnered, and in which man's spirit found repose on earth, have too often been trampled out of existence. On the religious plane this universalism can mask itself as a desire to transcend all cultural idiosyncracies and to acquire an angelic and suprahuman mode of existence. On the material level it is a false internationalism, to be attained through a self-stripping of all that makes one a member of a particular nation. In both cases it spells desolation and the utter impoverishment of the human spirit, providing fertile ground for further false universalisms, of which Communism may be the least.

We have felt it necessary to deal at some length with this particular psychology of the subhuman, because there is a very real danger in

Wales that it may be presented as an integral accompaniment of Catholicism. We have seen how this false approach has evolved out of purely temporal misfortunes. To achieve anything approaching the conversion of the Welsh the Church must herself cast her nets deeper, down to the roots of history. At the moment in Wales it is only a small minority of clergy who believe in this radical approach to the Welsh question. To the remainder, the argument for an appeal to the Welsh on their own grounds by a serious study of their religious involvements and culture is an argument for "narrow nationalism", and thus a question which far transcends the bounds of political expediency is repeatedly relegated to the cramping arena of a single political issue, especially and fatefully in the field of education. The tragedy is that the Catholic Church alone possesses the fructifying energy to assume this question and to recognize its full content as one of the gravest import to a society which, to be fully human, necessarily seeks its completion in the divine order.

In the Welsh religious scene there emerges a curious pattern. The Nonconformist purgation has released the Welsh soul from undue dependence on the mere externals of religion. It has, moreover, endowed it with the conviction that truth is to be known and experienced by the believer. The Welsh Nonconformist soul, deprived now of objective certainties, carries on its interior dialogue always within the area of this conviction: that even if final certainty is now obscured, it is somehow, sometime ascertainable.

The Welshman whose allegiance is to the Church in Wales is soon to be confronted with the need for a true assessment of the historical claims to apostolic succession. For him, too, will arise the necessity of deciding whether the exploitation of national language and customs, unless fostered within the Catholic context, does not run the risk of localizing and parochializing yet more the influence of the Church in Wales. He must realize that it is only the universalism of Catholicism, ever fructifying what is local and localizing what is universal, which can protect him from a naïve religious antiquarianism.

Meanwhile, what is being done by Catholics in Wales? A beginning there certainly is of a comprehensive approach to Wales, and this is being undertaken for the most part by Welsh converts, aided by a small body of clergy. With the blessing of both bishops in Wales *Y Cylch Catholig* (Catholic Circle) recruits its members from all those who truly desire the return of the Faith to Wales. The Cylch asks for prayer in Welsh from its members, who daily say the Prayer for Wales. It organizes pilgrimages, an annual triduum of prayer in the vernacular, and is responsible for a growing number of Welsh publications of devotional and theological import. It runs a highly successful bookstall every year for a week on the field of the Welsh National Eisteddfod where all the helpers, both priests and laity, must be in command of the Welsh language. So far, undoubtedly, the Cylch's chief impact has been not on Catholics but on Welsh non-Catholics, who have in many cases made their first contact with Welsh Catholicism through its activities. It now forms a liaison group of importance between the Church and Welshmen who would not, save in the most exceptional circumstances, ever come into contact with her.

In the last few years also, the Welsh Catholic group has been befriended from an unexpected source in one of those deeply satisfying ways which history sometimes has of repaying its debts. A group of Gaelic-speaking Irish scholars, clergy and laity of *An Realt*, have devoted a fortnight of their summer vacation to apostolic work in the wholly Welsh Catholic parish of Gelli-Lydan in Merionethshire. Some of these Irishmen are fluent Welsh speakers; others are learning Welsh in a Dublin night class which numbers about two hundred. All of them are fired with the desire to repay Wales for the gift of St. Patrick, by whose beneficent ministry they have so long profited. Our Irish friends do not limit their activities to purely spiritual matters. Welsh and Irish song and dance fill the evenings; non-Catholic Welsh fill the village hall; Welsh and Gaelic are intermingled. Because English is rarely used as an intermediary, both cultures make direct and immediate contact within the Christian context. After a fortnight's visit last summer our friends left behind them twelve new Welsh converts for instruction in this small parish. This is but one example of how much can be done in the rural and unspoilt areas of Wales.

Regarding the industrialized and *déraciné* South, we have said nothing. This is an area with its own special problems to be dealt with by particular measures. But these can only be effective within the larger context of national conversion. Can it be that, in contradiction to the abomination of desolation which present dehumanizing trends are creating, the ever-searching providence of God is raising up those "new harmonies" whereby all man's estate may be redeemed and the domain of the family (our Saviour's chosen sphere) extended in the revival of the nations? It is only *persons* who can withstand the impersonal monstrosities which threaten man's destiny today. And the sphere of the person is the family, and that of the family the nation.

Wales is greatly in need of help. We have not yet come within sight of the enormous work of teaching and explaining in Welsh; of patient exploration of the doctrinal position of the Christian sects in Wales, so that what is error may be discarded and what is truth filled out and completed. Catholicism in Wales is in dire need of a monastic house of studies where a beginning might be made of a serious study of the extensive Welsh Protestant literature of the last three centuries, but there is as yet no hint of an œcumenical approach to Welsh religious problems which must be made in the medium of Welsh in the numerous vernacular publications. There is no seminary specifically equipped to deal with Welsh religious vocations; they are scattered in every European seminary, and are thus prevented from being imbued with that particular ethos which would give them an intuitive insight into Wales, wherein God has called them.

The convert in Wales must draw upon consolations which lie beyond the sphere of the obvious. He must realize that he does not pray alone. The Communion of Saints is the interlocking in an unbreakable spiritual union of us and our forbears, Catholic and non-Catholic alike, who have died in the friendship of God; of that living ancestry of the flesh which now hears in its own tongue the intercession which we pour out for them. The gap between Catholic and non-Catholic is bridged and the language of St. David unites the past and present, containing also our intercession for the friends and relatives who have as yet not received the fulness of faith.

To see the apostolate in Wales in this way is to be free of the vanity of time, and our present cross becomes our secret consolation. For here *is* the entire Church, here and now *is* the entire Wales. Both *are* in God and it is *now* that matters. In this, our expression of hope, we bring God himself actually here and now into that point at which the future is conceived and takes shape. This great virtue of hope so enlarges our horizon that the Catholic ages gone and the Catholic age to come are fused in this point of time wherein we say our daily Prayer for Wales. This is the convert's true mode of existence wherein he comes to terms with God and Wales alike.

Bibliography

LLOYD, J. E., *A History of Wales*, vol. i.
EVANS, A. Wade, *Welsh Christian Origins*.
EVANS, David, *A History of Modern Wales*.
LEWIS, Saunders, *Williams Pantecelyn*.
BOWEN, E. G., *Settlements of the Celtic Saints in Wales*.
ATTWATER, Donald, *The Catholic Church in Modern Wales*.
BOUYER, Louis, *The Spirit and Forms of Protestantism*.
LUBAC, Henri de, *Catholicism*.
CHEVALIER, Jacques, *Essai sur la formation de la nationalité et les réveils religieux au pays de Galles*.

JAPAN

1. The Present Situation

YOSHIO KOBAYASHI

My aim here is to give a general picture of the present position of the Catholic Church in Japan. Japan was reopened to the Western world in 1873, the sixth year of the Meiji era. Since then the Church has been developing throughout Japan, principally through the work of missionaries of the Missions Étrangères de Paris, and has shown a very slow but steady progress. At present the Church here has fifteen dioceses, including more than 220,000 Catholics in all (about 0·2 per cent of the whole population of the country). There are 300 Japanese diocesan priests, 60 Japanese regular priests, and 1,039 foreign missionaries. There are, moreover, 208 Japanese brothers and 168 foreign brothers belonging to foreign missionary societies. Japanese sisters number 2,729, while the number of foreign sisters is 984. There are 241 diocesan major seminarians. There are 396 Catholic schools, which take 100,000 students. The oldest Catholic university, Sophia (Jochi Daigaku) has now been established for over forty years and has 1,800 students; it is managed by the Jesuits, together with the Tokyo diocesan major seminary. Compared with prewar figures, these figures are more than double.

With regard to the Catholic layman's activities, for example in the educational field, we find that coeducation was introduced into Japan after the War and is more or less general throughout all governmental, or public, schools, and now universities and high schools take boys and girls together, while Catholic schools remain as before the War, and take boys and girls separately only. From the standpoint of the Church girls' high schools are most successful, baptizing about half the non-Catholic girls during school years, while in the case of boys' high schools those who are baptized during school years are only 10-20 per cent. The missionaries give very solid preparatory instruction to those who wish to be baptized, so that

---

YOSHIO KOBAYASHI was born in 1902. He studied at Tokyo, Fribourg, Paris and Cologne, and has been since 1938 a Professor of Sophia University.

they keep their faith all their lives. But in parish churches on Sundays, we always find three or four times as many women as men. In Japan it is rather rare to find a whole family Catholic; to begin with only one or two members (wife or daughters) will usually be Catholics, probably through the influence of the girls' high school, the male members remaining non-Catholics, sometimes definitely anti-Christian. When the father of a family becomes a Catholic it is more often through the wife or daughters, and this is why the Catholic womens' clubs exert such an influence in Japanese society and exercise excellent social functions, such as financial and spiritual support for Catholic charitable institutions (hospitals, orphanages, leper hospitals, etc.).

Catholic men's activities are not so remarkable, except for the Catholic University Students' Club and the Jocists, both of which bodies are making good progress in both intellectual and labour circles, where all is in turmoil, even ten years after the War. Catholic influences in political and judicial circles are almost nil, in spite of the fact that the chief judge of the Supreme Court is a Catholic, Kotaro Tanaka, an ex-professor of the Imperial University in Tokyo, a world-famous scholar and a specialist in commercial law. However, one Catholic cannot do much, even if he occupies a very important position. Among Members of Parliament, too, only one is a Catholic, from Nagasaki prefecture, which occupies a very important place in the history of the Catholic Church in Japan since its establishment by St. Francis Xavier some four hundred years ago. Of course there is no Christian party in Japan, though there are a few Protestants in both the Conservative and Social Democratic parties. Recently, however, various means of mass-communication have become very important for the Church. Commercial broadcasting stations were opened after the War, and after heroic efforts the Church obtained the right to set up a station. After several years of struggle with the commercial stations it had to be handed over to them and religious broadcasting no longer exists. There are several Catholic publishing houses in Japan, mostly run by religious orders, who bring out many books every month, but they are strictly limited to devotional subjects, so it is seldom that these books are read by non-Catholics. Some religious orders publish periodicals (about five monthly, one weekly) but these also are seldom read by non-Catholics. On the other hand, the average Japanese is very fond of reading and very anxious to obtain information or news from abroad, so that each of the great Japanese papers sells more than four million copies a day and some magazines obtain more than a million readers each month. Compared with these results, we must admit our lack of effort. Thus the social influence of the Catholic Church in Japan leaves very much to be desired. These defects are most keenly felt with regard to social questions. The family system, emphasized so strongly by the Catholic Church as the basis of the social system, is going to collapse. Divorce is now fashionable among the Japanese upper classes, and the indissolubility of marriage preached by the Church is wholly disregarded.

The Japanese Government, along with doctors and intellectuals, is most energetic in advocating birth-control methods. Among the labouring classes Communist ideas, especially about the class struggle, are widespread, and there are not a few university professors who are sympathetic with, though not yet actual members of, the Japanese Communist Party, and who teach their students that Marxist theories alone provide the truth. Between those with a liberal or individualist view on the right wing, and the Communist sympathizers and "progressives" forming the left wing, Catholics must show a third way, which is the golden mean. This middle way, proclaimed by the Pope, is and must be the only one able to build up a truly humanistic community in any country, and to bring about a permanent peace among nations. In order to bring the Japanese to love the Catholic Church one must first show them what the Church stands for.

Although the Catholic Church in Japan enjoys a very fine reputation for its social work and schools, much is still to be done in the political, legislative and journalistic fields. For example, most of the sayings of the Pope concerning social questions should be translated into Japanese at once and widely diffused, at least among intellectuals. But little has been done in this respect, except a translation with commentaries of *Rerum Novarum* and *Quadragesimo Anno*, also a translation of Father Robert Kothen's work *L'Enseignement social de l'Église*, which is simply a collection of the great social encyclicals. We hope that through the efforts of its Catholics, Japanese society will come to know and take this middle way, and that Catholics in Japan will realize their function as the salt of the earth. Their numbers are only equal to a handful of salt among a population of more than 80,000,000.

2. The Church and Japanese Culture

THOMAS Y. TOMON

The task I have received is to explain the relationship of the Church in Japan to the national cultural tradition. Frankly speaking, Catholicism in Japan remains alien to its culture, while the cultural tradition has contributed almost nothing to the formation of Japanese Catholics. However, the problem of relationship does not only concern past history but also the work which lies ahead. Indeed, as the Church's mission has always to be carried out in an existing world, deriving from a particular historical process, the Church, by the very fact of her presence in a country, is bound to take up position with regard to its national tradition. The point here is not the number of the faithful, nor the question of reciprocal influences, but simply the basic fact that the Church is always within a situation which has been formed by history, and—in the case of a missionary country like Japan—formed with little or no Christian influence. Consequently, the problem of relationship does not only begin with the historical meeting of the Church and the country's culture, but it starts from the time when the cultural elements involved in that meeting were formed. I will try here to explain, as far as is possible, what these elements were, together with the meeting itself as seen within Japan's cultural history. Such an analysis should throw light on the actual situation which the Catholic Church has to face in Japan today.

I

The first written history of Japan dates from the beginning of the seventh century A.D. Using ancient Chinese and Korean documents, we can carry the story back to the first century, while according to the archaeologists metal was first employed in Japan some two centuries earlier. At that time a high civilization already flourished in China, destined to have an almost definitive influence upon the culture of Japan.

Communication between the two countries began in the Japanese prehistoric period, round about the first century B.C. On account of

---

THOMAS Y. TOMON was born in Shanghai in 1926. He studied pharmaceutical chemistry at the University of Kyoto; was received into the Church in 1949; and worked until 1952 in a penicillin factory, where he played a large part in trade-union activities. He is at present studying for the priesthood at the Pontifical College De Propaganda Fide, and is Japanese language broadcaster for the Vatican Radio.

its excellence, Chinese culture was always for Japan a thing to be embraced, yet throughout the long story of Sino-Japanese contact Japan has always maintained its political independence. No urge other than an internal one forced Japan to follow Chinese culture, and for that reason we can learn from this cultural contact of the very character of the primitive Japanese mentality, out of which—through the long story of Japanese culture—the modern mentality of Japan has been formed.

The importation of Chinese culture up to the seventh century was due to simple curiosity rather than to any conscious national act. Like children, the young Japanese people admired the products of the neighbouring civilization and wished to possess them. But from the seventh to the ninth centuries this importation was, we may say, on a national scale. The Chinese influence of those three hundred years was decisive for Japanese culture, and can be compared with that received by the barbarian peoples from the Roman Empire. Japan learnt the use of letters, laws, philosophy, religion. After this period there was still contact, still influence, but the age of education was over and the culture of Japan, still open to a completing influence from China, had now set out upon its own road.

Japan's adoption of Chinese characters poses a most complex problem, which derives from the very nature of the Chinese and Japanese languages; yet something must be said about it because of its immense influence on the formation of the Japanese mentality. The use of Chinese characters began about the third century. Japan had no letters of its own, and consequently learnt from China not merely Chinese writing, but writing itself. Chinese characters are not phonetic signs, but each has its own meaning and pronunciation, and consequently their number is horribly large, round about 100,000. The Japanese of that age either used them as phonetic signs for the transcription of Japanese words, or as a way of expressing a concept whose pronunciation remained quite different in Japanese from its Chinese form. Evidently, there were also many new words imported, and these held to their proper Chinese pronunciation.

The burden of these vastly numerous and complicated characters, specially for the transcription of purely Japanese words, was too great, and little by little the Japanese began to develop their own phonetic characters. This work was completed by the ninth century, and we now have fifty characters with two auxiliary signs which express, more or less, all the possible Japanese monosyllabic combinations (we use only five vowels and seventeen consonants).

However, the Chinese characters, and up to the end of the nineteenth century, the Chinese language itself, remained the language of intellectuals. When it was first introduced, Japanese was without the abstract and technical terms which Chinese possessed. The new terms were introduced with the characters, and with the use of these terms the Chinese language became that of the educated class. The process was quite natural and similar ones may be found elsewhere, for example in the relations between Latin and the other European languages.

But the result was a misfortune, almost fatal for the development of the Japanese language. Its grammatical structure was too different from that of Chinese. Japanese intellectuals could read and write Chinese well, but they could not speak it. They did not indeed have much occasion to do so, but the grammatical structure was, anyway, a great impediment; on this point it is enough to recall that this radical difference of structure prevents any so-called "simultaneous" translation of Japanese into either Chinese or any European language. The consequence was that the use of the new Chinese terms did not help much to develop the capacity of the Japanese language to express abstract concepts. Japanese is a language which expresses the refinements of the heart rather than those of the reason, and the use of Chinese characters could not change such a characteristic. Faced with Chinese reasoning, whose qualities were not found sufficient to express the heart of the Japanese people, the Japanese language itself insisted always more on its capacity to express sentiment—heart-knowledge. Even the members of the intelligentsia, with few exceptions, never ceased to compose Japanese poetry for the expression of their most intimate sentiments.

But we may apply here Pascal's remark about the heart's having reasons of its own; as a human language Japanese could not entirely lack a capacity of reasoning. However, due to the situation explained above, the Japanese way of reasoning has always laid the greatest stress on the logic of the heart; consent through the integral intuition of things, rather than on the formal logic of the intellect. This separation of reason and heart has had a great influence on culture, especially on its more spiritual aspect. On the one hand, the Japanese felt intuitively a certain weakness in Chinese culture, that is to say a "nihilist" neglect of personality, while they rightly knew that it is only the individual person who exists, lives, feels. To preserve the language of personal sentiment meant, in a certain way, to preserve personality itself. Both in the artistic and in the intellectual fields, the Japanese wished to maintain their "personalist" outlook, and in religion it is the person who counts. It is symptomatic of this that Shintoism, which has always remained the spiritual foundation of the people, has never—even to the present day—made use of Chinese terminology in its ceremonies.

On the other hand, because the use of Chinese characters has helped to separate the reason from the heart, Japanese people, when considering the world of sentiment, passion and intuition, do not envisage the possibility of a rational explanation or of the direction of passion and the practical judgement by a higher principle. The Japanese are as good as anyone in reasoning "horizontally", from point to point; what we lack is that reasoning which concerns the hierarchy of values. There has been no whole view of things. In practice, the dominant characteristic of Japanese history has been "the triumph of passion", though the manifestation of this has been quite different from anything in the Western world. Art has been well developed, but it has lacked synthesis, as also a sufficient intellectual basis. Another consequence of all this is that philosophy has never found a fruitful home in Japan. I don't deny that Confucianism was accepted by the Japanese intellectuals, but it only spread with the greatest difficulty among the people, and that only after the sixteenth century. Moreover, Confucianism was unable to solve the problem of the relation of mind and heart, and the Japanese did not come, after its spread, to place the Confucian moral values above the force of passion, though also not beneath. Many a time this clash of values has been resolved in death alone.

2

In the so-called Buddhist countries Buddhism has more or less destroyed the ancient pagan religions. But in Japan the old gods still live today, while Buddhism itself has taken on a very different form. Yet it has not been absorbed in the traditional religion, as in India; rather does it maintain a strange, peaceful coexistence with the old gods, so that today the majority of Japanese do not feel any contradiction in worshipping in the home at two altars, one Buddhist and one Shintoist. Of that we must now seek the reason by seeing how Buddhism entered Japan.

It did so, via Korea, in the fifth and sixth centuries. Buddhism arrived in its Chinese form, the Buddhist texts in Chinese translation.

At the beginning there was the usual clash. Conservatives feared the anger and curse of the old gods; but after a short conflict between progressives and traditionalists, the attack on Buddhism ended in the year 587.

The new religion was adopted especially by the nobles because it was understood to represent the foundation of Chinese civilization, and therefore also of the new Japanese civilization which they were intent on constructing. This was the time of the formation of a single Japanese nation, and the elaborated system of Buddhism captured the heart of young Japan; with youthful enthusiasm it was adopted as the foundation of the ideal order on this earth. In the Japanese appropriation of Buddhism we can see the joy of a young people conscious of its approach to the truth. "The world is vain, only Buddha is true", it has been said; but the Japanese of that time saw rather the possibility of founding a new and ideal society based upon the truth.

The passion and energy with which Japan embraced Buddhism nevertheless manifested at the very same time an attitude which has always since dominated the country. I am speaking of that attitude which recognizes in the State the supreme authority in matters religious. Before the shining superiority of Chinese culture, Japan wished to maintain its independence. As I have said, the primitive Japanese were very conscious of the value of the human person; this consciousness was without doubt the foundation of their desire for independence, and began—in the cultural contact with China—to have a social expression which finally so developed as to destroy the very sense of personality in a social totalitarianism. Japan wished to improve itself by means of Chinese civilization, but while appreciating the excellence of the latter, it was at the same time acutely conscious of the danger of losing its independence through the cult of civilization. No country is without stain, and the cultural attitude of Japan when faced with the developed civilization of a neighbouring country—to hold supreme the value of the State—was not without its reasons. But what consequences it has had! The supremacy of politics in the field of religion has from that time been almost always taken for granted.

The subordination of Buddhism to the State took various forms.

First, there was the very severe legislation concerning Buddhist priests and monks, which not only demanded of them a highly ascetic life but also prohibited all personal contact with the people. It was enough that the priest should pray; the Government would make itself responsible for religious propaganda. Secondly, there was what we may call the religious subordination of Buddhism to Shintoism. By Shintoism I mean the complex of cults of the ancient gods, of whom some of the most important were the ancestors of the Emperor and of the Japanese people. Shintoism is, doubtless, a species of religion, but to speak more precisely, it is a religious attitude towards one's own country and history. For Japan to affirm its own importance is more or less equivalent to maintaining Shintoism. Consequently, the subordination of Buddhism to statecraft involved its subordination to Shintoism, and even to Shintoism in its properly religious aspect. There is plenty of historic evidence for this subordination; it stands to show that Japan wished to use Buddhism as a political instrument, but it also shows, more profoundly, a defence reaction whereby Japan remained within the cultural and religious tradition which had been the foundation of its society. This was linked with an instinctive realization that Buddhism had not the required social character to provide a substitute.

When all is said and done, however, it has still to be admitted that Buddhism presented a higher culture with a force of its own, and the following period of Japanese history presents us with the gradual insertion of Buddhism in Japan's own national culture. It was concerned with that side of the human person which is unsatisfied with social development but is interested in personal salvation. Indeed, the social changes of that period, with the concentration of land in the hands of the nobility, and the impoverishment of the many who no longer enjoyed their primitive liberty, created the need for such a religion. Culture flourished among the nobles, but this was overshadowed by the sorrows of the common people.

In these circumstances Buddhism began to appear as a means of personal salvation. Certainly, it did not cease to be of social utility, but the common people wanted more than social utility. The ancient gods were sufficient for the granting of communal benefits, but they were not saviours of the individual person. Japanese Buddhism now began to take on its own characteristics. The Buddha too, it was said, could benefit humanity, and the people began to identify him with the ancient gods themselves. But, if he is a benefactor, the Buddha can be no more a philosopher who teaches the way of salvation; he must be a powerful divinity who saves man by his own salvific will. This line of thought developed in Japanese Buddhism from the ninth to the thirteenth century. Now was developed the theory of universal salvation—no one is predestined to be lost; and on this followed the devotion to the Buddha's salvific will. If we are sinners, the Buddha will save us in his infinite mercy. "If the good man will be saved", said Shinran (1175-1262), founder of the largest sect in modern Japanese Buddhism, "how can the bad man not be saved?" Others, like the great Dogen, insisted on the importance of human asceticism and the possibility of sanctifying oneself, and if all this seems very far away from the context of primitive Buddhism (or the modern Buddhism of, for example, Siam), we must still judge it to be a healthy change and due to a profound intuition. The Japanese were approaching a truer understanding of the relations between God and man. Yet this change was not made on account of intellectual reflection; the unique cause for religious certainty remained an interior conviction, and the whole religion was one of deep sentiment rather than of reason, more akin to Protestantism than Catholicism. It is perhaps a reason why in the last one hundred years the former has had greater influence on Japanese culture than the latter.

We must now return to the problem of the coexistence of Buddhism with the old gods. The subordination of Buddhism to Shintoism, of which I have already spoken, was not made only by the Government, but was often furthered by the Buddhists themselves. Yet if the juridical status of Buddhism was much inferior to that of Shintoism, it rose little by little through its Japanese transformation to the very throne of Japan's religious sentiment. But Buddha had to share his throne with the gods of the past.

Once the surpassing excellence of Chinese culture and Buddhism was admitted, the independence of Japan could only find its intellectual justification in the myth of the people forechosen by the gods. The central point and proof of the myth is the fact that the living god, descendant of the supreme goddess of the gods, is no other than the Japanese Emperor himself. That is Shintoism. The effort of importing a foreign culture always drew its strength from this myth: Japan could reach the level of China, and even rise higher, because it was the land chosen of the gods. Hence Buddhism could never really affect the supremacy of Shintoism, and it often even happened that the best Buddhists were the most devoted to the cult of the gods. From the tenth century the canonization (or posthumous recognition of sanctity) of distinguished Buddhist priests was made by the Emperor, who distributed this honour without prejudice among the different sects. He alone had an almost supreme authority over Buddhism, though he rarely intervened in questions of dogma. So the gods remained, and Buddha remained, but the Emperor ruled them both.

3

The arrival of Western culture in Japan is graced by the name of Saint Francis Xavier (1549), but to speak frankly, those hundred years of missionary work, rewarded though they were with numerous conversions (three to four hundred thousand, 2-3 per cent of the population) and crowned with the blood of martyrs, have left almost no trace upon the culture of Japan. The fiercest of persecutions completely uprooted the Church.

When we recall that martyrs are the very seed of Christianity, how are we to explain this wiping out of the Japanese Church? Let us repeat: a mission which was begun by a saint and crowned with the blood of martyrs has left hardly a trace in Japanese culture. Certainly, religion is not culture, yet up to a certain point we can measure the success of a mission in terms of culture. The reason is that our religion is something not only personal but social, and it finds its achieved perfection in the Christianization of the whole of society. The result of missionary work ought to be a genuinely Christian society, and hence, because culture is a spiritual expression of society, we can rightly judge the state of a mission by its influence on culture. But Christianity has left no mark upon the culture of Japan.

Notwithstanding the apparent results, Catholicism did not in fact penetrate the Japanese mentality. Why was this? Certainly, the martyrs did not die in vain, and one cannot deny the real enthusiasm with which Catholicism was accepted. Then why? To answer this question, a number of things have to be considered.

The mission supported itself too much upon the social system of that time, the missionaries concerning themselves principally with the nobles or minor princes. If one of these was baptized, at once and on his demand his subjects were baptized as well. Some among these princes were, without doubt, men of character. But too often their attraction towards Catholicism was far from being of a purely religious kind, rather was it accompanied by the hope of financial advantage, a desire to profit through contact and commerce with foreigners. As we know from the history of the West, enforced baptism produces many grave problems. A prince may certainly recommend baptism to his subjects, but not enforce it. Yet even the recommendation of a prince has often an almost binding psychological force upon subjects who have little awareness of any personal responsibility before God. Especially for the Japanese of that period, the moral foundation of submission to civil authority stressed the quality of a categorical obedience. Hence many were baptized, not only on the occasion of their prince's baptism, but *simply* because their prince was baptized.

This was to admit the superiority of the political order over the religious. Religion had to follow, not the will of the individual, but that of his superior—*Cuius regio eius et religio*! If, subsequently, these Christian princes were to submit to a supreme ruler who forbade his subjects to be Catholics, they would have difficulty in finding ground for objection, especially if they were still not well grounded in their faith. Unfortunately this was just what happened in Japan.

When Francis Xavier visited Japan, the country was divided between a large number of small independent princes; that was almost the only century in which we have lacked national unity. Yet the various rulers aimed at unification, which was natural and obvious, for there was only one country with one language and one culture. Unity was desired by all; its symbol remained always the Emperor, head of the most ancient family, the descendant of the supreme goddess; but at that time he had no political power, only a position of religious dignity. Unification could only be achieved by the domination of one among the princes, but also only beneath the imperial symbol sanctioned by the gods of the land. To be a Christian meant to abandon those gods, and therefore to abandon also the foundation of the Emperor's position and the whole social order of Japan.

It is not, then, surprising, that it was Toyotomi Hideyoshi, who finally unified Japan, who also in 1587 began the persecution of Christians, especially of foreign missionaries. The persecution, however, was not at first very severe; public missionary activity was forbidden, but personal faith in Catholicism was still allowed to common folk. Many Christian princes abandoned the Faith, or at least publicly denied it, and from that time the missionaries consequently turned to evangelizing ordinary people, from whom the greater part of the Japanese martyrs eventually came.

In this period of the unification of Japan and of growth in national consciousness, the Catholic missionaries were connected with a threat of attack from Spain. All Japanese desired to make use of Western technical progress, but they were not interested in the spiritual side of European civilization. Often the princes allowed missionary activity not out of any religious motive, but simply because they looked for technical and economic advantages. Immediately the Japanese saw the danger of losing their independence, their reaction was swift against foreign intrusion and its spiritual spearhead, the Catholic mission.

Christianity was not thought of as the possible means for a reformation of society and culture: not by non-Christians, nor perhaps even by many of the Christians. From 1614 the latter had simply to prepare for martyrdom, while for the Japanese non-Christian, Christianity remained a strange enthusiasm opposed to the whole Japanese tradition. And that judgement was a true one, not because Christianity was harmful, but because the tradition of Japan, especially its religious tradition, was not a right one.

In 1615 the government of Tokugawa set out to extinguish Catholicism. The national tradition remained unchanged, Catholicism disappeared. If the mission had concentrated in time upon the common people and then Japanese Catholics themselves had propagated the Faith among the upper classes, as in the case of Primitive Christianity within the Roman Empire, everything might have been different. As it was, the genuine conversion of the ordinary people came too late, and it was almost only such people that came to embrace the glory of martyrdom.

4

The subsequent centuries of separation between Japan and the Western world ended with the arrival of an American fleet under Commodore Perry in 1853. Japan was forced to open her doors; the Government had to make a treaty of friendship in 1854, and then also a commercial treaty. For thirteen years, from 1854 to 1867, the country was in a state of tremendous agitation; its outcome, in 1867, was the return of the Emperor to the fullness of his political power, which in practice he had not possessed for centuries.

The coming of the American fleet was truly "shocking" for the Japanese; it may be said to have determined their attitude towards Western civilization. The material force of the Western world was now a fact which no one could deny. Japan was threatened. Her future was in danger. Yet the existing feudal government could not guide the people because on account of economic development the whole feudal system was collapsing, and in these circumstances legislation alone had little force. On the other hand, everyone felt the need for national unity under a powerful government. From day to day the sense of national consciousness grew under the direct threat from abroad. That sense was based on belief in Japan as the kingdom of the gods. As in the past, before the threat of external force far superior to anything of their own, the Japanese had to convince themselves of their own religious and metaphysical value. But, faced with this new threat, it was not enough to affirm one's metaphysical superiority, it was also necessary to demonstrate the force and value of the Japanese State as such. The difficulty here lay in the very evident superiority of Western civilization, at least on the material side. Only spiritually could the Japanese claim superiority; this was a type of superiority unmeasurable and even unknowable. Rationally, doubtless, it could not be proved, but that did not matter, for the determining proof of it was not reason, but traditional religion, which taught the value of the country given by the gods. Japan was the kingdom of the gods, and she was ruled by the descendant of the supreme goddess. This type of racial-religious nationalism grew ever stronger.

On the other hand, two hundred and fifty years of peace had encouraged the study of the ancient cultural tradition of Japan. The classics dating from the eighth to the tenth centuries returned to favour, and the value of the ancient Japanese who had known neither Buddhism nor Confusianism was again recognized. There was some gain in this, for the primitive people of Japan had lived nearer to the natural law than their descendants; nevertheless, in the actual circumstances of that moment of crisis, it further encouraged the nationalism which looked for a new national unity under the effective rule of the Emperor.

This tendency grew from the national desire for a political change but also from the accepted philosophy, which insisted on the supremacy of the political. It being agreed that there was an authority —the Emperor—which sanctioned the acts of the Government, and that that authority, although religious, sanctioned also non-religious political acts, it was almost inevitable that there should be a movement to give back to the Emperor effective full political authority. Indeed historically his power had certainly been of a politico-religious type, not religious only.

Consequently, after the coming of the American fleet, the activity of the loyalists continually grew, until, fifteen years later, it brought about the revolution of 1867.

At first the loyalist movement was simply anti-foreign. Its aim was to drive out the forces from abroad, but, when this proved impossible, the policy became rather one of civilizing Japan by means of contact with foreign countries. Consequently we have to understand that contact between Japan and Western civilization came to be caused and promoted precisely by that type of nationalist sentiment, rooted in the country's Shintoist consciousness, which had now become a recognizable ideology. This approach was decisive as regards the formation of the Japanese attitude towards the civilization of the West.

5

Here is the beginning of modern Japan. We must reach the standard of the West—this was the theorem which dominated all the activity of the new government of the Emperor Meiji, dating from 1867. It was an exaggerated, and yet an almost necessary, political attitude: exaggerated, because literally every side of life was now developed according to its dictate. It is incredible, and yet true, that even utilitarianism and rationalism were imported into the country because it was thought that they would make Japan more civilized and stronger. It was also a necessary attitude—necessitated by the need to maintain national independence in the era of colonialism. Once we have understood the origin of the revolution and the cause of its internal energy, it is not difficult to grasp the resultant situation.

One of the historical events which best illustrate the character of the Government is its tactics in the field of religion. As nationalist Shintoism had been a dominant element making for the 1867 revolution, it was natural for the Shintoist ideologists, at the beginning of the new regime, to try and insert their own views in Government policy. The ministry of the cult of the ancient gods was raised above that of the political ministries, manifesting the Government's desire to establish a Shintoist theocracy. In 1868 began the separation of the gods from Buddhism—in the past, as we know, they were much mixed up. After this the attack on Buddhism grew stronger. The temples were destroyed, many Buddhist statues and religious ornaments carried off for use, ironically enough, in armament manufacture, and the lands possessed by Buddhist temples were taken over by the Government. By 1873 the separation of gods and Buddhism was completed.

Also in 1870 there was issued the imperial decree for the Shintoist "Great Mission", and it was repeated in the following year. Shintoism was to be strictly the national religion.

This policy was not a great success. In 1871 the ministry of the cult of the gods lost its superiority over the other ministries, and in 1872 it was renamed the Ministry of Shintoist Education. In the following year the Government promulgated the three chapters of the so-called "Great Mission", at the same time choosing its ministers among Shintoist and Buddhist priests, Shintologists and Confucianists. The three chapters were the following: (1) All must learn to fear the gods and to love the homeland; (2) The way of the gods and the moral life of man must be made clear; (3) All have the duty of supporting and defending the land of the Emperor and obeying the will of the Emperor.

The duty of the ministers was simply to preach these three ideas. Buddhist temples became branch stations for the "Great Mission". In them was also begun the new cult of the gods of Shintoism. The Buddhist priests had to preach the cult of the Emperor as well as that of Buddha, while often, after listening to a Buddhist priest, the people would have to listen in the same temple to the sermon of some Shintoist priest telling them to observe the cult of the Emperor and the national gods but not to take part in other religions.

It can be understood that the confusion due to all this was very great, and many sincere Buddhists protested vigorously. In 1875 the centre of the "Great Mission" was consequently closed down, while Shintoist and Buddhist priests were allowed to preach apart. In 1877 the very Ministry of Shintoist Education was abolished, its work passing to a section of the Ministry for Internal Affairs. In 1884 the obligation of teaching the "Great Mission" was also removed, and so ended the Government's attempt to make of Shintoism the unique national religion.

After such a failure the Government no more attempted to impose a national religion on the people; instead it stressed that Shintoism—the cult of the ancient gods—was not a religious but a national act. It had had to recognize, at least to some extent, that religion was something above it, something more than an instrument of policy.

Nevertheless we must not attach too much importance to this failure. The Buddhists who criticized the Government were not against the substance of governmental policy—the deepening of the national Shintoist consciousness of the people—but against the method by which this was being done. Each religion, Buddhists thought, ought to teach Shintoist nationalism—on this point no one had any doubt at all—but this teaching would be effective only if in conformity with religious dogma. Each religion has its own dogma, different from the others, and Shintoist nationalism should be preached upon this foundation. There can be no organization above the Government, but the work of teaching must be left to each religion.

The Japanese liberals, too, had protested that if Japan wished to be a civilized country it must have "freedom of religion". Religion is a private thing, not to be touched by the Government. But they too had nothing to say against the Shintoist approach to the Emperor.

Substantially, the Government never abandoned its design. It had been the purpose of the "Great Mission" to form a new social mentality. Besides the three foundamental chapters, it had propounded the teaching of twenty-eight theses. Among them we find the virtue of the gods and the benevolence of the Emperor (no. 1), love of country (5), of the Emperor and his subjects (8), attitude to other countries (19), to civilization (23), state laws (25), the enriching of the homeland and the increase of military strength (26). The Government had desired to make use of the Shintoist and Buddhist priests for the formation of this new national mentality; failure had shown only that they were not suitable instruments. It is too difficult to re-educate the old. Henceforward the Government turned instead to the schools. No one was to be forced to believe, and the traditional religions were to continue to enjoy complete liberty. But all must go to school, and more than 90 per cent of the schools were run by the Government. This solid foundation for nationalist and Shintoist education was established by 1890 and continued substantially unchanged until the end of the Second World War.

Christianity could not be so easily assimilated in this mental climate, and it remained a great problem for the Government. Its prohibition by law remained, and in 1869 those Japanese Catholics who had maintained the Faith in secret—though most probably they were denying the Faith before public authority—and had now been rediscovered by French missionaries, were persecuted by the new Government. The Western ambassadors protested, but their protests were disregarded. But when the Government sent a delegation abroad to procure a change in the treaty between Japan and the Western powers, the delegates encountered strong criticism of the persecution. While this continued, they were told, the treaty could not be changed. After 1872 there was no more public persecution and the imprisoned Catholics were released. But persecution persisted in more subtle forms until 1887. Up to 1884 Christians had not been allowed to bury their dead in their own way, and if we remember that for the Japanese burying the dead is the most important religious act in life, we realize that such a prohibition was tantamount to the prohibition of Christianity itself.

The Government could not long continue with this anachronistic policy. After 1883 it began to show favour to Christianity, not indeed because Christianity was true, but because such a course would facilitate the changing of the treaty. If Christians in Japan are more numerous, it argued, foreigners will cease to feel so hostile towards us. Basically, the attitude of the Government never changed, as appears quite clearly in the "liberty of religion" clause of the new constitution.

This new constitution was promulgated in 1889. By it freedom of religion was granted in so far as this should not disturb social order or be contrary to the duty of the subject. It was the first official permission of Christianity. Until 1889 Christianity had only been tacitly allowed, for the law of prohibition had never been publicly withdrawn. But we must not forget that this same constitution defines the Emperor as a person sacred and inviolable (art. 2). Such words had a more than legal sense. The very next year a Protestant teacher who failed to make an act of adoration before a copy of the imperial rescript on education, but only inclined his head a little, was widely accused of *lèse-majesté*, and a Protestant journal which defended him was immediately prohibited by the Government. Until the abolition of State Shintoism ordered by the Allied forces in 1945 and the denial of his divine personality by the Emperor himself in 1946, there was never freedom of religion in the full sense, and Christians were constantly made aware of it.

6

It is generally true that nationalism has two sides—one conservative, the other progressive. Based on a firm belief in the country's traditional values is the equally firm desire for improvement. National self-confidence was already clear before 1867, and under the new Government it brought forth a wonderful effort towards modernizing and renewal. The motto was "civilize and enlighten". Modernization was not understood merely as material improvement, but also as a real "enlightening" of the old mentality. The men of this new Japanese Enlightenment wished to educate the people, and their books were widely disseminated. For example, a popular work on Western civilization was published in 1870 and sold more than 300,000 copies, although at that time elementary education was still not compulsory in Japan. It was not the Government which distributed the books, but the people who bought them. The passion for improving Japan was an entirely popular one.

But this at once presents a problem. It was the nineteenth century, the age of modern nationalism, when European civilization no longer maintained its previous unity. What culture did the men of the Japanese Enlightenment in fact understand by Western civilization? How did they think of it, and what did they want to do about it?

As we already know, their psychology was more or less nationalist. Their great desire was to improve their country. They fiercely attacked the old superstitions, customs and ways of thought; they were rationalists, insisting on the natural science of modern Europe and deriding the old-fashioned *a priori* metaphysics of Buddhism or Confusianism. Even Shintoism, in so far as it was a superstitious cult of the gods, was criticized. Rationalist, nationalist and loyalist, they did not attack the imperial system, although they all more or less looked for a democratic system under the Emperor.

For us the important thing is what sort of a culture they were importing into Japan. The first thing to come was English utilitarianism. Fukusawa Iukichi, who was the leading figure of the time, spoke of liberty, personal independence and the importance of positive and useful study as a means to liberty. He insisted that the criterion of morality was utility, and there can be no doubt that it was the vision of Victorian England in all her splendour that had risen before his eyes. But his utilitarianism remained nationalist. He believed it in no way contrary to the Emperor; on the contrary, the unique practical way to glorify him. His starting point was always the need to improve the country, and for this end he insisted on the importance of liberty. From 1868 to 1880 English liberalism was dominant. Numerous works of Mill and Herbert Spencer were translated, while all spoke of liberty, of reason and of the parliamentary system. In place of the old feudalism they were going to establish a new society, reasonable and free.

This period of Japanese history reminds one of the optimism of the eighteenth century in Europe. Like Europe, people thought, we can found a new society by use of our reason and our human capabilities; and we must do it. With this affirmation of the intellectual value of man went belief in human freedom. Hitherto Japan had had no concept of liberty, and the very word now used to express it was a new one formed in the 1850's as a translation of the "liberty" of European languages. It was Western liberalism which taught the Japanese the idea of freedom as a fundamental value of life, and it is only their discovery of this idea which can explain the novelty and vitality of what they were doing at that time.

Nevertheless they failed to penetrate to its metaphysical and Christian foundation, and many, for instance, spoke of freedom of religion simply as a mark of a civilized country, without grasping its deeper significance. As has always happened in Japanese history, the new movement—this time liberalism—did not overcome nationalism but rather tended to strengthen it with a modern form; its aim, furthermore, was political rather than spiritual, the development of a parliamentary system for the improvement and modernization of Japan.

Liberalism, as appears from its classical texts, is quite unable to determine the duties of government towards society, aiming as it does in leaving the maximum of freedom to the people. But in Japan at that time the duty of government was inevitably very great. The civil development of the country could only continue and be perfected under the strongest of governments. Consequently, in spite of the enthusiasm of the people, Liberalism was not very pleasing to the Government.

This explains why after 1880 Germany became the Japanese Government's ideal. It was the age of Bismarck, and the growing glory of Germany fascinated the Government of Japan: here was a successful statolatry which seemed to resemble Shintoism. In 1879 began the teaching of Hegelian philosophy in the University of Tokyo. An absolutist theory of the State began to take the place of English liberalism, and this was what the Government wanted, because it corresponded with Shintoist sentiment and the need for a strong hand in civil development. But it represented a fatal turning-aside for modern Japan. Setting aside freedom and the development of personality, Shintoism took on the appearance of a modern absolutism. The constitution, made on the German model in 1889, sanctioned a complete autocracy under the disguise of an up-to-date form. Although the sacred and omnipotent Emperor did not himself exercise his full authority, it was this constitution which legitimized the later military Fascism carried on in the Emperor's name.

Very significant in the period 1880-90 was the growth of traditionalism, both cultural and moral. It began as a reaction to the democratic movement. Liberalism, in spite of its nationalistic flavour, could not help but be in some way the negation of Shintoism. The Emperor could not be omnipotent in a democratic regime, and to limit the imperial power in any way whatsoever was, for the out-and-out Shintoist, a blasphemy against the Emperor. Once the danger was felt the reaction set in. The traditionalists vigorously insisted on what they held to be the fact that it was the same God who had created the whole world who was the Emperor's ancestor; the Emperor's rule depends on the will of God, not on that of the people; and even freedom, being a gift of God, is also in the gift of the Emperor. If we set aside the identification of god and emperor, we can feel that the traditionalist opinion was reasonably correct: at least it touched on the metaphysical origin of freedom and authority, which the liberals ignored. Nevertheless, on account of the theocratic absolutism of Shinto, this right intuition served only as an instrument for the oppression of human liberty.

Traditionalism received authoritative approbation in the imperial rescript on education (1890) which, until 1945, was always held to be the last word on Japanese morality. The foundation of education, it declared, is the tradition of Shinto. It commended many virtues, but only if they were concentrated on glorifying the Emperor. Together with victory in the Chinese war of 1894-5, this contributed to the even more secure establishment of Shintoist absolutism.

7

The only force which could have re-established a right hierarchy of values was Christianity. It alone could have maintained the value of the human person and—recognizing the supreme authority of God—have stood up to the absolutism of Shinto. But Japanese history has taken a different road.

As we have already seen, the Government was very hostile towards Christianity, and the common people shared this hostility. Such an attitude had its foundation in truth, because Christianity is certainly incompatible with any form of absolutism, and what was needed from Christianity was precisely enlightenment about the true character of human society, and in particular what the end of society is. The Japanese had rejoiced on first hearing the word "liberty"; it was for Christianity to tell them what the true meaning of that word was. Unfortunately Christianity did not appear equal to its task. The missionaries who worked and had the greatest influence among the intellectual class were Protestants. They, of course, knew that the cult of the ancient gods was contrary to Christianity, and they did not need to be afraid of saying that the Emperor was not God because, at least from 1868 to 1898, foreigners were privileged by treaty and the Government did not dare to touch them. But what was needed was more than this; it was rather a complete vision of human and social reality which was required, and this the Protestant missionaries did not seem to have. At least, they did not communicate it to the Japanese Christians.

Between 1870 and 1890 many and distinguished were the Japanese who came under the educational influence of the Protestant missionaries. That influence was good, without doubt. They did many good things. Yet from their activity and way of behaviour we can see what their mentality was like. Strange as it may seem, the greatest effect that they had had on Japan was to inspire the Socialist movement. From 1895 to 1905 the greater part of the first Japanese Socialists were Protestants. Again, their influence on the purity of matrimonial life (hitherto the possession of a second or third, non-legal, wife had not caused much scandal) and on the freeing of prostitutes (especially the work of the Salvation Army) is undeniable. But one might say that it was not so much Christians who did these things, as that those who did them were Christians. Certainly it was from a motive of Christian charity that such things were begun, but the means taken to realize the end were often hardly Christian. Again, such activities often became an end in themselves, and many of these first Christians came to abandon their Protestant faith as their social or socialistic activity intensified.

Furthermore, all this activity tended to be a matter of politics rather than of the spiritual reform of the individual. With regard to Socialism, that is obvious enough. But equally in the campaign against polygamy or for the liberation of prostitutes, the aim was to have a law passed which would realize their end. When we consider that the number of Christians in Japan never arrived at 500,000, and that all the rest—99 per cent of the nation—disagreed with their Christian principles, we cannot help feeling that such a desire to reform society by means of law and the State was rather inspired by rationalism than by Christianity. Can law really change morals? In the end it was rather the Shintoist supremacy of State policy over the individual person which found its strange expression in all this. We ought to say that this failure was not just that of the Japanese Christians, but of the very Protestantism which they had been taught. Anyway, after 1910 Protestantism ceased to have any powerful influence on Japanese culture.

We cannot deny that Protestant activity had its true merits. First among them is the diffusion of the Bible. I believe that the majority of Japanese intellectuals, though not Christians, have read the Bible. The name of Christ has been made known. Secondly, they introduced a more serious approach to life, especially among the young. It could easily become a type of hypocrisy, yet it had its value: serious personal quest for one's own *Weltanschauung* began after 1890. Thirdly, on account of the Protestant missionaries, Japanese Socialism for long had a very humanitarian character. It was a movement of the educated youth who felt social injustice and their, almost Christian, duty to change it. It was an expression of active charity. These three points are undeniable and they witness to the force of Christian truth or, better, of the Christian tradition.

Catholicism, on the other hand, never had a social influence like that of Protestantism. The reason was a chance one. The Protestant missionaries, being for the most part Americans, could become teachers in the schools—even the State schools—and were thus able to influence the future leaders (at least until 1890). The Catholic missionaries, on the other hand, were French, were not specialists, and had not the same opportunities. Up till about 1930 they had absolutely no contact with the intellectual classes, unless it were the odd personal one. Practically speaking, Catholicism in Japan has until now contributed nothing to Japanese culture, except that its suffering and persecution facilitated the grant of freedom of religion. The Catholics have not compromised with the national tradition, but they have always remained an isolated, local and closed group. Probably the missionaries had little understanding of the spiritual state of Japan, and their formation was not adequate to enable them to give the required Christian lead to a country in the midst of an immense material development. To have asked such things of the missionaries of the last century would not have been reasonable. Even the Japanese lack of a metaphysical mentality, as also of a sense of the historicity of religion, helped to prevent fruitful missionary work. At that time it was certainly easier for Protestantism to penetrate the Japanese mentality, but the advantage was superficial, and it even points to a certain dechristianization of Protestantism. Many a time Christian activities initiated by Protestants failed to remain Christian; thus, charity became philanthropy or socalism, while the reading of the Bible became part of the culture required of a member of the intellectual class.

8

Although Shinto had become Japan's official morality, taught through the centralized educational system, it had never had a complete doctrinal system of its own, and the Government had consequently to borrow the substance of Confucian moral teaching. This latter has many admirable doctrines in full conformity with the natural law, but it lacks any theory of freedom or of personality; consequently it was not adequate as a moral foundation for Japan's new civilization, which, being of Western importation, really required something more. In spite of official Shintoist education, some Japanese never ceased to seek a satisfying philosophy of life. They had learnt something of freedom, of the power of mind, of a serious personal approach to life, and they could not again forget these things: they sought for a whole view of reality, a new philosophy.

Japanese intellectuals could not be satisfied with traditional Confucian morality, and they sought for some solution in the contemporary culture of the West: Dostoievski, Tolstoi, Zola, Strindberg, Nietzsche, Bergson, Gide, etc. . . they have all been tried and found wanting. If they did not satisfy their own fellow-countrymen, how could they satisfy the Japanese? Meanwhile, there was another and equally important motive behind this search for a personal *Weltanschauung*.

Reliable historians tell us that it was really the war of 1894-5 which made of Japan an industrial and capitalist country. Nationalism willed it, the Government furthered it. But under the surface of its Shinto ideology this industrial revolution brought terrible suffering to the working class. In the fine-sounding name of sacrifice for the Fatherland the workers had to rest content with the lowest possible pay. The population was rapidly increasing (from 1867 to 1957 the population has grown from 25,000,000 to 90,000,000; before 1867 the number had remained constant for three hundred years), and the vast urban proletariat was formed. The growth of industry did not benefit the common people but gave glory to the Emperor and put money in the pockets of the capitalists. Production overtook need, but instead of cultivating the internal market the industrialists set about selling overseas, and this meant competition with industrial countries possessing a far higher technical ability. The only way to compete was to underpay the workers, and to justify this they incessantly spoke of sacrifice for the Fatherland—but it was always to be the workers' sacrifice, not the capitalists'. Over-population strengthened the latter's position, while the need for raw materials from overseas seemed to justify their fierce export drive. The amorality of Japanese capitalism was truly terrible; its products were gaining world markets on account of their low price, while at home the workers could still not afford them even at that price. One may say that the same has been true in every country, but in Japan we lacked a Christian conscience with which to criticize it. The Government imitated Bismarck's policy against Socialism, but in Japan there was no Central Party to criticize the Government from a Christian point of view.

It is not, therefore, difficult to understand the growth of Japanese Socialism. Faced with such grave social injustice, men were forced to an examination of conscience. Why this injustice? And what can I do about it? Not all but many of the intellectual class became

Socialists. After the First World War the economic crisis became worse, and in 1922 the Japanese Communist Party was founded.

Whatever his personal solution to the problems of life might be, every Japanese intellectual had to take up some attitude with regard to Shinto. Those who sought their solution in the spiritual culture of the West kept more or less to a respectful silence. They did not believe, but they did not resist either, and on the whole they had little trust in politics. Equally, they distrusted Socialism on account of its neglect of the deeper problems of personal existence. Through reflection, and with the assistance of Western culture, they rediscovered the true values of traditional Japanese culture hidden behind the prejudices of nationalism. Steeped in the learning both of Japan and of the West, they began to ask for the first time—especially in the years after 1930—where really lay the difference between Japanese and European culture, and still more recently they have come to discover the essential importance of Catholicism in the culture of the West.

These, however, were few. It is always difficult to maintain an attitude of enquiry, while the circumstances of the time seemed especially a call to action. From the end of the First World War until 1937 many young men at the universities threw themselves into the Socialist movement. They fiercely criticized Shinto and even the Emperor himself. Yet they shared with Shinto belief in the supremacy of politics and the State. They had not changed the old hierarchy of values in which politics took the first place, they had simply put in place of the Emperor some imagined Socialist Government of their own. This may explain the very rapid diffusion of Socialism in Japan and also give the reason why it was attacked by the Government. The difference between Socialism and Shinto was material, not formal, and the Government could easily see its danger. The threat from the personalist current of thought was more profound but less obvious. The persecution of Socialism, and even more of Communism, was very violent. As a result, from '37 to '45 Socialism was almost entirely suppressed. Of this period there are two things to be noted.

The first was the so-called conversion of the Communists (Tenko). To be a Communist was by law a crime, and the Government wanted imprisoned Communists to deny their ideal publicly; to obtain this end every means was used, often including extreme torture. Some resisted to the end, but many gave in. There was also a great number of people, formerly Communists, who without imprisonment abandoned Communism.

Certainly torture and imprisonment were a powerful cause of this abandonment, but one cannot deny that with many it was also a matter of internal reflection. The principal reason was the feeling that they had neglected to be Japanese. In the years from 1920 to 1940 Communism had opposed itself to nationalism and insisted on being international. To become a Communist was often equivalent to denying one's patriotism. In the solitude of prison a nostalgia for the old tradition of country and family returned. Why should we deny the old gods and loyalty to the Emperor? These things are necessary for the common people and hold society together. Should they not be the foundations for our new social order? Thus some of the Socialists became National-Socialists, and the military Fascism of modern Japan has been supported not only by the traditional Shintoist feeling of the people, but also by a new ideology of National Socialism.

The second was the growth of fanatical Shintoism. Shintoist sentiment had always been strong, but after the economic crisis of the inter-war years (1922, 1928, 1932) a deep distrust of Western civilization grew in the Japanese mind. Every evil was attributed to the new spirit imported from Europe, and not unreasonably in that the West too suffered from the effects of capitalism. But it was anachronistic to seek a return to some sort of divine patriarchalism. With Shinto, it was said, stands history, tradition, peace of mind. In the years from 1930 to 1945 the Shintoists did all in their power to stress the Emperor's divinity: he is god in person, father of the whole Japanese family, he loves us, suffers for us . . . Empty words, but they meant a lot at the time.

9

In 1946, after Japan's defeat, the Emperor himself denied his divinity. That may cause a smile, but for the Japanese it was full of meaning. For the first time in history the Japanese have abandoned Shinto in so far as it concerns the Emperor. The pressure of extreme nationalism has declined, and we can think about the true meaning of life without prejudice. Moreover the destruction of the chief traditional view has forced us to seek this meaning in earnest.

Without prejudice—a nice phrase, but not an easily attained state of mind! In fact, the post-war period has been one of a good deal of intellectual confusion, increased by the bad economic situation. Not vast numbers, but still a good number, of young Japanese have become Catholics. They were looking for a spiritual strength which could no longer be found in Shinto or in Buddhism, but which must be something new, something connected with this Western civilization which had defeated the Emperor. General MacArthur's insistent praise of the Christian spirit had its psychological effect, and it became a fashion to go to Church. All this was spread abroad by missionaries across the Christian world in a slightly exaggerated way. But the Hegelian view of history which is still dominant in Japan prevents any great number of young men from discovering the permanent truth of Catholicism. They look on it as something which was outdated by the Lutheran reform and as not in conformity with modern science and civilization. Far greater numbers turn towards Socialism and Communism. I don't say that all Japanese youth is Communist, but there are very few who are capable of criticizing the Socialist view of things. Quite apart from the actual state of the Communist party, there are very few young men who do not agree with the social-economic theory of Marxism. In order to obtain a good job many hide their sympathy for Communism and do not take part in Communist activities, but privately they admit finding the theory of Marxism irresistible.

Though it may seem strange, I must also say that few really share the Communist view of life. This must be explained by the old dichotomy between heart and reason. Theoretically convinced, they still feel almost instinctively that human life has elements which have escaped the Marxist analysis. It is a true intuition but it lacks theoretical support. The feelings of the Japanese may be strongly anti-Communist, but his arguments are very weak.

In short, after the War Japan still stands on her traditional road. Now, as ever, the supremacy of politics over the individual, and the lack of metaphysics, are the key principles of the situation. The principle of the supreme State has lost its god-Emperor, but it cannot so easily accept a new society which would recognize the full dignity of man. The Japanese, because he is a man, may feel unhappy about this, but he lacks the metaphysics to critize it.

Yet history always brings something new, and in many ways the post-war situation is a very favourable one. At least Socialism is more reasonable than Shinto, while there is freedom to speak and act against both. We know that there is no situation better for the Faith than one of freedom and reasonableness.

There are still scholars and thinkers who seek to relate Japanese tradition to Western civilization, and their numbers are increasing. If the War silenced them, it also gave them a chance to think and study more deeply. It was during the War that a critical version of many of the classics of the Western world was prepared. Works of Aristotle, Plato, Sophocles, Euripides, Aeschylus, Augustine, Anselm, and other more modern or contemporary authors have been translated with care. These were published during the War or after, and they have begun to form a new intellectual situation. The Japanese are beginning to understand better the tradition behind Western civilization and the place of Catholicism within that tradition, though not yet its supernatural worth. Without doubt there is precious fruit ripening.

The old gods are not dead, the old malformed mentality remains, but truth also is always strong. If the position of Japan does not allow us great optimism, we can still see the hand of Providence in our history. Endless the errors and turnings aside, yet the Japanese have remained men, sons of Adam, blessed, fallen and worth redeeming at the price of the Son of God's death. In spite of all the shadows truth also has never ceased to shine. But what shadows there were, and how obscured the truth!

As I said at the beginning, this study has been rather a reflection on Japanese culture in the light of Catholicism than one on the relations between that culture and Catholicism. Such relations, alas! have hitherto hardly existed.

My judgement on Japanese culture may seem too severe. I have noted failings, but almost no positive value, and I have not spoken at all of those things which foreigners are accustomed to praise, such as serenity, simplicity and refinement. For my part I see them as deriving from deeper principles which we cannot sanction. It is those fundamental principles which we must purify. To Christianize the very heart of a people and its way of life, to transform its inner principles, we must not fear even the destruction of its traditional culture, especially if it is grounded on a vast absence of revealed truth.

The history of Japanese culture has developed on two basic elements: lack of metaphysics and of the true notion of the dignity of the human person. Primitive Japan possessed these two things far more than the Japan of today; but little by little the development of the language killed metaphysics, while the idea of the person was lost in nationalism. These failings presupposed, the Japanese have done all they could to satisfy the existential and spiritual needs of man. Intuition was honoured, art flourished, manners were refined. By divinizing the Emperor the Japanese sought to satisfy their desire to have a living god to guide their lives. But the failings remained, and in spite of many attractive details which can excite the admiration even of Christians, they were disastrous.

There is no room for pessimism about the future of the Church in Japan. Indeed, we know that the Church alone can solve Japan's problems, and that in solving them she will Christianize its people. The road is long but the victory is certain. Certain, because it will be the victory of charity which no man can resist. Certain, because man is naturally Christian and cannot not accept the Saviour's gentle invitation. Let us beg the Lord to grant us always to work in the light of truth and in the love and comprehension of our neighbour. In our case that means loving the Japanese and their culture and understanding them in the light of truth.

THE NETHERLANDS

H. J. Dekkers, C.SS.R.

1: The Historical Background

To understand the geographical division of the Catholic population of the Netherlands it is necessary to know something about what happened at the Reformation, which took place at a time when our country was a part of the Spanish Empire, in which Church and State were inseparably bound together. The consequence of the Dutch revolt against Spanish rule, finally terminated by the Treaty of Münster (part of the Peace of Westphalia) in 1648, was the complete collapse of the structure of the Church in the Low Countries. Bishops and priests, who had been in large part officials of the Spanish Empire, had fled the country. New religious leaders had come in their place, and these also, as a matter of fact, were civil servants. The adage *Cujus regio, eius religio* held good for our country just as it did for the rest of Europe. Nevertheless, the process of "Protestantization" in the Netherlands took a course of its own. This was so first of all because it started relatively late in history, after the Council of Trent. The new doctrine found for its opponents men who already knew the dividing line between orthodoxy and heresy, and there was therefore no question of that unsuspectingness and ignorance which elsewhere caused an unnoticed transition to Protestantism. Secondly, the early days of Protestantism in this country were ones of a very fluctuating political situation, the civil authorities in towns and counties being at one moment Catholic, at another Protestant. Where the public authority was republican—in other words, anti-Spanish—it would suppress all Catholic services, assign church buildings and revenues to the Reformers, and put pressure on children, as on officials and magistrates, to conform to the new religion. But the most important factor of all was the large-scale exodus of Catholic clergy from the country, so that positive resistance was badly lacking.

FR. H. J. DEKKERS, C.SS.R., was born in Groningen; he studied theology at the University of Nijmegen and the Angelicum, Rome, and then returned to Nijmegen to study sociology. From 1952 to 1957 he worked for the International Catholic Institute for Social Ecclesiastical Research. He is now Professor of Religious Sociology at the Redemptorist Seminary at Wittem.

In those districts where the public authorities were extremely intolerant towards Catholicism and where also the Catholic ministry was interrupted for a long period, we find nowadays an almost homogeneous Protestant population, e.g., in the north-east provinces of Groningen, Friesland and Drenthe. In contrast with these, the parts of the present Kingdom of the Netherlands south of the rivers Rhine and Meuse did not come under the influence of the North Netherlands Republic until the reforms of the Council of Trent had taken their full effect, and they have never been deprived of their Catholic clergy. Consequently in these southern provinces (Brabant and Limburg) we find an almost homogeneous Catholic population. In the other parts of the country the picture is much more varied; the same influences made themselves felt but within a smaller geographical compass. It is estimated that in these parts one-third of the population remained Catholic. Between 1648 and the middle of the nineteenth century no considerable change took place in the geographical distribution of Catholics and Protestants.

Since the Treaty of Münster there has also been no question of any bloody religious persecution of the Catholic body; nevertheless anti-Catholic edicts remained in force until the end of the eighteenth century by which Catholics were excluded from all official positions and were only allowed to practise their religion after the payment of heavy fines. They were treated as second-class citizens and their contribution to public life was insignificant. Numbers remained proportionately the same throughout this period. It is obvious that Dutch Catholicism still bears the stamp of its struggle for life in the seventeenth and eighteenth centuries. Its militant character is evident and is due to its adherents' having had to hold their own as an unprivileged minority for years. This is most noticeable in areas where the population is multi-denominational. In these parts one may note on the positive side a more conscious personal belief, but against this must be balanced the fact that the Catholics are more reserved and seem to have secluded themselves from society and from much of value which is to be found elsewhere. It is not to be wondered at that the continuous influence of Calvinism made these Catholics less cheerful, lacking the optimistic spirit of the south, but at the same time freed of its nonchalance and carelessness. Emphasis has been laid on a strong inward piety which is not unlinked with a tendency to puritanism.

When, about the beginning of the nineteenth century, Catholics began to emerge from the long isolation which had been imposed on them, they naturally lacked breadth of outlook. Moreover, the Liberalism of that time, ever pushing forward—especially in the field of education—drove Catholics and Protestants alike into a still more isolated position. To resist Liberalism the religious bodies set about strengthening their own fortifications and internal concentration, and the consequent isolationism has had a marked effect on the whole political, social and cultural structure of the country. A remarkable division into three groups, based on philosophical grounds, appeared in Dutch public life:

1. Roman Catholic
2. Protestant
3. Neutral

Although there is at times a stronger, at times a weaker, effort to "break out" of this isolation, adherence to it still remains very characteristic of official Catholic religion in the Netherlands.

2: The Roman Catholic Church in the Netherlands Today

From the second half of the nineteenth century the population became less static with the result that purely Protestant and purely Catholic areas have come to obtain a mixed character. Nevertheless, in broad outlines the old division has not disappeared; the south remains on the whole Catholic, the west and middle parts of the country are mixed, the north and north-east are still "diaspora areas" as far as the Catholic Church is concerned. Moreover, if the local distribution of the Catholic population has undergone some changes, the total percentage has not: in 1849 Catholics totalled 38·2 per cent of the population, in 1947 38·5 per cent. The Protestants, in contrast, were 59 per cent of the population in 1849 but only 41 per cent in 1947. As Catholics have bigger families the future may well be promising for them. Indeed, 45 per cent of Dutch children of school-age are Catholic.

One finds Catholics in nearly every stratum of the population, but their number is highest among farmers and workers. Among the ranks of civil servants and intellectuals they have still a long way to go to catch up. This of course points to a weakness in the position of Dutch Catholics, as these latter classes have the greater influence on the future development of the country as a whole.

Until this century Dutch people could be divided into two groups —Protestants and Catholics, the latter forming an obvious minority;

in the last fifty years a third group has emerged, the non-denominational. They accounted for only 2 per cent of the population in 1889, but today their number may well be estimated at some 20 per cent, and this figure only refers to those actually registered as without religion. Needless to say, this group is largest in the bigger towns: in Amsterdam nearly 50 per cent, in the Hague—the Government centre—30 per cent, and in Rotterdam 31 per cent. In former times Protestantism, in one form or another, was the one and only opponent of Catholicism, but in the new situation of today there is a strong tendency among Dutch Catholics towards a more ecumenical attitude. The desire grows stronger and stronger to live down the past tragic cleavage and face together the danger of a growing dechristianization.

In actual fact, the greater number of apostates have come from the Protestant Churches, but in the last decades apostasy has affected the Catholic and Protestant Churches almost equally, and the rather sharp absolute rise in the numbers of Catholics should be ascribed to a high excess of births over deaths rather than to a small number of apostasies. That, however, applies to the mixed rather than to the purely Catholic areas. The following figures may be noted:

Towns in mixed areas:

20,000-50,000	19·8%	no religion
50,000-100,000	23·1%	,, ,,
100,000-200,000	27·6%	,, ,,
500,000 and more	34·6%	,, ,,

Towns in a Catholic area:

20,000-50,000	1·1%	no religion
50,000-100,000	2·5%	,, ,,
100,000-200,000	3·8%	,, ,,

It is among the most influential groups that irreligion is highest. In Amsterdam, for instance, 50 per cent of all the leading people in the intellectual field have severed every outward tie with Christianity. In the Hague this figure is somewhat lower, 36 per cent. But it is clear that in this most influential group of the population Catholics are relatively weak and non-Christians strongest, whereas in the more easily influenced sections of the population Catholics are relatively more numerous.

It would be a mistake to think of Dutch apostasy as the same sort of thing as the passivity which is to be found widespread in South European countries such as France, Spain and Italy. The latter phenomenon does not necessarily imply the loss of Christian faith, while it is characteristic of apostates in the Netherlands that practically nothing remains of any belief in Christ as the Son of God. Undoubtedly there remains a difference between apostasy in the first and in subsequent generations, but in the Netherlands one does not often find people who stop for years half-way between renunciation and complete recognition of the Church.

Although one cannot measure inward devotion, we shall try to get an impression of the general climate of Catholicism in the Netherlands from quantitative data about three things which can be called qualitative as well, viz. the Paschal precept, Holy Communion, priestly and religious vocations.

1. *The Paschal Precept.* The average figure for Roman Catholics in this country who do not fulfil their Easter duties is 11 per cent. In some areas, such as the provinces of the south, the figure is only 1 per cent. In Amsterdam, the Hague and Rotterdam on the other hand, the situation is much worse (30 per cent or more). The figures for regular Sunday churchgoers are somewhat lower than for those who make their Easter duties, as may be learnt from a recent census of Sunday worshippers; but a striking fact is that there is no marked minority of men or of certain age groups, as is the case in Marseilles, Lyons and Grenoble, where similar Sunday censuses have been held.

2. *Holy Communion.* It is characteristic of Dutch Catholics that they responded immediately and universally to the decrees of Pope St. Pius X about frequent Communion and children's Communion. This is typical of their loyalty to Rome and their readiness to listen to the Pope's voice. (We may also remember the many Dutch Zouaves who marched to Rome in the second half of the nineteenth century to defend the Papal States). The average of Communion figures per annum was 9 or 10 in Pius X's time; this figure rose to 25 for the Archbishopric of Utrecht between 1906 and 1918, and to 35 for the other bishoprics. At the moment it stands at 42. This throws some light on the fervour of our Catholic religious life.

3. *Vocations.* A reliable guide to the religious vigour of any given group is the number of persons belonging to it who enter the ministry and monastic life. In the Netherlands, as in a good many other European countries, vocations for the priesthood have become

a problem, not because the number of students entering seminaries is falling off, but mainly due to a decrease in the proportion of those who finish their studies. In the last twenty-five years this has dropped to about 35-50 per cent. This of course means that a start must be made with twice the number of students previously admitted, if the same number of priests is to be provided. The following survey shows that from a European standpoint we cannot be said to have a superfluity of priests.

Number of Catholics per active priest in some European countries:[1]

Scandinavia	300
Luxemburg	701
Great Britain	746
Switzerland	766
Ireland	917
Belgium	974
France	1,090
Italy	1,109
Netherlands	1,300
Spain	1,336
Portugal	2,311

In the Netherlands there are more than 30,000 nuns; in this respect she surpasses most other countries, as may be seen from the following list:

Country	*Census year*	*Number of nuns per 10,000 Roman Catholics*
Netherlands	1953	70·3
Great Britain	1953	55·2
Belgium	1953	54·9
Ireland	1953	37·9
Germany	1950	35·7
France	1948	28·6

Nevertheless, it is a serious fact that the number of female vocations has dwindled to about one-third of what it was twenty-five years ago.

In the political field a sense of isolation still dominates Dutch Catholics. As we have seen, this sense is due to the defensive position which has been theirs on account of their political, social and cultural minority status. The bulk of Dutch Catholics are organized in one

[1] Cf. Dr. J. J. Dellepoort, *Priestly Vocations in the Netherlands*, The Hague, 1955.

party, which polls 80-90 per cent of all Catholic votes. In this country religious convictions weigh heavier in the political field than do economic convictions, unlike England or America. While in other nations the principle of political organization seems to lie chiefly in a community of economic interest, the Dutch still find in their religious beliefs or philosophy the deepest motive force of national life. It has been truly said that the Dutch, thanks to their history, have been transformed into a philosophical nation.

Besides the Catholic People's Party, which is the biggest political group, there are two important Protestant political parties, together with the non-denominational Labour Party, which has strong socialistic tendencies. Since the War a fairly strong group of Catholics has come to feel that Catholic political unity is no longer necessary, and many of these are now to be found within the ranks of the Labour Party. However, this decline in the Catholic United Party seems for the time being to have come to a standstill—at least it seems so. The shape of our political life is evidently to continue as it has these last seventy-five years.

In the field of work, as well, there is the same keen contest between denominational unions of Catholics, Protestants, Socialists, and Communists. On the Catholic side each class has its own organization: one for employers, another for farmers or market-gardeners; there is no common overall organization in which all the separate classes can co-operate.

The unfinished state of Catholic emancipation in the Netherlands finds its expression in the cultural field. This is especially obvious when one examines the number of Catholics receiving higher education. Here a great deal of leeway has still to be made up. The situation may be summed up in the following figures.

44 per cent of the younger generation is Catholic.

42 per cent attends Catholic primary schools.

36 per cent attends Catholic modern schools (3-4 years after primary school).

26 per cent attends Catholic secondary schools (5-6 years after primary school).

The higher you go up the educational pyramid the smaller is the proportion of Catholics. It should be noted that only a very small number of Catholic children are sent to neutral (non-denominational) schools to receive compulsory education.

Undoubtedly, however, the situation is far more favourable than it was at the beginning of this century. In those days only 7 per cent of Dutch school children were Catholic and only 2 per cent of the teachers. Of 162 secondary schools existing in 1910, only 7 were Catholic. In fact, at that time the cultural and intellectual emancipation of Catholics was only just starting. It has still not finished, and this has consequences in every field of public life. The fewer the number of Catholics leaving secondary and higher schools, the fewer also will be found in senior public positions. This is something of a vicious circle, for the consequent lower social status of parents is itself an important factor influencing the education of the next generation.

In brief, it is evident that in the political and general fields Catholic emancipation is almost complete, but culturally and educationally much has still to be done. Though it has not been possible to give here a complete picture of Catholicism as it exists in the Netherlands, the salient points have been picked out. At present society is in motion and everything seems to change, yet the future direction which our Catholic community will follow in the Netherlands is bound to be determined by the outstanding features set out here.

VIETNAM
Nguyen Huy Lai

On the 11th June, 1933, when Pope Pius XI consecrated Mgr. Nguyen Ba Tong first Bishop of Vietnam, His Holiness said: "Indo-China is the eldest daughter of the Church of the Far East." It was an expression of fatherly affection which was received with pride and gratitude by Vietnamese Catholics. It did justice to three centuries of work and struggle and suffering endured by generations of missionaries and Christians for the victory of the truth. It also struck a note of warning for the Catholics of Vietnam who have received the priceless heritage of the Catholic faith from their forefathers, for, from the moment when their foreheads are signed with the sign of the Cross, they are committed to preserving, defending and if necessary dying for that faith.

Despite the tragic events which have wrecked our country since the Second World War the Church of Vietnam is still there, alive and strong as ever, with its bishops, priests and faithful. It was built by our missionaries and our ancestors with huge efforts and sometimes at the cost of their lives. It is for us to consolidate it, so that it shall flourish on Vietnamese soil. In order to convey an idea both of the greatness of their work and of the task devolving on us in the present and the future it is absolutely necessary to recall the history of the Church of Vietnam from its origins to the present day.

The beginnings of Christianity in Vietnam are not known with any precision. We do not know the date of the first conversions. It seems that at the beginning of the fourteenth century a Franciscan, Odorico Pordenone, came to Central Vietnam, but he does not appear to have made any converts. A royal edict of 1533 forbade the spread of "the false doctrine of Gia-To" (Jesus) which was being taught in secret by "a man of the sea named I-Ni-Khu" (Ignatius).

What is certain is that the effective evangelization of Vietnam

---

NGUYEN HUY LAI was born in 1908. He has been both Counsel of the Court of Appeals at Hanoi and Vice-President and Minister of Finance in the Government of Viet-Nam.

began only in the sixteenth century. Thanks to the work of Father Marcos Gisbert, *Historia de las Missiones dominicanes en Tung-Kin*, we know of the work of the Portuguese Dominicans. In 1550 Father Gaspar de Santa Cruz, from the Mission of Malacca, came to evangelize South Vietnam. About 1558 came Fathers Lopès and Acevedo. From 1580 to 1586 Fathers De Fonseca and Grégoire de la Motte preached the Gospel in the province of Quang-nam, Central Vietnam.

The seventeenth century was a time of very active evangelization. The missionaries have left us plenty of written records of their activities and of the birth of the Church of Vietnam. This was the great period of the Society of Jesus, the successors of the Portuguese Dominican Mission. In about 1564 the Jesuits had come to Macao, a concession obtained by the Portuguese nine years earlier. From there they went to Vietnam. In 1615 Father Francis Buzomi came to Cochin-China, now South Vietnam. He was the apostle of Cochin-China, working there with energy and courage for twenty years. In his first year he baptized three hundred Vietnamese and built two churches. Seeing the scope of this apostolic work, the Mission at Macao soon sent him two brave companions, Fathers Francis Barret and Francis de Pina. The latter was the first Westerner to possess a thorough knowledge of the Vietnamese language.

Other Jesuits were soon to come to swell the number of missionaries in Cochin-China, thanks to certain developments. As is well known, St. Francis Xavier reached Japan in 1549, and not only the common people but also members of the Nipponese feudal aristocracy, the Daimios, embraced the Catholic faith with enthusiasm. But this promising beginning to Japanese Christianity lasted only forty years. An edict of 1613 expelled the missionaries and ordered the Catholics to destroy the churches and to apostatize. Since Japan was, at least temporarily, closed to missionaries, five Jesuit priests, amongst whom was Father Alexander de Rhodes, who had been destined for the Japanese mission, were ordered in 1624 to go to Cochin-China.

The name of Father Alexander de Rhodes deserves particular mention, bound up as it is with the history of Vietnam. Born at Avignon, on 15th March, 1591, he entered the Society of Jesus at the age of eighteen. He went successively to Goa, Malacca and Macao, and arrived in January 1625 in Cochin-China. He was at once struck by the state of Christianity there. "It was not the fertility of the soil which seemed so great to me," he said, "it was the great fruits which the preaching of the Gospel had produced here in a short space of time. I have witnessed them, and, having been sent there five times, I can say that I have seen always the blessings of that fruitful land, of which David says that heaven pours its dew upon it and all the fields bear every kind of fruit in abundance." Father Alexander preached in Cochin-China for eighteen months; then, in 1627, he was sent by his superiors to Tonkin (now in Northern Vietnam) where he worked till 1630, when he was banished by Trinh-Trang, Lord of Tonkin. After fleeing to Macao, he went back to Cochin-China in 1640. This second visit lasted five years. In 1645 he was finally expelled from Vietnamese territory.

Father Alexander realized that to conquer souls for Christ he must first win men's hearts. By tact and understanding he had avoided all that could conflict with the manners and customs of the country. For this reason his preaching affected not only the masses of the population, to whom he had entirely devoted himself, but also members of the aristocracy. One of the King's aunts, known as Madame Marie, was converted and built a church in the grounds of her palace, which, unfortunately, her son, who was hostile to the Faith, had destroyed. "The fruit that we gathered from our labours," wrote Father Alexander, "and from the seed of God's word which we sowed, was so great that we had to spend two days of the week giving baptism to those who asked for it: normally to twenty, sometimes forty, people, among whom were men of every condition, even of the Royal House." At this period there were about 82,000 Christians at Tonkin and 39,000 in Cochin-China (Georges Bois, *Les débuts du Christianisme en Annam*).

The evangelization of the country was too recent for Father Alexander to fulfil his desire to ensure the continuance of Christianity by forming a Vietnamese clergy. He was, however, able to build up a group of devoted catechists. One of them, named Andrew, nineteen years of age, was martyred at Quang-Nam, Central Vietnam, in July 1644. He had been converted three years previously, and was the first Vietnamese to shed his blood for the Catholic faith. His death was a heavy grief to Father Alexander and the whole Christian community, but it infused into the Church of Vietnam a strength in which she could henceforth neither grow old nor perish.

As a missionary Father Alexander helped to build up the Church of Vietnam. As a scholar he contributed to Vietnamese culture and civilization. He was both a great mathematician and an astonishing linguist. Besides French, Italian, Latin, Greek and Portuguese, he acquired, during his thirty-four years in Asia, a knowledge of Hindustani, Persian, Japanese, Chinese and Vietnamese. When he first heard Vietnamese women speaking it sounded to him like "the twittering of birds", and he admitted that he lost all hope of ever learning so difficult a language. But he set himself to study it "as seriously as he had learnt theology at Rome", and in six months he was preaching in Vietnamese. Together with Fathers De Pina, Borri, Gaspar de Amaral, Barbosa and others, he rendered incalculable service to the Vietnamese nation by inventing the *Quoc-Ngu*, the phonetic transcription of Vietnamese, using the Latin alphabet supplemented by five signs corresponding to the five tones. It has been universally adopted in Vietnam, though the ancient characters are preserved as the medium of classical study. An adaptation which China and Japan have still not succeeded in making took place in Vietnam three centuries ago, thanks to the missionaries. Two works by Father Alexander, written in *Quoc-Ngu*, were printed in Rome in 1651, the Catechism and a Vietnamese-Portuguese-Latin dictionary. It is easy to understand how his memory is revered in Vietnam, by non-Catholics as well as Catholics. When he left the country, his heart was "breaking with sorrow". Later on he wrote: "My body left Cochin-China, but certainly my heart did not, nor Tonkin either. Indeed, the whole of it is in both of them, nor do I think it can ever leave them." A monument was erected in 1941 as a token of gratitude to this great missionary and scholar, and stands under a pagoda beside the picturesque little lake of Hanoi.

When his body left Cochin-China and Tonkin, Father Alexander continued to serve the Church of Vietnam. In 1649 he went to Rome to inform the Holy See of the possibility of spreading Christianity in Vietnam, and to appeal for missionaries. With the same purpose, he went to Paris in 1652. He did not spare his efforts to interest the court of Louis XIV, for he felt that "the glory of bearing the torch of Christian truth beyond the ocean ought to belong to the most pious kingdom in the world". But in 1655 he was obliged, by order of his superiors, to leave for Persia to direct the Jesuit mission there. He died at Ispahan on the 16th November, 1660.

He witnessed the success of his efforts before he died. In May 1658 Pope Alexander VII appointed Fathers Pallu and Lambert de la Motte bishops *in partibus infidelium*. They became vicars apostolic of Tonkin and Cochin-China respectively. Their nomination marked the foundation of the Société des Missions Étrangères, of which Father Alexander de Rhodes was the chief promoter. A seminary was founded in Paris, in the Rue du Bac, in July 1663, from which missionaries went out for three centuries, many of them never to return. The Society is at present under the authority of Monsignor Lemaire.

The first man to go out from the Société des Missions Étrangères was Monsignor Lambert de la Motte. He left France in July 1660 with Fathers De Bourges and Deydier, and arrived in Siam in August 1662. Monsignor Pallu was not able to leave Marseille until 2nd January, 1662, with nine missionaries, of whom five died worn out by the two-year-long voyage. At first the two missionary bishops waited in Siam, the only country where they were safe from persecution, trying to find a way of getting to their mission in Vietnam. But the Jesuits in Cochin-China advised them to delay their departure, since their arrival might provoke still worse persecution of Vietnamese Catholics. A document of 23rd January, 1664 testifies to the hostility of the Vietnamese authorities: "We have expelled, and we do in perpetuity expel from our kingdom these Fathers, who, being fugitives from their own lands, have come to instruct rude and unlettered folk and women in a law which is without foundation and is all the more pernicious and ridiculous in that it teaches that neither heaven nor earth is to be adored." In these circumstances Monsignor Lambert de la Motte sent Father Chevreuil into Cochin-China in August 1665 as pro-vicar; he remained there for five years. He could not get into Central Vietnam until July 1671, while Monsignor Pallu was never able to go to Tonkin.

The greatest achievement of the two founders of the Société des Missions Étrangères was the formation of a Vietnamese clergy. This was in fact the chief aim of the Society: "To work for the conversion of the Gentiles, not only by preaching the Gospel to them but especially by preparing by the best possible means and raising to ecclesiastical status such of the new Christians or their children as may be judged fit for this holy estate, so as to form in each land a clergy and hierarchy as established in the Church by Jesus Christ and the Apostles." In 1666 a seminary for native priests of the Far East was started at Ayuthia, the old capital of Siam. In 1807 it was transferred to Penang. Since it was very difficult, in the midst of the persecution, to send students to Siam, each of the missions managed to found a small undercover school for their training. The first seminary in Tonkin, started by Monsignor Deydier, was a boat on the Red River, reminiscent of that boat on Lake Genesareth manned by the first of the fishers of men. It was not long afterwards that the two first Tonkinese priests, Benedict Hien and John Hue, went "in unto the altar of God", to the great joy of the Church of Vietnam.

From the very beginning of the Society, Monsignor Lambert de la Motte and Monsignor Pallu had intended to hand over the Church of Vietnam to Vietnamese bishops. In 1678 they asked the Congregation of Propaganda to appoint four Vietnamese bishops in Tonkin and two in Cochin-China, so as to "show the unbelievers our high opinion of their nation and to allay the doubts and suspicions which the princes and their ministers may have that the missionaries, under the cloak of religion, intend to assume control of their dominions and subject them to the kings of Europe". Their desire was not fulfilled until 1933, when Monsignor Nguyen Ba Tong was appointed Vicar Apostolic of Phat-Diem (Northern Vietnam).

The Société des Missions Étrangères continued to send missionaries to the Far East. By 1685 sixty-nine priests had set out from the Rue du Bac. According to Monsignor Laneau, the Church of Vietnam now numbered 200,000 Christians in Tonkin and 60,000 in Cochin-China. But the Society alone, fruitful as its efforts were, could not suffice for the vast field of action now opening up. At the request of the Society, the Spanish Dominicans from the Mission of Manila came to help in the evangelization of Vietnam. In 1693 they took charge of eastern Tonkin, while western Tonkin remained under the Society.

In the eighteenth century the Church of Vietnam went through one of its worst times of trial. There was a series of persecutions in town and country. Many missionaries and Vietnamese Catholics were arrested, tortured and beheaded. But under the pressure of these difficulties the Faith increased, and so did vocations to the priesthood. In 1763 there were thirty Vietnamese priests working in western Tonkin. It was not till the end of the eighteenth century that there was a respite in the persecution. In about 1770 the revolt of the Tay-Son (the western hillmen) broke out in Cochin-China. After gaining control of the north and centre the rebels wrested the southern province from the reigning dynasty, represented by the young prince Nguyen-Anh. In 1777, a fugitive from his kingdom, the prince met on the island of Puloway in the Gulf of Siam a missionary of the Société des Missions Étrangères, Monsignor

Pigneau de Béhaine, Bishop of Adran, who gave him asylum and helped him to reconquer his kingdom. From 1788 to 1802 Nguyen-Anh fought the Tay-Son, finally achieving the unification of Vietnam with the three *Ky* (north, centre and south) united under the Crown. After winning back his empire he took the name of Gia-Long. When Monsignor Pigneau de Béhaine died in 1799 the Emperor made a moving funeral oration: "I had a wise man by my side, the close sharer of all my secrets, who, over thousands upon thousands of leagues, had come into my dominions and who never left me, not even when fortune had turned against me. And now today, when she is ranged once more beneath my standard, now when we are more united than ever, why must a too early death come suddenly to separate us?"

During the reign of Gia-Long, from 1788 to 1820, the Church of Vietnam was no longer persecuted. But neither was it favoured. In 1792 Father Lavoué wrote: "Though the King does not persecute our religion he lets it be seen at every opportunity that he is displeased when anyone embraces it, and there seems no likelihood that he will ever be a Christian." Like most well-educated Vietnamese, Gia-Long was an eclectic. He loved to learn of different beliefs. He had not neglected to ask the Bishop of Adran to explain Catholicism to him; he acknowledged the beauty of the doctrine but suspected that it would sap the foundations of Vietnam's political and social institutions. He was neither a Buddhist nor a Taoist. He mocked at all who believed in superstition and magic. His only doctrine was Confucianism, his only cult the worship of his ancestors.

If Gia-Long had shown no hostility to Catholicism, his successors, Minh-Mang, Thieu-Tri and Tu-Duc were worthy rivals of Nero and Diocletian. From 1833 to 1862 the Church of Vietnam underwent the worst persecutions of its history. Father Gagelin, strangled at Hue on the 17th October, 1833, and Father Peter Tuy, beheaded at Tonkin on the 11th, were the first in a glorious series of martyrs. From north to south missionaries and Vietnamese Catholics fell under the swords of Minh-Mang's executioners. Among the priests of the Society who died were Fathers Marchand, Cornay, Jacquard, and Monsignor Dumoulin-Borie. The Spanish mission had its martyrs too, as for example Monsignor Henarès and Father Fernandez. And the Church of Vietnam offered a holocaust of her own sons: Fathers Diem, Nam, Ngan, Thinh and many others. The fury of the persecution was such that on 4th August, 1839 Pope Gregory XVI sent a pontifical brief to the Christians of Tonkin and Cochin-China to assure them of his paternal encouragement: "We have felt deep sorrow, most dear sons, as we contemplate the peril in which you stand . . . You are not delivered over for ever to this atrocious persecution. A day will come when, released from your tears and escaped from the fury of the storm, you will worship the true God in peace, and render endless thanks to him for the restoration of tranquillity."

When Thieu-Tri ascended the throne in 1841 the persecution abated to some extent. But it redoubled its vigour at the accession of Tu-Duc (1847-83). The edict of March 1851 ordered that missionaries and Christians should be hunted with the utmost rigour. At Tonkin Fathers Schoeffer, Bonnard, Vénard and others were beheaded, as well as Father Tinh, director of the Junior Seminary of Vinh-Tri. The Spanish mission recorded the martyrdom of Fathers Piaz, Garcia Sempedo, Hermosilla, Ochoa and Almato. In Cochin-China Fathers Minh, Loc, Qui, Luu, Hoan and others suffered the same fate. Before his execution Father Tinh wrote to his students to tell them of his joy at sacrificing his life for the Church of Vietnam: "I give thanks with all my soul to divine Providence, praying ardently for the salvation and holiness of our bishops, our missionaries and all our priests, for the prosperity of our Tonkinese Church . . . I have kept the Faith, I have finished my course, and I hope that the just Judge will give me the crown of justice, not only to me but to all those who love his coming. I am writing these few words, on the point of suffering martyrdom, so that you shall know how much I love you. Love one another . . . "

How is one to estimate the profit and loss from these thirty terrible years of persecution? The number of Vietnamese Catholics who died for the Faith has been put at 100,000; more than a hundred Vietnamese priests and twenty missionaries were martyred, and two thousand Christian communities destroyed. A hundred and twenty of the martyrs have been beatified. But *sanguis martyrum, semen christianorum*. The Church of Vietnam triumphed over persecution. Love was stronger than hatred.

That Church now numbers about 1,600,000, with 1,500 priests and 400 missionaries, divided into seventeen vicariates apostolic. There are ten Vietnamese bishops. From the rice-fields to the mountains the bells of five thousand churches each evening ring the Angelus and proclaim the reality of Vietnamese Christianity. One landmark of history, the glory of the Church of Vietnam, is the Cathedral of Phat-Diem, the episcopal see of the first Vietnamese Vicar Apostolic. It was built in 1891 by "Father Six" (his real name was Tran-Luc) who, by his priestly and social activity, was one of the great figures of the Vietnamese clergy. With its fine roof resting on majestic columns of lacquered wood and its stone façade sculptured in the purest traditional style, it looks out over the peaceful Vietnamese countryside. Built in the land of persecution, it is the symbol of the Church of Vietnam.

After a long period of peace the Church of Vietnam is now going through a new period of trial. It is now the Communists who are the persecutors. The Geneva Agreement, signed on 21st July, 1954, brought to an end a seven years' war against the Viet-Minh by dividing Vietnam into separate territories north and south of the Seventeenth Parallel. Northern Vietnam has a Communist régime, while Southern Vietnam remains nationalist. The reader will remember the exodus from Northern Vietnam which took place after the signing of the Agreement. Nearly eight hundred thousand Vietnamese, of whom the majority were Catholics, left their country and their possessions to escape from Communism. The Catholics of the three vicariates of Bui-Chu, Phat-Diem and Hai-Phong, together with their bishops and priests, took refuge in the south.

Has the Church of Northern Vietnam become a "Church of Silence"? The Viet-Cong (Communists) love to disguise their hostility to Christianity under an appearance of complete tolerance. At Hanoi, where there are foreign observers, orders have been given that no hindrance is to be placed in the way of Catholic worship. The sight of Vietnamese Catholics fervently celebrating Christmas and Easter gives the impression that they enjoy complete religious liberty. But the Viet-Cong do not forget that the majority of Catholics are opposed to their régime. Communist intolerance appears most openly in the countryside. Priests do not have the right to move freely about their parishes in the exercise of their ministry. The sick often die without a priest. In some villages religious marriage is forbidden. Public meetings are arranged to coincide with the Sunday services so as to prevent the faithful from attending Mass. Catholics who react against these arbitrary measures are declared "enemies of the people" and thrown into prison.

Nevertheless, behind the Bamboo Curtain the Church of Northern

Vietnam maintains its strength and vitality in the midst of its many difficulties. The faith of the Catholics in the north is as deep as in the days of the martyrs. Neither war nor famine nor the hatred of the Viet-Cong has weakened it. Heroic acts, attributable only to a burning faith, are of constant occurrence. Catholics refuse to go to meetings so as not to fail in their religious duties. Priests prefer to be arrested rather than to forego their ministry. The dying ask to be taken to church to receive the sacraments, if the Viet-Cong prevent the priests from coming to them. And in Christian homes the crucifix looks down from the wall upon those who believe in him, sharing their joys and sufferings and consoling them in their hours of distress.

Why is the Faith so vigorous amongst Vietnamese Catholics, despite their overwhelmingly painful circumstances? How has Catholicism managed to take root in Vietnam and adapt itself to Vietnamese social institutions? To what degree has a faith born on the shores of the Mediterranean proved capable of supplanting another faith, older than itself, on the shores of the China Sea? By what miracle have two different moralities achieved a reconciliation —the Confucian morality of the East and the Christian morality of the West? The problem is an old one, dating from the time of the first Vietnamese convert. But it keeps its interest today and will do tomorrow. We shall try to resolve this grave problem, upon which the fate of the Church of Vietnam depends, by first giving a general outline of the three principal institutions upon which Vietnamese society is based: ancestor worship, paternal authority and polygamy. We shall then see in what conditions Vietnamese Catholics are obliged to break certain traditional rules established by these institutions. Finally, we shall examine the burning question of whether Catholicism has sapped the foundations of Vietnamese institutions, as some maintain, or whether it has, on the contrary, strengthened them while adapting itself to them.

What is ancestor worship? It is one of the most important social institutions of Vietnam. Confucius said: "To honour and serve one's parents after their death, as during their life, is the first obligation of a man." According to the generally accepted idea, a Vietnamese family consists both of the living and of the dead. Like the ancient Romans, the Vietnamese believe that after their death the ancestors continue to live in the family with their descendants and take them under their protection. "This survival of one's ancestors," writes Father Cadière, "and their presence in the family is not just a manner of speaking, no mere poetic figure. It is a profound reality recognized by all." The spirits of the ancestors lead not only a supernatural but also a material life. They eat and drink and share in all the family activities. During the days of *Tet* (New Year) they revisit their descendants and celebrate the feast with them. They join in marriage and funeral ceremonies celebrated in the family. Parents do not always remain upon the altar after their deaths. They readily take their places among the living, with due attention to degrees of kindred and the family hierarchy. Thus those of the living whose rank is superior to that of the dead do not pay them the honours of the cult.

It is the duty of the descendants to give their ancestors a peaceful and happy life. If they attend devotedly to the cult, the spirits of their ancestors will be well-disposed towards them and accord them protection. But woe to those who neglect to honour them! Deprived of their proper sacrifices, these restless spirits will torment the family and visit every kind of malediction upon it.

In the higher levels of Vietnamese society, however, we find a different conception of ancestor worship. According to the opinion expressed by the intellectual minority, it does not rest upon any system of belief. It is simply an expression of reverence and gratitude. It is based on filial piety and free from all superstition. A pious and grateful child can never forget his parents after their death. He honours them, not from fear of punishment or need of protection, but out of affection and gratitude. Ancestor worship is then elevated in character, despite the popular beliefs about it. It is noble, pure and entirely disinterested.

Whatever may be one's conception of ancestor worship, it demands the performance of certain rites. There are two great rites: sacrifice and mourning. As everyone knows, every Vietnamese family has an altar, varying in richness according to its means. On anniversaries and feast-days the members of the family gather before this altar. They lay offerings upon it and meditate or prostrate themselves before it in honour of their ancestors. Each individual attaches to these ceremonies a meaning corresponding to his particular conception of the worship due to the dead.

But these offerings, and the upkeep of the altar itself, cost money. Hence there exists in Vietnam a custom connected with ancestor worship called *Huong-Hoa* (the Portion of Fire and Incense). It consists in transmitting part of the family property to the ritual heir, who must be the eldest son of the eldest branch of the family, together with the duty of maintaining the cult. As for mourning, ancient laws and customs determine in detail what clothes must be worn and for how long a period. Confucius, when asked why mourning for one's parents lasts three years, replied: "Parents carry their children in their arms for three years, and it is in recognition of this benefit that such is the length of the period of mourning."

Paternal authority, *Gia-Truong*, is that of the head of the family over all those who live together in one household, whether as relations by blood or marriage or under the terms of a contract, such as domestic servants, apprentices and workmen. (*Civil Code*, article 204.) It is based on the same principle as ancestor worship, i.e., filial piety. Filial piety obliges children to honour, respect and serve their parents, and to remain under their tutelage, even when they have attained their majority and are married.

As for polygamy, law and custom still recognize its existence. It has a special cause which appears to justify it: the necessity of having male posterity to maintain the worship of the ancestors. The head of a family whose wife does not give him a son has not only the right but the duty of marrying another to provide an heir for the cult. In the words of Mencius: "The worst of all failures in filial piety is to die without leaving any posterity." In Vietnam, polygamy is strictly hierarchical. There is the principal wife, or wife of the first rank, and there are the wives of the second rank. Society and law both recognize this hierarchy. In all social relationships the principal wife is regarded as a person equal to her husband. She is the mother of the family, not only of her own children but also those of the other wives. The same distinction is found in law, which in general reflects manners and custom. The principal wife shares her husbands rights, including the control of the family property. On her husband's death she takes his place as head of the family. (*Civil Code*, article 344.)

Such, in brief outline, are the three chief social institutions of Vietnam. What effect has contact with Catholicism had upon them? We know what Christianity teaches about our dead parents. We must indeed honour them after their deaths as during their life-time. But all the beliefs and superstitions connected with ancestor worship are forbidden. Suppose we go into the house of a Vietnamese Catholic family. An altar still stands in the principal room, but its appearance is different. The crucifix has taken the place of the tablets bearing the names of dead members of the family. The sticks of incense, the plates of rice, fruit and flowers have been replaced by pious pictures. On the fifteenth day of each lunar month, on the days of *Tet* and on family anniversaries, a Catholic family does not make offerings to its ancestors nor burn sticks of incense in their honour, nor prostrate itself before the altar, but it prays and has Masses celebrated for the repose of the souls of its dead members.

A blow may seem to be struck at the prerogatives of paternal authority by the Christian doctrine that the father must exercise his authority for the common good of the family. It follows that the head of the family loses his rights over his children, notably that of determining their marriages. Polygamy, of course, is excluded.

The changes caused by Catholicism in Vietnamese institutions have considerable social significance. Those who have no understanding of the Catholic religion insist that it attacks the very basis of the Vietnamese family and society. If children no longer give worship to their deceased parents they will fail in their duty of filial piety, which is the basic rule of the Vietnamese family. Again, if paternal authority is reduced, order will no longer reign in the family, since the latter is patriarchal in character. And if the head of a family whose wife does not give him a son cannot take another, there will be no one to carry on the worship of the ancestors. What will become of Vietnamese society if it no longer recognizes Confucian morality, by which it has been governed for centuries? In consequence many Vietnamese, while paying tribute to the Catholic faith, refuse to embrace it, since this would mean giving up ancestor worship. Others are hostile towards it because it comes from the West.

Now, while it is true that Vietnamese Catholics no longer observe certain rules demanded by usage and tradition, there is on the other side of this question a solid, incontrovertible historical fact: the existence of a vast Vietnamese Catholic community, a multitude of believers, of priests, of churches, and of martyrs who were willing to suffer and die in witness to the truth. Is it conceivable that this could have happened if the Catholic religion were really prejudicial to Vietnamese institutions and incapable of adapting itself to our manners and customs?

Let us now consider our social institutions in themselves. It was the teaching of Confucius that one must "honour and serve one's parents after their deaths as during their life-time". The Fourth Commandment of God is, "Honour thy father and thy mother." There is no difference between the two precepts. Filial piety has the same moral value for us, whether we are Confucianists or Catholics. Obviously Catholics cannot fall into the error of believing that their dead relatives have become spirits to whom they must pay ritual honours in order to receive graces and benefits from them. They venerate their parents after their deaths as during their lifetime, but they wish their filial piety to be founded upon truth. Hence their prayers rise from the family altar to God, praying that he will grant their ancestors eternal happiness. If it is true, as is claimed, that ancestor worship has no religious or superstitious character, and that the offerings and prostrations before the altar are only an expression of respect and gratitude, a demonstration of filial piety, then they are perfectly in harmony with Christian principles.

Three centuries ago the question of Chinese Rites was a centre of controversy. It may be useful to recall it. It arose in China about 1631 between the Jesuits on the one hand and the Dominicans and Franciscans on the other. Bent on adapting Catholicism to the many-thousands-of-years-old wisdom of China, and thus enabling many conversions to be made, the Jesuits were convinced that the honours paid to one's ancestors were purely civil ceremonies without taint of idolatry, still less superstition; and further, that the celebrations in honour of Confucius were simply an expression of official admiration, veneration and gratitude to the great Sage and supreme Teacher of the Far East.

The Dominicans and Franciscans did not share this opinion, which they regarded as an over-subtle interpretation. They maintained that these practices, as observed by the Chinese people with whom they were in daily contact, were in fact idolatrous. The echoes of the dispute reached so far that Pascal referred to it in the fifth of his *Provincial Letters*. It was submitted to Rome and examined under successive pontificates, many factors combining to prolong the dispute immensely. But on 28th May 1935 the Congregation of Propaganda gave permission to Manchurian Catholics to join in the honours paid to Confucius. On 26th May 1936 it authorized the official ceremonies venerating the Emperor and national heroes of Japan. The final solution was given by the Congregation in its Instruction of 8th December 1939, which applied to the whole of

China and to all countries of Chinese culture. According to this instruction, Catholics are allowed "to take part in ceremonies in honour of Confucius, before his picture or the tablet bearing his name, in shrines and in schools". It also approved as "licit and suitable the inclinations of the head and other manifestations of public respect before the dead or their pictures, and before the tablets which bear their names". The Chinese Rites dispute was over at last. The Church's solution has shown once more that her insistence on spiritual unity does not mean that she aims at the uniformity of all peoples, but respects their spirit and traditions. "Everything in these uses and customs which is not indissolubly linked to religious error," said Pius XII, "is always to be examined with sympathy, and when possible protected and encouraged."

It is to be hoped that the decision of the Holy See in this matter may be applied in large measure to Vietnam. This would allow a large number of Vietnamese, till now held back by their fear of failing in their duty towards their deceased parents, to embrace the Catholic religion, whose beauty and generosity they admire. It would dispel the prejudice which holds that Catholicism has no respect for one of the most beautiful of Far Eastern institutions, the rites of ancestor worship. This was the wish of the Emperor Gia-Long. In one of his conversations with Monsignor Pigneau de Béhaine he told him that "he was convinced that the souls of our deceased parents do not return, and that their children cannot obtain anything from them, but that he regarded this ceremony simply as a proof of the memory which a grateful son is bound to keep of his ancestors". And he added: "It is greatly to be hoped that this custom may be reconciled with Christianity, for, as far as I can see, there is no other real obstacle to my whole kingdom's becoming Christian."

Has the Catholic religion diminished the father's authority in the Vietnamese family? I think not. Catholicism, like Confucianism, asserts that children have duties towards their parents, for the maintenance of the structure of the family, the cell of society. In asserting likewise that they have rights attaching to their own persons, it is not weakening paternal authority but determining its true nature. For paternal authority is not so much a privilege as a function to be exercised by the father in the interests of the children, whose membership of the family is bound to take precedence of their membership of any other society. It is hardly necessary to add that the greatest benefit which Catholicism has brought to our social institutions is the recognition of the human person, sometimes sacrificed upon the altar of patriarchal authority.

Moreover, if we examine the development of Vietnamese law in regard to the family, we shall see that it has been in a Christian direction in the sense of enhancing the importance of the individual. According to ancient Vietnamese law, the head of the family held exorbitant powers. He had the right of tutelage and ward over his children at all ages (Code of Gia-Long, article 82); the right to marry them at his pleasure (ibid., article 94); the right to put them in pledge and to repudiate them if they failed in their filial duties or created fraternal strife (*Code of the Le*, article 311). But the ancient legislator seems to have established these rigid rules and then left it to custom to temper their effect. In practice, despite the absolute rights which the law gave him, the head of the family very seldom exercised his prerogatives. They have completely disappeared in modern legislation.

Law and custom have evolved in an even more striking manner in regard to polygamy. Under the influence of Western ideas deriving from Christianity, Vietnamese women are becoming more and more conscious of their personal rights and their role in society. They are not prepared to tolerate the sharing of their husband's affection with other women. Again, the difficulties of modern life give little encouragement to polygamy. Added to this, modern law gives the father of the family full freedom in the matter of choosing his ritual heir. In these circumstances the duty of marrying a wife of the second rank in order to have a male heir to maintain the worship of the ancestors has no longer any foundation (*Civil Code*, articles 409 and 410), and the Government of South Vietnam has recently published a law forbidding polygamy. It is consoling to see how in this matter the evolution of ideas and conditions of life in our nation has confirmed the soundness of Christian doctrine.

After studying the points of contact between the principal Vietnamese institutions and Catholicism, we see that the Catholic faith can claim full citizenship in Vietnamese society. It is not a religion of which the West holds a monopoly. It opens itself to all men on earth, of whatever race or country they may be. There is only one truth, under whatever sky. "Go and teach all nations," was Christ's command to his disciples. Far from destroying the foundations of our Vietnamese society, Catholicism has adapted itself to our institutions, filling up the gaps in them and strengthening the basis on which they rest. Who would dare to dispute the high moral value of Confucianism and its vast influence on the whole of the Far East? Such a morality was sufficient in an age when everything was concentrated within the patriarchal family. But our society has evolved, our knowledge has expanded, our economic activities have developed. New problems are posed by a new age. Confucianism, for all its beauty and strength, could not meet these problems. It was then that Christianity rose above our horizon, and we gazed upon it with a certain apprehensiveness. A voice spoke to reassure us: "I am come not to destroy but to fulfil." From that day onwards new life has been breathed into Confucianism, for its doctrine has been complemented by Christianity. It is within this union of Christian and Confucian civilization that we are called to become "perfect as our heavenly Father is perfect".

Now that Catholicism is rooted in our soil it exerts an ever-increasing influence throughout all classes of society. But Vietnam is still a missionary country. The Church of Vietnam, even though ten of its vicariates are headed by Vietnamese bishops and the number of priests tends to increase, still needs missionaries to spread the word of God. Their presence in Vietnam, as in other missionary countries, raises the difficult problem of their relations with the nationalist movements coming into being amongst the peoples to whom they preach the Gospel. Have they been sent to distant lands to carry the Gospel to them, or to serve the ends of the countries from which they came? It is a question that has arisen in the course of the history of the Vietnamese Church, especially in connection with the last war fought in our country. Not only the Viet-Minh but Vietnamese Catholics as well were demanding the expulsion of the missionaries, on the ground that they were a hindrance to the nationalist movement.

It is a grave problem, and demands a solution if we are to safeguard the honour of the Church of Vietnam and of our missionaries. We must let all Vietnamese know the unchanging attitude of the Catholic Church; in propagating the Faith, she scrupulously insists upon her Founder's precept: "Render to Caesar the things that are Caesar's, and to God the things that are God's." It is necessary, too, to show them the meaning of the vocation of a missionary, who devotes his life to the good of the country which he has adopted as a second native land and who, as a soldier of Christ, seeks no conquest but that of a kingdom which is not of this world. Vietnamese Catholics cannot be indifferent to this problem. Have they not been accused of being accomplices of the missionaries? Have they not been regarded as traitors to their country, simply because they are Christians?

Let us first see what instructions the Church has given to missionaries in their apostolate. As far back as 1657 the Congregation of Propaganda issued instructions concerning the respect due to the usages and customs of countries to be evangelized: "Make no attempt, either by persuasion or otherwise to make these people change their rites, customs or manners where these are not plainly contrary to religion and morality. What indeed could be more absurd than to introduce France, Spain, Italy, or any other European system, into China?" Thus, the missionary must not only respect the social and family traditions of the country to which he goes, but even adapt himself to its customs and usages. If any of its customs are contrary to Christian morality, he must modify them only with the greatest prudence. Further, the Instruction of 18th October 1883 requires missionaries not to meddle in political questions. "Any interference in political affairs or interests of state must be regarded with horror." Persecutions in missionary countries have often been occasioned by the fear of such interference. Pope Pius XI made the supra-national position of the Church clear in his message of 15th June 1926 to the people of China: "The Church is careful not to interfere or involve herself in civil and political affairs; she has never permitted missionaries to act in such a way as to favour the plans or interests of foreign powers. Nor is there anyone who does not know—for the whole of history testifies to it—that the Church adapts herself to the laws and constitutions belonging to each nation or state; that she practises and teaches respect for lawfully constituted governments; and that, for those who work faithfully preaching the Gospel, she asks nothing but the common law, security and freedom."

Have the Church's instructions been carried out in Vietnam? If we are to pass an objective judgement on this question we must be careful not to take a few individual cases and make hasty generalizations from them. If one missionary does something which he, in good faith, thinks legitimate, but which is liable to be adversely commented upon and criticized, his conduct does not alter the attitude of other missionaries who know how to remain faithful to their vocation. Still less does it modify the position of the Church. We have seen our missionaries at work. They, in their modesty, would not wish us to speak of their merits. But who could justly deny the benefits, in the spiritual, intellectual and material order, which they have conferred upon our country? Let us recall the memory of Father Cadière, of the Missions Étrangères, who died at Hue on 6th July 1955 after having been interned for six and a half years by the Viet-Minh. In 1942, when celebrating the fiftieth anniversary of his arrival in Vietnam, he said: "Once having studied and understood the Vietnamese, I loved them. I loved them because of their fine intelligence and quick wit. I loved them for their moral virtues. I loved them for their character. And finally, I loved them because of their sufferings." Father Cadière was not content to restrict his missionary activity to Christian circles, whose material conditions he strove to improve. He left a considerable body of scientific work, the fruit of a lifetime of linguistic, historical and ethnological research occupying no less than 250 articles in the *Bulletin des amis du vieux Hue* and the *Bulletin de l'École française d'Extrême-Orient*. His studies of the "Beliefs and Religious Practices of the Vietnamese" are particularly striking. Here is one missionary who has a right to the grateful homage of all Vietnam.

Events in Vietnam after the Japanese *coup* of 9th March 1945 proved that our missionaries had worthily fulfilled their role as messengers of the Faith and were fit successors of those who had shed their blood for the Vietnamese Church. No one could accuse them of having said or done anything which could in any way favour the interests of their country of origin. Nor could anyone accuse them of having prevented the Vietnamese nationalists from defending the national cause. Their best reward has been to see the Vietnamese Church, upon which they have laboured, come forth from her trials more glorious than ever.

It is now the splendid task of Vietnamese Catholics to serve the Church of which they are members. One generation of Christians succeeds to another, each contributing something to the work of construction. Though Catholics are a minority of the population, they are nevertheless a living force in Vietnam. Their wish is to be the salt of the Vietnamese earth. Their action and influence upon their surroundings are by no means negligible. Non-Catholics often ask for their co-operation in social action, recognizing the effective quality of Christian charity. During the last twenty years, in obedience to the directives of the Popes, Vietnamese Catholics have devoted themselves to Catholic Action. Their finest achievement has been the formation of the various Young Christian groups—workers, farmers, etc. They have had a good effect on Vietnamese youth. We have also had Social Action Days, devoted to seeking solutions to the country's social problems in the light of the Church's teaching. Finally, Vietnamese Catholics have taken a particular interest in works of charity, especially in the St. Vincent de Paul Society, whose object, of course, is to relieve the sufferings of the poorest classes.

After the Second World War, when nationalist movements came into being and demanded the independence of Vietnam, Catholics had a part to play in their country's politics. This raised the new problem of how Catholics in political life ought to act towards the Vietnamese Church. We scarcely need to be reminded that the Church, while maintaining Catholic Action in the purely religious field, sets no limits to our civil and political liberty but those imposed by natural and Christian morality. We are free to have our preferences in political affairs, to form parties to work for the victory of our ideas, and even to refuse to support the existing régime or to give it merely *de facto* recognition. Pius XI gave formal expression to this principle: "While Catholic Action, being of its very nature alien to political parties, cannot be limited within any faction, there is nothing to prevent the faithful from belonging to political parties, on condition that the action of such parties is not opposed to the laws of God and the Church" (*Letter to Cardinal Segura*).

But the Church has been careful to put Catholics on their guard against two errors concerning the relation between religion and politics. The first consists in separating political life from the moral law laid down by religion in such a way that the Christian and the citizen are separated from each other in the same person: the Christian, in his private life, professing his belief in the teachings of the Church, while the citizen, in his public life, denies those teachings and regulates his conduct according to interests which ignore moral considerations. In his Encyclical *Immortale Dei*, Leo XIII wrote: "It is not permissible to follow different rules of conduct in private and in public life, respecting the authority of the Church as an individual while rejecting it as a citizen. This would be to combine good with evil and to put a man in open conflict with himself, whereas he should be always at peace with himself, and never swerve from Christian virtue in any activity or circumstances whatever." The second error is to identify religion with one political party. It was again Leo XIII who taught: "There are those who confuse and so to speak identify religion with one political party, to the extent that they hold that the members of any other party have practically given up any claim to be Catholics. This is a clumsy introduction of political factions into the august field of religion; it also means breaking the bond of brotherhood as well as opening the door to numerous deplorable consequences." (Encyclical *Cum Multa Sint.*)

Those who love the Vietnamese Church and desire to serve her trust that Vietnamese politicians will have enough discernment and Christian spirit to avoid confusing the Catholic religion with their own political parties. In a country of several beliefs, like ours, any such identification would risk arousing anti-Catholic political feeling. A still graver consequence would be to make the various political parties regard the Vietnamese Church as a politico-religious sect, when she is in her essence divine and set above all political parties and activities. Vietnamese Catholics have an absolute duty to preserve her true character and nature. Does this mean that they ought to abstain from politics? That too is an error. Let us refer once more to the teaching of the Church. "It is for the public good," said Leo XIII, "that Catholics should lend their wise co-operation to the administration of the affairs of the community and take part in the government of the State. Generally speaking, to refuse to take part in political affairs would be as reprehensible as to do nothing at all for the common good, all the more so as Catholics, by virtue of the very doctrine which they profess, are obliged to carry out this duty with all conscientious integrity." (*Immortale Dei.*) Vietnamese Catholics are, then, under an obligation to descend into the political arena to defend the Church of Vietnam, to bring about the triumph of social justice and charity, in short, to establish a Christian social order in Vietnamese society.

In the dawn of our independence, and faced by the Communist menace confronting our country, what is to be desired most of all is the union of all Vietnamese, without distinction of religious conviction or political tendency. By uniting ourselves with our non-Catholic compatriots in public life we shall be giving proof of our patriotism, our solidarity, and our Christian charity. If our words and acts are a reflection of Christian virtue we shall have the merit of winning their sympathy and esteem for the Vietnamese Church. All Vietnamese, being in the service of the same cause, should take their place in the national community and work together for the solution of our country's problems. No patriot could fail to be moved at the fate of our Vietnam, lacerated by war, split into two territories, riddled with political dissension, and impoverished by economic disaster. No Christian could fail to be troubled over the future of the Vietnamese Church, threatened both by the Communist danger and by the hostility of the religious sects.

In the midst of our daily anxieties and sufferings, and writing at a time when hosts of pilgrims from all over the world are flocking to Lourdes in memory of the centenary of the apparition of our Lady, we cannot do better than address a humble prayer for our country to her:

> Queen of Vietnam, cast your gentle and compassionate gaze upon our country and our Vietnamese Church. Kissing the earth, and with our arms outstretched in the image of your crucified Son, we beg you not to abandon us. In your love and mercy, bind all Vietnamese together. You have said that if we knew how to pray, those who do not believe in the common Father of all mankind would one day win grace to know the truth. Teach us to pray, and protect us under your kindly mantle. Queen of Vietnam, be our Queen always; be with us and amongst us. Be the Mother of our great Vietnamese family. May the words of our Saviour be echoed in the hearts of all Vietnamese: "You have but one Master and all of you are brothers."

BRAZIL

Alceu Amoroso Lima

The history of Brazilian Catholicism can be divided into three periods: the early period, from 1500 to 1759—that is, from the first Mass said by a Franciscan, who came with the fleet of the Portuguese Admiral, Pedro Alvares Cabral, up till the expulsion of the Jesuits; the central period, from 1759 to 1875—that is, up till the trial, condemnation and amnesty, after two years' imprisonment, of two bishops, Dom Vital Maria de Oliveira and Dom Antonio de Macedo Costa, who defended the Church's freedom against the Empire; and the present period, from 1875 till now, which shows a trend of religious renaissance and the coming of heretical beliefs.

Early Period (1500-1759)

It was the missionary spirit that characterized this period. During the first century of the colonization of Brazil by the Portuguese, four great religious orders became established there: the Franciscans, Jesuits, Carmelites and Benedictines. It was the Franciscans who first took possession of our land for Christ by saying the first Mass in 1500, and by the end of the century their missionary activity was quite important, especially at Pernambuco, which, with its cultivation of sugar-cane, was the economic centre of the new Portuguese colony.

But it was the Jesuits, who first came in 1549, who became the founders of the first schools of Christian training in Brazil, for both rich and poor, with what were called their *collegios*, which were to some extent comparable with the universities the Dominicans founded in Peru and Mexico.

What the sons of Saint Ignacius brought to Brazil was the spirit of the Council of Trent and the Counter-Reformation, together with a discipline of conduct of which they themselves were an excellent example throughout the colonial period.

ALCEU AMOROSO LIMA was born in 1893, and holds professorships in the University of Brazil and the Pontifical Catholic University. He is a member of the Brazilian Academy of Letters and the Brazilian National Council of Education, and was Director of the Cultural Department of the Pan-American Union in Washington from 1951 to 1953. He is a regular contributor to many Latin American periodicals, and the author of numerous books.

The coming of the secular clergy and the setting up of the first bishopric at Bahia, independent of the Portuguese jurisdiction from the island of Madeira, in the first century of our history, marks the establishment of the ecclesiastical organization which was linked with the political organization in that close union of Church and State which had always been one of the characteristics of peninsular Catholicism, whether Spanish or Portuguese.

One may therefore say that the two badges of early Brazilian Catholicism were the missionary spirit and a close union of Church and State.

This missionary spirit, very much bound up with the Jesuits' catechetical training in the strict spirit of the Counter-Reformation, firmly established, from the beginning, that Catholic unity which has been such a marked characteristic of our religious history. Our Catholicism most certainly came to us through tradition, since Portugal had long practised the strictest obedience to the Holy See and the teaching of the Catholic Church. But in Brazil it came as one of the first attempts at *conquest* and the expansion of the new missionary spirit was similar in nature to the spirit of the Renaissance and the great maritime discoveries of the time.

The transplanting of the seeds of Catholicism in the New World did not take place without a struggle. The missionary work of the great religious orders, especially of the Jesuits and the Franciscans, had to contend not only with the polytheism of the Indians, as was the case also in Mexico and Peru, but also with that of the African population who had early on been brought to Central and South America by the slave trade.

This spirit—of conquest and self-discipline—of the orders did not always correspond with the ideas of the secular clergy, who tended rather to lean on the State and establish themselves in the shadow of the various political institutions. This does not mean that there were no martyrs among the secular clergy: Dom Pedro Sardinha, for instance, Bishop of Bahia, was killed by the Indians. But the dynamic missionary spirit came more from the regulars, whereas the secular clergy had a greater spirit of organization and of co-operation with the State. This sometimes led to quarrels between the two bodies of clergy. But the greatest conflict was between the missionaries (especially the Jesuits) and the *colonos*, whose object was to exploit the country to the utmost, to find gold, and to get cheap labour by keeping the slaves, rather than to Christianize the developing colony.

In any case, we can say that the first two centuries of our religious development established our Catholic unity, and offer an example of the purest missionary spirit and an expression of the Church as she was throughout the world at the dawn of modern times. It was the new era in which Catholicism, obeying the demands of its nature, was setting out to bear the banner of Christ from Europe both westward, as in our case, and eastward, to India and Japan.

The expulsion of the Jesuits, who had until then been the incarnation of the missionary spirit and almost the only ones to offer education to the masses, was a hard blow, and can be considered as marking the end of a splendid age—an age decisive in establishing Catholicism not only in the institutions, but even more in the habits and the hearts of the new nation that was growing up.

Central Period (1759-1875)

The event which marks the dividing line between the two first periods of our Catholic development is the expulsion of the Jesuits from Portugal and her territories abroad. It showed how events in the wider world affected the colonies, just as the coming of the Society of Jesus had in the sixteenth century. The Church had then been at the beginning of her great modern movement of world-wide expansion. Now, in the eighteenth century, the reverse was happening, as the power of states was growing, and the political role of the Church was gradually weakening. The struggle between the two powers is a perennial one, and will go on till the end of time. In the eighteenth century the secularist spirit was spreading over society as a whole. The Society of Jesus had based their missionary work on the closest collaboration with the State, and the price of that collaboration, as far as Portugal was concerned, was what was called Pombalism, after the Marquis de Pombal, King José's Prime Minister, famous for his authoritarian and anti-Jesuit attitude. Pombalism in Portugal was the same sort of thing as Josephism in Austria and Gallicanism in France, none of which had the disastrous spiritual consequences that religious nationalism had in England or Germany, leading to the destruction of the whole of Western Christian unity. But this notion of the primacy of civil power over religious characterized the new era which started in Brazil—still colonial, and soon to be independent (1822)—with the expulsion of the Jesuits.

The missionary spirit gave way to what we may call the "sedentary spirit". The Church rested upon the State. The State paid the clergy, just as it paid civil and military functionaries. The colonial Church in Brazil gradually changed from a fighting militia into an established, settled, conventional institution. Religious education went downhill, with the men who had run most of the schools expelled. The lack of properly-trained priests and the decline in the work of catechesis owing to the absence of any sense of apostleship and the lack of religious instruction, gradually resulted in the disappearance of the missionary spirit of conquest and its replacement by a policy of staying still. Religious nationalism appeared, and with it a growing suspicion of the great religious orders, which were of their nature Catholic, in the sense of being international. The secular clergy were actively involved in the movement towards independence, but their political enthusiasm was not matched with an equal fervour for religion. When the first Constituent Assembly met in 1823, there were more than a dozen priests among its members, all with a very strong spirit of liberalism. I will not say that all priests were like this, but most were. Even Diego Antonio Feijó, who was a priest with a good knowledge of theology, a great politician, a great statesman, the Regent of the Empire during the minority of the Emperor Don Pedro II, had such an independent attitude towards the Holy See, and was so opposed to the religious orders, that he even started a campaign in favour of permitting ecclesiastics to marry, and would allow no religious to stay in Brazil except the Capuchins, who served as Army chaplains.

This concern of the clergy in active politics, and increase of hostility between the seculars and regulars, was the strongest characteristic of this further period in the history of Brazilian Catholicism.

Another characteristic was the growing drift of the laity, men in particular, away from the sacraments. In fact, there had always been very few men seriously practising their religion; but now came a time when all external prayer and religious practice was carried out by women and children. The spirit of the eighteenth century, and the influence of what were then called "French ideas", coupled with the narrowness of the traditional religious outlook and the change from a missionary to a "sedentary" attitude, were a first preparation for the decline of Catholicism in the nineteenth century.

Religion, thanks to the work of the missionaries, who were concerned as much with the pagan Indians and Africans as with the colonials, remained an important element in the life of everyone, from the upper classes to the most destitute. It had been a major element in the historical development of the Portuguese, and they brought it to the Brazilians. It was by no means an enlightened faith. It was not an intellectual faith gained in religious controversy or persecution. It was an established religion, meeting no obstacles, handed down from father to son as an unquestioned patrimony, and not without superstitious elements, owing to its contact with the aboriginals and above all with the African slaves. It was a religious outlook which permeated the whole mind of the nation, but which, although accepted and practised in childhood, was given up, at least in any practical sense, by the ruling classes, especially the men, in youth. It was a vague and a latent religion, but it was ingrained in the very fibres of the Brazilian soul. In this sense, the Brazilian people may be said to be religious even now. We are religious by *instinct* rather than by *reason*. As with our ancestors, it is a religion taught in our homes through the faith of the women and the respect of the men. Catholicism is officially recognized by the Constitution as a state religion and state-supported, in the secular tradition, as it has been since the Visigothic kings of the Iberian peninsula.

Among other traditions there are some laws, no longer effective, which gave the State certain powers over the Church, and especially over lay societies of a religious nature, that have never been officially recognized by the Church, but have not been repealed. Thus, in the mid-nineteenth century, a great Bishop of Northern Brazil (the State of Pernambuco), Dom Vital Maria de Oliveira, and soon afterwards another, Dom Antonio de Macedo Costa (State of Pará), tried to prevent certain interferences from the Imperial State in the internal administration of various religious associations (*Irmandades*, Fraternities), and caused a collision between Church and State which resulted in both bishops' being sentenced by the Supreme Court to four years' hard labour.

This struggle, which lasted from 1872 till 1875, marks an important moment in the history of Catholicism in Brazil. It was the high point of the influence of Freemasonry in our country. Masonry played an important part in the events leading up to our independence, from 1822 up till the Constitution of the Empire. Brazilian Masonry was related to the French, and took from it a strongly anti-clerical flavour. It was the political and ideological influence of the Masons on the Imperial Government which opened up this whole "religious question" which stirred public opinion so deeply in Brazil. It was certainly behind the fall of the Empire and the separation of Church and State. Since 1855 the Imperial Government had been trying to get an increasing hold upon the Church. In that year the Minister of Justice made it law that orders and congregations could not run seminaries. It thus became legal to intervene directly in the internal affairs of the Church, and in particular to weaken the religious congregations and orders, who had gone from strength to strength since Brazil was first discovered. The Society of Jesus had been driven out in 1759. Now came the turn of the other orders—Benedictines, Franciscans, Capuchins, Dominicans, Oratorians—who stood for the Church's independence in relation to the State far more than did the secular clergy.

This anti-monastic policy of the Empire, together with the dissemination of the new European philosophies—the positivism of Auguste Comte, the evolutionism of Spencer, the monism of the Germans—which led to religious scepticism among the intellectual and governing classes from 1870 onwards, made the nineteenth century in Brazil a time of decline for the Church. The masses kept their traditional faith. The ceremonies took place with their accustomed splendour. The devout pursued their own spiritual lives. Missionaries went quietly about their work of self-sacrifice among the Indians. Convents had their quota of vocations, and still were used as of old by those who wanted to amend their ways or take refuge from the disappointments of the world. Monasteries were almost totally deserted and vocations practically ceased for them. The religious schools carried on their work. But the general atmosphere reflected the breakdown of religion in both political and intellectual circles. The sedentary spirit I mentioned earlier became a conventionalism which impoverished the Church and gradually destroyed her influence over the upper classes.

We come now to the third period I spoke of.

The Present Period (1875-1959)

The courage and self-sacrifice of the two great bishops paved the way for a new era in the development of the history of Catholicism in Brazil. The time of decline was to be followed by a renaissance which is still going on, though naturally there are ups and downs. To put in a nutshell the contrast between the two periods, and indeed the two centuries—nineteenth and twentieth—I would say that in the nineteenth century the masses remained Catholic and the upper classes left the Church, whereas in the twentieth, the latter are returning to the Faith while the masses are undergoing a religious crisis. This is a sweeping statement, and needs qualifying, but it is in general the picture we get from a bird's eye view of both centuries.

In the nineteenth century, the mass of the people held on to the traditional Catholic belief which had become part of their national life, as we have seen, during the three centuries of colonial life. It was not perhaps a very well-reasoned faith, but it grasped the essentials, and was simple and fairly pure.

The upper classes, on the other hand, not only the intellectuals, but also the political and social leaders, quickly became imbued with the theories of the time, and came more and more to think of religion as a philosophical anachronism and nothing more than a familiar ritual.

But now, ever since the "religious question" was raised, with such startling effects, it is the upper classes who are returning to the Faith, or at least becoming sharply divided into believers and unbelievers, while the masses are drifting with two streams which flow against their Catholic upbringing: the upsurge of polytheistic African cults and also of modern spiritualism, and the spread of materialism and revolutionary expediency. The upper and lower classes are passing each other in the doorway! In a century their positions have been reversed. Their problems have been reversed. That contradiction which is at the root of Christ's mystery (*signum cui contradicetur* (Luke ii. 34)) has changed sides but not weakened.

This crossing of the streams began, as we have seen, with the bishops' resistance. This pricked the religious conscience of the upper classes. When the collision occurred, the people were still on the side of the bishops and the ruling classes on the side of the State. But when the Empire came to an end—precipitated by that religious crisis—the renaissance among the upper classes had begun. It was launched, in one sense, by a convert from positivism, Julio Cesar de Morais Carneiro; he was a great lawyer, and after the death of his second wife became a priest and shortly afterwards a Redemptorist, taking the name of Julio Maria.

His sermons, around the end of the Empire, used always to end with one phrase (rather like Cato's *Carthago delenda est!*)—"We must make Brazil Catholic"; and this gave a spur to the religious conscience of the educated classes. It was a new *voice*. And it was with this new voice that the young "missionary of Brazil" as Pius IX called him, touched the whole religious conscience of the country. His conversion and his apostolate coincided almost exactly with the fall of the Empire, and this reawakening of Catholicism which he effected brought with it two new changes of direction: the altar became independent of the throne, and democracy was seen to be compatible with the teaching of the Gospel.

In the nineteenth century, in both attack and defence, the Church had more or less stood by the same premisses: the indissoluble union of Church and State and the incompatibility of democratic ideas with Catholic teaching.

The words of this young convert opened new vistas, and ushered in a new era in the history of Brazilian Catholicism. The upper classes began a *volte-face* movement back to the traditional faith. This young positivist's conversion was soon followed by the conversion of another representative of the highest intellectual group, Joaquim Nabuco (1849-1910). Nabuco was to tell some time later (1900) in his autobiography (*Minha Formação*) the story of his religious development and his return to the Faith, which was tremendously influenced by Newman and English Catholicism in general. *Pensées détachées*, written in French, gives us the kernel of his religious thought.

These two conversions were the starting-point for a religious revival among the intellectuals, and at the beginning of the century various movements sprang up, not as yet very clearly defined, among the young men in the colleges, with such names as the Catholic Union. In political circles, a few isolated voices began talking an entirely new language—for, in 1891, when the Constitution of the Republic was put to the vote, there were so few Catholics in Parliament that certain anti-Catholic measures—such as divorce and the dissolution of the religious orders—were chiefly attacked by the positivists!

The beginnings of a Catholic party were apparent in the early years of the century, and in 1907 a Catholic deputy, Andrade Bezerra, put the first of our "social laws" before Parliament. Another early sign of a religious revival was the meeting of various Catholic congresses to consider the problems of education, of the family, of social legislation.

The general state of mind, however, was unchanged from that during the Empire. And once again, as with Dom Vital in 1872, it was a young bishop who stirred up the religious conscience of the country. This was the future Cardinal D. Sebastião Leme, like his predecessor, Dom Vital, Bishop of Recife and of Olinda. In 1916, the young bishop issued a pastoral letter deploring the apathy of Catholicism in the country. "We are a majority who count for nothing", he said. We have a traditional faith, but are satisfied with the mere externals of worship. To counteract this state of mind he launched a programme of Catholic Action, an early precursor of the world-wide movement started by Pius XI.

His call did not go unheeded, particularly in intellectual circles. During the nineteenth century, philosophical thought in Brazil had moved gradually from spiritualism to naturalism, under the combined influence of French positivism, English evolutionism, and German monism.

At the end of the century, the Bergsonian revolution and return to Kant had a profound influence on a philosopher called Farias Brito (d. 1917). One of his disciples, Jackson de Figueiredo (1891-1928), went one step further; impressed by Pascal, and with the same feeling that led Kierkegaard to turn away from Hegel, he heard the young bishop's words in 1916, and the following year made his submission to the Church.

Some years later, in 1922 (the same year in which the Brazilian Communist Party was founded), this young and enthusiastic convert set up the Dom Vital Centre with the martyred bishop for its patron —the Brazilian Thomas à Becket, he was called. He had earlier started a periodical, *A Ordem* (*Order*).

This was no coincidence. The generation that came after the 1914-18 war were starting to lose the state of mind Gide defended as *disponibilité*, which had affected young intellectuals in general from the start of the new century. These young minds, greedy for positive statements, after the cult of doubt which had possessed them at the start of their intellectual lives, were turning either to Rome or to Moscow. At one time it looked as though it was a century fated to swing between the Church of Rome and the Party in Moscow—which after all is a sort of Church in reverse. In 1922 this was certainly the case: the only possible answer to the revolution seemed to be the counter-revolution. Fascism had only just appeared, and its doctrines seemed to coincide with those of the young Brazilian convert, who was indeed attacking liberalism and the *bien pensant* middle class as much as the Marxist and Leninist revolutionaries. His premature death in 1928, at thirty-seven, prevented his doing full justice to his ideas, which derived politically mainly from Joseph de Maistre and Donoso Cortès. At the time of his death, the condemnation of the Action Française in 1926, and the first brushes between the Church and Fascism, had just begun to show how wrong it was to set Rome and Moscow up on the same level, as adversaries—in a Cartesian, or perhaps even a Manichean dualism. The enemy of Communism, on the same political level, and using the same methods, was Fascism, and later on Nazism and neo-Fascism. The Church's whole spirit was entirely different from either, though her positions might occasionally coincide with Fascist or reactionary positions; they will also sometimes coincide with conservative, liberal or even revolutionary ones. The only truly revolutionary force in history is the Judaeo-Christian revelation.

This recognition of the Church as beyond and above all civilizations and political parties, all races and continents, and as finding concrete expression in social, political, economic and cultural life through the lay apostolate, was Jackson de Figueiredo's underlying idea in founding the Dom Vital Centre. After his death, this idea became fully explicit in the intellectual and social life of the centre he founded and of the group which came together from all points of Brazil's social and cultural horizon as a result of his work.

The political revolution of 1930, which brought the first Republic of 1889 to an end, and opened a new era in Brazilian political life, found Catholicism in a very different position from the one it held in the first Republic. While, as we have seen, it then looked as though the fall of the throne must mean the fall of the altar too, and Catholic ideas found only a few scattered voices to defend them in Parliament, the intellectual and political leaders were so changed by 1930 that the new Constituent Assembly of 1934 approved the Catholic programme as it stood.

Instead of the Catholic party which had once been hoped for, or the indifference of 1889, Cardinal Leme (the same who in 1916 had launched the appeal to a dormant Catholicism) was able to set up a League of Catholic Electors, quite outside any political parties, and with a social programme based on the defence of the natural law, with no reference to any one class or party.

This alone shows the tremendous change that had taken place in Brazilian Catholicism in two generations. The separation of Church and State in 1891 had taken place in perfect peace and justice. Under the Empire, the juridical and political union of the two powers, far from indicating that the Church had any profound spiritual influence over the State, meant rather that the Church was under the thumb of the State, as the "religious question" plainly showed. After 1891, her liberty won, the Church developed so much that if we are to take the number of dioceses and archdioceses as any indication of religious life, we need only mention that whereas in 1889 there were twelve religious districts in Brazil, there are now more than a hundred and twenty—ten times as many for a population no more than three times as large.

Catholic Action was officially founded in 1935, and from 1932 onwards, individual groups of students and workers, under the names of "Catholic University Action" and "General Confederation of Catholic Workers", had begun the work of assembling their scattered forces. The special result of the Catholic Action movement was to increase religious and sacramental life, particularly among the young. The Jesuits' movement for Marian Congresses has been especially important in this. And there is also a liturgical revival, led chiefly by the Benedictines and Dominicans. In this whole renaissance of the twentieth century, the work of the religious orders has been quite outstanding. At the close of the Empire, as a result of the law of 1855 which I mentioned before, the decline of the religious orders was one of the clearest indications of a decline in religion as a whole. In 1889, when the Empire fell, the Jesuits had barely returned to their educational work, which had ceased with their expulsion in 1759 and started again in southern Brazil in 1847; the Franciscans had only a few old priests left; the Benedictine monasteries were empty, and so were the Carmelite. The absence of vocations made it seem as though the great religious orders were doomed to total extinction. Since then, with the reopening of novitiates, and an influx of vocations, the monastic movement and the growth both of the traditional orders and such new congregations as the one founded by Père de Foucauld, are among the most outstanding features of Brazilian Catholicism at the present time.

In *Modernismo*, the literary movement which has been growing since 1922, we can also see a reflexion of this same wave of religious revival that is to be found in the specifically religious sphere (1922 was the centenary of our national independence, which may help to explain the fact of the renewal of activities in the various fields of national life).

In the same way, if one compares our situation in mid-twentieth century with what obtained in the middle of the nineteenth, one soon sees the essential difference. Whereas in 1880, for instance, all educated Brazilians, with one exception (the journalist and polemist Carlos de Laet), were agnostic or anti-Catholic, we find, between 1920 and 1950, more than two dozen first-class writers, in prose and in verse, Catholic by inclination if not by profession, like Jackson de Figueiredo, Jorge de Lima, Mário de Andrade, Antônio de Alcântara Machado, Oliveira Viana, Jose Lins do Rêgo, Perilo Gomes, among those now dead; and among the living, Sobral Pinto, Hamilton Nogueira, Alexandre Corrêa, Murilo Mendes, Manuel Bandeira, Roberto Alvim Corrêa, Agripino Grieco, Tasso de Silveira, Renato Almeida, Augusto Frederico Schmidt, Dom Marcos Barbosa, Cassiono Ricardo, Octavio de Faria, Plínio Salvado, Antônio Callado, Oscar Mendes, Abgar Renault, Guimarães Rosa, Joao Etienne Filho, Murilo Araújo, Ariano Suassuna, Andrade Muricy, Sérgio Buarque de Holanda, Ribeiro Couto, Luís Delgada, Barreto Filho, Jose Paulo Moreira da Fonseca, Aires e Edgard da Mata Machado, Henriqueta Lisboa, Osman Lins, Fernando Sabino, Oto Lara Rezende, Odill Costa Filho, Antônio Vilaça, Jose Carlos Barlosa Moneira, to name only some of the best-known who represent all branches of literature and fields of theology. And there is a whole new generation coming forward. One of the most notable figures in present-day intellectual circles in Brazil is Gustavo Corção, thought by some non-Catholics to be the greatest intellectual descendent of our most important national writer, Machado de Assis. He has already been translated into French, English, Spanish, Dutch and German, and is a convert and a most enthusiastic Catholic. Such a thing would have been unheard of at the end of the nineteenth century, when the Brazilian intelligentsia seemed to have finished with Catholicism forever. None of this had happened before Jackson de Figueiredo was converted, and in this case it would be true to say *post hoc ergo propter hoc* . . .

Does this mean that Brazil has reached a high point of Catholic life and thought? Alas, no. It is not hard to show the reverse of the picture.

I have shown the two simultaneous movements going on in the nineteenth and twentieth centuries. In the last century, while the masses in general kept their traditional faith, the intelligentsia lost it. The opposite is happening now. The mass of the people have been overwhelmed by heretical movements, and particularly by the growth of spiritualism and the traditional polytheistic religions of the Africans. Protestantism has gained a lot of ground of late. But the gravest consequence of this invasion of heresy, chiefly from the United States (who have sent us, be it also said, missionaries and teaching congregations too), is not the coming of Protestant sects. It is the weakening of all religious faith, and the opening of the way for spiritualism and other cults, both in the lower and middle classes. Generally speaking, Brazilians will be Catholics or vague spiritualists. They will never make good Protestants.

The greatest enemy of Catholic belief in Brazil is still religious indifference. Catholicism remains the national and traditional religion. But for that very reason its roots are not deep. It may be that the recent growth of Protestant, spiritualist and polytheistic sects among the lower classes is an indication of a return to the Faith, just as the loss of their faith, among the upper classes in the nineteenth century, led to the Catholic intellectual revival we can see in the first half of the twentieth. Faith is often deepened by contradiction. Unanimity paves the way for indifference. It was the shock that came from the "religious question" at the end of the last century, which sowed the seeds of the religious revival in the intelligentsia at the beginning of this. It may be that the downfall of the Catholic faith among the middle and lower classes at the moment heralds a revival.

At the moment the situation is the reverse of what it was in the last century. But there is always religious superficiality to contend with.

The greatest problem is still the lack of vocations to the priesthood. For almost sixty million people we have no more than ten thousand priests, including foreign ones. Compare this with the United States, a country with a Protestant majority, which has more than forty-five thousand priests for a Catholic population of under forty million. Need I comment?

Here then, side by side, are the two lots of evidence; pessimism and optimism seem equally justifiable. To compare the present situation of Catholicism in Brazil with that of a century ago, we see an extraordinary change which seems favourable in quantity and quality.

And yet religious indifference is steadily growing; the younger generation are less concerned with the religious problem than were the generation of thirty years back; exotic cults proliferate and the level of priestly vocations is dangerously low, so that Catholic Action bears a burden that it should not, and indeed cannot cope with.

Personally I cannot feel pessimistic. I can only compare our state with that of a century back; I see monasticism and liturgy flourishing, the tremendous increase in Communions, and the welcome given to every true form of apostolate; and the present situation seems to offer more than an equal chance for the future. But grace must always have the last word!

EGYPT

Henry Ayrout, S. J.

Christianity can be said to have begun in Egypt before the preaching of the Gospel, with the arrival of Jesus, Mary and Joseph, fleeing Herod's persecution. Because of the hospitality given to the Holy Family on the soil of the Nile Valley, between Heliopolis and Babylon, and because the first human words of the Word of God were pronounced here, his first steps taken here, Egypt became a holy land.

A very old tradition attributes to Mark the Evangelist, the disciple of St. Peter, the first preaching of the new Gospel in Egypt, and still today the head of the Church of Alexandria is officially called "Patriarch of the Preaching of St. Mark".

Already in the third century the Church in Egypt had obtained maturity, and the radiance of its life enlightened the whole of Christendom. The doctors of the *Didascalia* contributed to the development of theology. Origen, Didymus, Clement, Cyril, remain shining lights. Monasticism was born in Thebes and Nitria; there, in the desert, the fundamental laws of the spiritual life were worked out, and for the first time religious communities were constituted according to the evangelical counsels of poverty, chastity and obedience. Nor did the ancient Church of Egypt fail to witness even unto death; so abundantly was blood shed, especially in Diocletian's persecution, that the Coptic calendar begins with this "era of martyrs".

Unfortunately, Egypt was also the first to start a great schism. Elder daughter of Rome, she separated herself from Rome at the Council of Chalcedon (451). The Monophysite Church, now called "Coptic Orthodox", dates from that year. The political isolation resulting from the Moslem invasion which came soon after (641) made this rupture final.

FR. HENRY AYROUT, S.J., was born in Cairo, where his father was a civil engineer. He studied at the University of Lyons, where his doctorate thesis was on the sociology of the Egyptian fellah, and was the first Jesuit to be ordained in the Melchite Rite. He is the founder and director of the Catholic Association of Egyptian Schools, and has published many studies of Egyptian affairs both in book form and in French and Egyptian periodicals.

More than a thousand years later, when Egypt reopened its gates to the West, indigenous Christianity was dying, yet not dead. The wick was still smoking, saved from extinction by Upper Egypt. This was in contrast with the position in North Africa where, in spite of the brilliance of a St. Augustine and a St. Cyprian, Christianity disappeared completely, perhaps because it had never taken root in the rural areas.

As for the Egyptian Catholics, in spite of the efforts of the Council of Lyons and Florence, and later the Franciscan and Jesuit missions, they remained scarce, and only began to reappear at the beginning of the nineteenth century with the settling of the European colonies called for or accepted by Mohamed Ali. In contrast with, for example, Lebanon, there is no organized Catholic Church in Egypt which dates from before this period.

The present structure of Catholicism in Egypt is very composite. First of all, a few statistics will clarify its position in relation to the whole: of the twenty-two million inhabitants of Egypt, four millions are Christians, of whom all but half a million are Coptic Orthodox. Of this half million 100,000 are Greek Orthodox, 200,000 are Protestants of different denominations, and 200,000 are Catholics. These are approximate figures.

The 200,000 Catholics are divided into seven different rites. Egypt is perhaps the only country in the world where these seven rites coexist. In this she surpasses Paris, New York, and even Rome. In fact, in these three capitals the Coptic rite is not represented, although all the other rites are. Each rite follows its own special liturgy, sharing it with its own community, and possessing its own hierarchy. From a canonical point of view this leads to a multiple jurisdiction, more personal than geographical, exercised in one and the same territory.

The Latin rite has three vicars apostolic, at Alexandria, Heliopolis and Port Said.[1] There were 100,000 faithful, among whom less than 10,000 Egyptians. In the past twenty years there has been a rapid decrease in numbers; more than 40,000 Italians, Maltese, French and others have left Egypt for good. Until 1937 this rite was the most privileged, thanks to the "Capitulations". It is still the best organized, but also the least integrated one. There is no secular clergy, but there are forty religious congregations (mostly French and Italian),

[1] The Vicariate of Port Said was suspended after the Anglo-French invasion of November 1956 and joined to the Vicariate of Alexandria.

three-fourths of which are women's communities and one-fourth men's. Their arrivals in Egypt were spread out over the last century, the first to come being the Brothers of the Christian Schools and the Daughters of Charity. For the most part these missionary teams are concentrated in the cities, and a certain lack of proportion can be noticed in their geographical distribution: in some places there are none to be found, in others too many. This is due to the fact that these foundations sprouted up according to circumstances, without a pre-established plan or a common direction, or any awareness of the situation seen as a whole. Whereas Protestantism became synonymous with "English-speaking", missionary Catholicism was identified with France and Italy. By 1956, the Catholic schools of Latin jurisdiction numbered 50,000 students, of whom 17,000 were Moslems.

There are five Oriental rites of Asiatic origin, together numbering some 40,000 members who have settled in Egypt during the last century, and of whom most have become Egyptian citizens. We list these rites here, beginning with the least important in Egypt:

(1) The Chaldean Catholics number 1,000; they are governed by a Patriarchal Vicar. They were little known until the recent erection of the Sanctuary of Our Lady of Fatima in the neighbourhood of Heliopolis.

(2) The Syrians, or Syriacs (the exact title is the subject of unending discussion) are about 5,000 in number. They have one bishop, three churches, one school, a few millionaires.

(3) There are about 8,000 Catholic Armenians, most of whom speak Arabic, whereas in the Orthodox branch of this rite the faithful as well as the clergy speak Armenian. They have one bishop, three churches, and Mekhitarist congregations from Venice and Vienna.

(4) The Maronites number 13,000 and are chiefly of Lebanese origin. They have one bishop, ten parishes, and an important college at Cairo.

(5) The 23,000 Greek Catholics or Melkites are governed by the Patriarch of Antioch, who is also the Patriarch of Alexandria and who divides his time between Syria and Egypt. He is represented by a resident bishop. The clergy are numerous; there are fifteen parish churches and two colleges. Socially and financially they are the most influential of the communities, and perhaps the most integrated with Egypt's economic life.

These groups have certain characteristics in common: because of their *savoir-faire*, and also because of the fact that they possess a double culture, they are often the link between the Europeans and Egyptians. They are found only in the cities. Those families that owed the acquisition of their fortune to the country have now abandoned it for the city. These groups are also, willingly or not, more and more cut off from Government service and increasingly engaged in commerce and industry. On the whole they have grown richer. There have been no new immigrants in the last twenty years, and the birth rate of these communities has decreased. Since they are grouped around their religious leaders rather than grafted onto the national life of Egypt (though they have acquired Egyptian nationality), and since the present situation is less favourable to them than the past, many think of leaving the country in order to ensure for their children greater chances of success.

The Coptic Catholics number about 100,000 faithful. The total increases each year, owing to the conversion of many Coptic Orthodox, especially in the villages of Upper Egypt, where they feel themselves abandoned and in danger of losing their Christian faith. There is a Patriarch, five bishops, and a national seminary. There are no orders of priests but there exists a Congregation of Egyptian Sisters, numbering eighty nuns. This is also the number of the priests in the four dioceses of Alexandria, Minia (Hermopolis Magna), Assiout (Lycopolis), and Sohag (Thebes).

The educated elite is very small, and there is no great wealth. There is a large rural concentration. The Coptic Catholic population, even in the cities—especially the slum parishes of Cairo, Alexandria and Port Said—is of Upper Egyptian origin. From a social point of view this is the weakest of the Catholic communities (it has still no cathedral in Cairo) but it is the most deeply rooted in Egypt. Whether because of its rapid growth, or its poverty, or because of its situation as a minority within a minority, or again because of the mortgage of a long past of suffering, fear, and division, the Catholic Coptic Church needs help from others. It is helped by various missionary congregations, by Rome, and by the Catholic Association for the Schools of Egypt, which supports and maintains all its schools.

The Coptic liturgy, known as Alexandrine, is the same for both Catholics and Orthodox. It is remarkable to see how, through fifteen centuries of Monophysite heresy in the Egyptian Church, its *lex orandi* has remained unaffected. The language in use was at first exclusively Coptic, a dead language, but Arabic is now more and more often used, as is happening in all liturgies in the Middle East, and in spite of the efforts of the purists. The Coptic alphabet is composed of Greek letters to which five demotic letters have been added. The singing is diatonic and somewhat plaintive. The church, a square building, has a choir separated from the faithful by an iconostasis less open and ornate than in the Byzantine rite, a fore-choir for the cantors, whose leader is usually a blind man, and a nave, part of which is reserved for the men, the other for the women. The priest conducts the service barefooted, and his head is covered by a mitre whose ends hang loose, as they were worn by priests of the Old Testament. In the Coptic liturgy, as in its spirituality, the predominating influence of the Bible is striking, and the attitude which comes foremost is that of faith, constantly expressed by both celebrant and people: "I believe . . . I believe . . ."

The Coptic Catholic Church may still not be able to glory in the present state of affairs, but it is a Church with a past, and—very certainly—with a future.

In pre-revolutionary Egypt Catholics were able to boast, if never of a minister, at least of several representatives in Parliament, of some high State officials, and even of the first Egyptian ambassador to Washington. Today they are absent from Government service, even from the economic and financial councils and from the Foreign Service, for which they are particularly qualified. Although the Orthodox Copts are conscious of the isolation of their situation, this is still more emphatically felt by the Catholic Copts. As a consequence a very definite, though rather tardy, tendency is developing in the Catholic educational programme towards a more Egyptian formation and a more thorough knowledge of the Arabic language. Young Catholics who in the past went rather to foreign universities are now registering more and more in the Faculties of Cairo and Alexandria. Others, willingly or unwillingly, are aided in the process of assimilation to the Arabic-speaking world by the military service which has now become compulsory.

Missionary mentality has also undergone an evolution in regard to Egypt. There is now much less of the patronizing and protective attitude, which may have been justifiable fifty years ago, and there is more of an effort towards co-operation and assistance on lines similar to those of the U.N.O. or of Point IV—helping Egypt to help itself and to perfect itself within an Egyptian framework.

Our great problem can now be stated: If Catholics, in their effort to become more Egyptian, plunge completely into the Egyptian culture (that is, in fact, an Arabic, Islamic culture), they will surely be assimilated, but perhaps also dissolved, with the great danger of watering down their Christianity. If, on the other hand, they remain connected with the Christian culture of the West, they will be renewed and broadened, but also cut off from the real Egypt. Can we avoid the choice between being a feeble leaven within the bread and a strong leaven separated from the bread?

It is, however, an encouraging fact that there still exist today in our country Christian traditions which are also authentically Egyptian and which have continued in spite of thirteen centuries of Islam. Examples of these are the Feast of Spring, "Sham El Nessim", on the Monday after Easter (following the Julian calendar), and the pilgrimages in honour of our Lady and of St. George, in which Moslems and Christians alike take part, by tens of thousands, sharing the same ceremonial rites: vows, meat, the fair.

Monastic life, impoverished and anaemic, survives in seven monasteries in the desert, all of them Coptic Orthodox, and in that of Sinai, under Greek jurisdiction. This survival, without renewal since the initial impulse, is almost miraculous.

Unfortunately, the Catholics of Egypt have not been, in either their private or their collective devotion, faithful to the legacy of Egypt's traditional piety. In imitation of their Latin teachers, they have substituted Western practices: the month of Mary is celebrated in May, whereas the Coptic liturgy places it in December, "the Virgin's Expectation"; so, too, the Tuesdays of St. Anthony of Padua have been observed, and devotion to the latter has replaced that to Anthony the Great, the sixteenth centenary of whose death was celebrated by the West in 1956.

However, in Upper Egypt the Catholic Copts have kept the Julian calendar with the Orthodox, and they celebrate with them and like them. In recent years their liturgy, as well as their churches, has tended to return to primitive purity; European missionaries who have become Coptic priests are helping in this "return to the sources". The first of these *coptisants* was the well-known and holy Father Yacoub Muyser, a Dutchman of the African Missions of Lyons, who became entirely Coptic, "body and soul", as Father Lebbe had become Chinese. He died in Rome in 1956.

The Orthodox Copts look on this change with mixed feelings.

Some are proud of it, seeing therein an expression of esteem and union, others believe that it is a danger capable of overthrowing their last resistance. The daily newspaper *Masr*, a Coptic paper, often prints these protests. It is true that the National Church of Egypt finds itself in a very serious position. Though it is in fact the most important Christian group in the Moslem world, with a solid structure made up of sixteen dioceses with a numerous clergy, indigenous if not instructed, it sees each year its faithful turn by thousands to Protestantism, to Catholicism, or to Islam. Actually, no one can gain from this weakening.

The great Coptic problems of the past, present and future are being studied in a friendly fashion at the Institute of Higher Coptic Studies, at the Coptic Archaeological Society, and in other specialized groups where Catholics and Orthodox meet, which they do whenever some common danger threatens Egyptian Christendom, as happened recently over the free schools, and the laws of Christian marriage.

The problems which Catholics have to face in modern Egypt are problems of inter-relations.

The first point of difficulty lies in the relations among Catholics themselves. As has been pointed out above, they are of various origins and of multiple jurisdictions. From this has risen a parallelism, not to say a divergence, of efforts. There is no common denominator except their faith and the Apostolic Internuncio. Individuals do not feel strongly enough that they are parts of one whole, for each community presents itself to its members as a self-sufficient island. Here the solution would be to simplify the hierarchies, or at least to unite for the tackling of general problems: Catholic Action, education, personal status, civic rights.

A second set of problems concerns the relations between Catholics and other Christians: the Coptic Orthodox (the most numerous), the Greek Orthodox, and the Protestants. Not enough effort is made to know one another. Either other groups are seen through a thick haze of prejudice, or they are ignored, or again just quietly tolerated. They dwell passively side by side without any co-ordination, and yet there are so many resemblances, so many possibilities for mutual help and common action. The National Coptic Church is especially sensitive to good will and sympathy, and there is nothing to be gained if it is weakened.

Thirdly, there are the relations with Moslems. The Catholic Church, through its many schools (especially its girls' schools), has left the imprint of its spirit on many Moslem souls. But after and beyond this, there is little contact on the human level, the level of friendship, between Christians and Moslems. It is bound to be a difficult matter owing to the difference in family structure; it is rendered still more difficult by the question of mentality and language. Catholics who would appreciate a contact do not know Arabic well enough; others prefer to keep to themselves, justifying their attitude with a series of excuses.

Finally, there is the relationship with Egypt as such: evidently the existence of a State religion[1] tends to make those who do not belong to it seem less patriotic; their education, with an insufficient emphasis on the social aspect, strengthens this impression. This social aspect is now particularly important, because, if the way to participation in political life is closed, there is still an immense field of social work to be realized. To work in this field unselfishly would be a wonderful expression of patriotism. Here the way is open to research, action, and co-operation. Of this I can speak from experience.

In the Egypt of 1959 the Church is hardly represented, either in the Government or in diplomacy, in the magistrature or in the army. If its influence is not altogether absent from the Press, it is less than it used to be. For this reason Catholics are being more and more drawn, almost against their will, to the liberal careers, to commercial and industrial ones, to immigration, and, from a social point of view, to a new ghetto. This will continue to happen if they refuse to make the effort to infuse into this new Egypt the Christian way of thinking and to live in closer contact with their Moslem brothers. Any kind of work, in the light of faith, may turn into a vocation. Placed as we are by Providence, and even without any official position, we may still become indispensable to the progress of the nation.

The Catholics of today will have to remain "just men" in the biblical sense of the word, that is loyal, patriotic and co-operative on the one hand, firm, courageous and united on the other, in order to maintain both their faith and their rights as Christians and citizens.

1 Though the Constitution of the new United Arab Republic does not mention it.

To hold to this twofold position requires—especially at the beginning—a profound understanding of the Gospel and the serene renunciation of certain comforts and privileges. To sum it up, it is necessary to die a little in order to live and give life. That is the challenge of a game we must win for the greater benefit both of Egypt and of the Church.

SOUTHERN AFRICA

Harold Jowitt

Thirty-one ecclesiastical territories comprise the organization of the Church within the Apostolic Delegation of Southern Africa.

This enormous sub-continent is nearly three times larger than Nigeria, Britain's most extensive dependency. It is not a political entity, containing as it does widely varying forms of government. The Union of South Africa is a dominion which, under the Statute of Westminster and the South African Status Act, has parity of polity, not only with Canada and Australia, but with the Mother Country herself, so that for fifty years there has been no question of disallowance by the Crown.

South-West Africa, a mandated territory of German origin, after a history containing dark pages of ruthless severity, now has a destiny merged in that of the Union, of which she may be regarded as the fifth province. When taken over by the Union, the words "incorporation" and "annexation" were diplomatically replaced by the more euphemistic term "closer association". This gave her over-generous representation in both Houses of South Africa's bi-cameral system.

The High Commission Territories of Basutoland, the Bechuanaland Protectorate and Swaziland are administered by the Commonwealth Relations Office through the High Commissioner, who holds a double portfolio, diplomatic and political. In the former capacity he is the High Commissioner for the United Kingdom in Pretoria; in the latter, the officer administering the three southern protectorates over each of which is a resident commissioner, with powers comparable to those exercised elsewhere by provincial commissioners.

HAROLD JOWITT was born in 1893 and educated at Southampton University College. He was Headmaster of a training college in Natal from 1913 to 1917; 1918-27, Inspector of Schools in Natal; 1927-34, Director of Native Development, Southern Rhodesia. From 1934 to 1945 he was Director of Education and a member of the Legislative and Executive Council in Uganda. From 1945 to 1950 he was Director of Education, Bechuanaland, and since 1951 he has been Dean of Education at Roma University College, Basutoland.

He has written a number of standard works on African Education and also other more specialized South African studies.

Periodically since the Act of Union, but with growing insistence and occasional querulousness, successive Union prime ministers have pressed for the incorporation of these territories, and have even threatened sanctions. This, stripped of the parliamentary language normally used in these exchanges, would mean starving the people into submission, thus adding to the growing Fifth Column of disaffected Africans in the Union, a course inconsistent with the honour of either power.

With the fullest evidence in support it can be claimed that in these territories today there is a genuine concern for African interests; that the administrations have accorded their people the dignity of human personality, and that they are encouraged to grow up and stand on their own feet—such things having no cash equivalent.

As this article is being written the radio announces the passing in the Union Parliament of the bill ironically entitled "The Bantu Self-Government Bill". This proclaims 90 per cent of the Dominion a white area, comparative population figures being ignored; it "allows" the Africans to labour in the white area whilst affording them no political rights there; it abolishes completely the representation of Africans by elected Europeans in both Houses—so competently and conscientiously discharged by members of distinction during the past twenty-three years; it takes away long-established rights without replacement. It then includes enabling provisions for Africans to have defined powers of local government—called self-government—in the remaining 10 per cent of the Union.

This is mentioned as part of the political background against which the Church must continue to operate in South Africa, to which the High Commission Territories are contiguous, and by which Basutoland, the senior of the three, is completely surrounded.

Finally, Southern Rhodesia, which also belongs to the Southern African Delegation, is a member of the Central African Federation; she has had responsible government for a third of a century, with her own territorial parliament for that length of time, but now, with her two northern neighbours of Northern Rhodesia and Nyasaland (which belong to the Apostolic Delegation of East and West Africa), looks forward to the revision of the provisional Central African Federal Constitution in 1960, the year of crisis in Africa. Whatever form this takes, it will profoundly affect Church policy and administration.

Meanwhile Southern Rhodesia inclines to complacency; prides

herself on being far superior to the Union in racial policies; like the Union, resents outside criticism, however informed and well-meaning; is buoyant and confident; has done admirable work in African agriculture, land tenure, health, housing and so on; has been increasingly generous in aiding mission work and in her steeply rising expenditure on African education.

To her credit, by and large, is the absence of the degree of unrest and dissatisfaction which has gathered such momentum in the Northern Territories, but, in spite of the liberal pronouncements of the more progressive European politicians, qualified African leadership has not been promoted—a need they will come to feel acutely in the near future and will find difficulty in meeting.

Mr. A. A. J. Van Bilsen, Lecturer at the Antwerp University of Overseas Territories, has defined nationalism as "the political expression of a consciousness of solidarity amoung a group of people who live in the same territory". Apart from its basis in the acknowledgement and idealization of one's own values and culture, he held that, generally, the consciousness resulted from frustration, a feeling of inferiority or of a threat.

The almost fanatical emotional growth of the political consciousness of the South African Dutch, with exactly these origins, has led to their solidarity, their insular cohesion, their exclusive nationism, vigorously promoted by the "asperity of Voortrekker Calvinism". Dr. De Kiewiet, President of the University of Rochester, New York, who has been described as writing with the subdued intellectual fervour of a man whose passions are aroused, but whose reason is still under control, says that "Afrikaner nationalism is an instrument of cultural defence against the English, and of racial defence against the natives", that it is a war on two fronts, against domination from above, and invasion from below.

African nationalism, which is spreading across the continent like a prairie fire, is a dramatic departure from the days when tribalism, now on its death-bed, made nationalism impossible, so that inter-tribal raids were common, but inter-tribal co-operation non-existent. In its various forms and degrees of intensity, it similarly derives from mounting frustration, fears and threats, but—unlike Afrikaner nationalism—it has no spiritual cohesive force.

Joseph Murumbi, formerly a Joint Secretary of the movement for Colonial Freedom, now with the Moroccan Embassy in London, describes himself as an African nationalist. He attended the Accra

Conference in December, 1958 and is a Catholic. Speaking in London the same month, he said trenchantly, "Nationalism is useless unless it has a more solid base, some guiding spirit that will unite the peoples after their independence has been won." Its absence he found discouraging in Ghana, since "there is no ideal to keep the people together".

If this be not a ringing challenge to the Church, it is a doctrine of despair.

Yet the inevitable tendency in Southern Africa, excepting the High Commission Territories and largely excepting Southern Rhodesia, is towards two clear-cut colour fronts, constant appeals being made by politicians to weld together a white nationhood *against* the non-white, which is not admitted to nationhood, with the logical consequence of its conversion into an anti-white front.

And the Church is commissioned to serve in both camps, and does so valiantly, although neither faith nor tolerance flourishes smoothly when opposed by fear and insecurity. But when did our divine Lord promise that her commission would be easy? In Southern Africa today she ministers to a strained and anxious generation hungry for relief. To lighten their stress European Catholics must share it, and show forth the supreme worthwhileness of loyalty to faith, loyalty to death if need be.

Our period of quietude is ended, giving place to one of militant action on all fronts. It must be so when the primacy of Christian values is challenged and allegiance endangered.

Throughout the great Southern Africa Apostolic Delegation, in the absence of a distinct race or people of common descent, a common language and culture, a common history and shared political institutions, the unity of a strongly held nationality cannot yet be expected, although its emergence is essential to survival.

It follows that within this ecclesiastical area and organization one cannot speak validly of the Church being integrated with "the" national life and culture, for no such unit exists. There are so many different patterns contributing to this many-coloured tapestry that a central pattern dominating the whole is not discernible. And yet "in my Father's house there are many mansions", and those admitted will have the threefold unity of those who share a common vision, have fed on the same Life and have come through these means to attain a common likeness.

With local differences of application inevitable to changing circumstances, an attempt will be made to show certain characteristics of the Church's contribution to the various communities in the territories concerned. Merely a representative selection of activities will be possible, together with some of the problems and weaknesses which remain.

At the beginning of 1952, South Africa celebrated the tercentenary of the arrival at the Cape of Jan van Riebeeck, inaugurating the establishment of the Dutch East India Company there. It is of interest that a century and a half before his ship's bell in Table Bay sounded the death-knell of tribalism in Southern Africa, the first place of Christian worship in that land should have been erected—namely the little Catholic chapel built at Mossel Bay in 1501.

An unobtrusive Press paragraph in January 1951, three centuries after Van Riebeeck's arrival, made known to any who might be interested, that by decree of His Holiness, the Hierarchy had been established in South Africa. To understand this delay one must remember the sparseness of the early population; the fact that the Catholic Church practically disappeared from the pages of South African history from 1685 until 1804; the further fact that in the old South African Republic, now the Transvaal, it was not until 1870 that freedom of worship was extended to Catholics; that as the early Colonists opened up the continent they were engaged for many years in one frontier war after another, and that, for an area almost 200,000 square miles larger than that of the Belgian Congo, the religious were always pathetically inadequate in numbers. Moreover, the Church came to a pagan country, where the isolated groups of settlers were largely of northern European Calvinist stock, to which were added French Huguenots and a small number of Germans.

Whatever weaknesses, tensions and unresolved problems the following pages may reveal, one remains humbled before the great men and women throughout the Delegation, who laboured so strenuously and so sacrificially to build up the Faith in the pioneering days, and those who, today, loyally uphold that tradition amid even greater difficulties.

Established in 1947, the Southern African Bishops' Conference, a permanent executive body, co-ordinates and organizes various aspects of Church activity within the Delegation. It gives effect to decisions of regional assemblies, and deals authoritatively with important matters arising during the five-year intervals between conferences. It is thus more than a consultative body.

Under the *ex-officio* chairmanship of the Apostolic Delegate, the work is entrusted to an Administrative Board of five members of the Hierarchy, aided by a General Secretariate with permanent headquarters in Pretoria, the portfolios being distributed as follows :-

Archbishop Hurley, O.M.I., Chairman and Director of the African Affairs Department

Archbishop McCann, Director of Catholic Action Department

Archbishop Garner, Director of Church Affairs Department

Archbishop Whelan, O.M.I., Director of Education Department

Bishop Van Velsen, O.P., Director of Social Welfare Department.

The awareness of the Church of her responsibilities on all fronts is clearly shown from this representative organization, so that matters may receive intensive and specialist attention before *corporate decisions*, with resultant action, are taken. What is not so clear, except to Catholics and a growing number of non-Catholics within the Delegation, is Southern Africa's good fortune in possessing so distinguished a hierarchy, capable of supplying an Administrative Board at once eminent, fearlessly outspoken and fully competent in any grave situation to uphold the sword of the spirit to the confusion of the enemy. To this the English, Afrikaner and vernacular Press bear witness, as does the Hansard of Parliament.

In Bantu education especially, but also in other issues, the Government, often reacting querulously, has ensured that in more directions than were at times anticipated, and at a quicker rate, the Church has lost ground to the State. Unflinchingly, the Hierarchy, however bitter the blows, have sounded in clarion tones the continuing challenge of higher loyalties. This outstanding leadership will ever be needed in the hierarchical order and for Church government, not only among the senior European members of that order, but among the twenty-seven Africans—and others to follow them—who have been raised to the episcopate in this continent.

This latter fact is richly significant and a source of inspiration to the indigenous Church throughout the land, especially at this time of emerging nationalism and political expression. By itself, however, it is incommensurate with the challenge. That they should be men of marked courage and personality is essential, but also inadequate. They must also be men of distinction and that such will be found, we need not doubt.

In the Delegation of Southern Africa, in 1953, Bishop 'Mabathoana was consecrated Bishop of Leribe in Basutoland before a large gathering which included the Resident Commissioner and the Acting Paramount. Under the famous Chief Moshoeshoe, the founder of the nation, the Bishop's great-grandfather occupied the post of what, today, would be termed Minister of Finance and of Agriculture. Because of loyal and outstanding services, he received a State burial at the royal cemetery, an honour given to no other Mosotho outside the royal house.

Claiming proficiency in eight languages, the Bishop, before his consecration, specialized in comparative African languages, studying at the School of Oriental and African Studies, London; he wrote an accredited Sotho grammar, and lectured in this, his mother-tongue, at Pius XII University College, Roma, Basutoland. A gifted musician, he plays the organ well; has composed a polyphonic Mass, and published a book of Sotho hymns.

Cardinal Constantini said that his appointment was "a sign of the recognition of the most fruitful work accomplished by the Oblates, particularly in Basutoland". The Bishop derives from such work, but is not limited by it. Those who know him would describe him as a humble, devout, charitable man, possessed of a pleasant and friendly personality. He has an outstanding desire to serve his people as their shepherd, consistent with his early vocation as a boy, when his appropriately episcopal nick-name was "Motjoli" or "the Shepherd Bird", by which name he is still remembered.

By virtue of his ancestry, Bishop Dhlamini of Umzimkulu, Natal, belongs to the Zulu nobility, claiming descent from the great chief, Nomagaga. His mother was sister to the second Zulu priest who, over half a century ago, was sent to Rome by the Mariannhill Trappists to study for the priesthood.

Known among his confrères, European and African, as a man of action, prayer and discipline, he enjoys their respect and confidence. When he received his preferment as first Zulu bishop, he had to face the prejudice and opposition of many European Catholics (not only laymen, one fears) in his new diocese, but they have come to appreciate his solicitous care for his flock, and his personal worthiness.

This has been treated rather fully to illustrate that within the Southern Africa Delegation these two African bishops rightly share in their own characteristic way in the distinction of the Hierarchy. The importance of this cannot be measured.

The Church in Basutoland has a special importance in Southern

Africa; it is the majority Church there. Without retracing the dramatic history of mission development in that High Commission Territory, a geographical enclave within the Union, a country which has never known European military conquest, it should be noted that Bereng, the Paramount, first educated at the Sacred Heart College, Roma, then at Ampleforth, and at present at Oxford, is a devout Catholic, as is the Regent Mantsebo, who will relinquish her position as soon as he completes his studies.

Among the members of the National Council, or Pitso, have always been many Catholic chiefs. Such representation will undoubtedly remain when, in the near future, this body is reconstituted with defined legislative powers.

Of the three political parties electioneering in Basutoland, the Congress Party states in its manifesto: "It shall be the Party's policy to strive for the maintenance and enhancement of the position, status and dignity of the Paramount Chief as the sole ruler of Basutoland"—somewhat difficult to promote when, under a new democratic policy, the National Council is to be vested with powers of legislation.

They recognize also "freedom of worship" and will "work for keeping religion out of the political arena", a gesture of tolerance towards the Catholicism of the Paramount on the one hand, and, towards the Protestantism of the large minority on the other. Concurrently, it appears to be an attack on one of the opposing parties, which, unfortunately, to my mind, is avowedly Catholic. I say, "unfortunately", because of the handicaps involved when spiritual values tend to become confused with political and material interests in a country predominantly Catholic, where it is not necessary to protect the claims of the Church in education, for example.

In 1852 Bishop Allard and his Oblate Missionaries of Mary Immaculate established themselves in Durban, and, crossing the Drakensberg, spread to Basutoland ten years later, Moshesh (popularly so spelt) receiving them in a most friendly fashion. In 1864 they were joined by the Holy Family Sisters, the pioneer nuns among the African peoples. At St. Mary's, Roma, they still run most competently a high school and teachers' training college, together with a related system of girls' schools and homecraft centres. In this work they are assisted by an African sisterhood of their own foundation.

In October 1937, when the celebrations at Roma commemorated the seventy-fifth anniversary of the establishment of the Church in Basutoland, there were 3,000 communicants each morning during the novena. When the centenary is reached in three years' time, the enthusiastic response will be territory-wide.

In the meantime this small but attractive mountainous country possesses four seminaries, nine novitiates, six high schools, five training schools for teachers, three hospitals, two industrial schools and a system of primary schools co-extensive with the country, the reference being only to Catholic institutions.

It possesses, moreover, Pius XII University College at Roma, at present an associated college of the University of South Africa. At present it offers degrees in arts, science, commerce and sociology, and the post-graduate diploma course in education. Its students are drawn from South Africa, the High Commission Territories, Central and East Africa.

Of this college, Professor Lewis, formerly Director of the Institute of Education, Ghana, now holding the Chair of Education in Tropical Areas at the University of London, reported as follows:

> In all my 25 years of experience as an educationist, I have never found anything in Africa as vital as the Pius XII University College at Roma. It could, in certain respects, teach educationists in Ghana and in other African countries a great deal.

One is grateful for his informed comment.

God dwells in high places, and here in the midst of the silence of ancient mountain ranges this small college may help many students to new points of vision for his greater glory. That must remain the criterion of success rather than the number of graduates produced. Of great importance has been the raising of academic and administrative standards and the rejection of earlier and unwarranted complacency. Enduringly urgent must remain the need to ensure commensurate spiritual standards, without which there is no *raison d'être* for the college.

Of Basutoland it can definitely be said that it has a pronounced Catholic character, the Church being integrated with national life and culture. How extremely favoured it is! Nevertheless, it suffers from the defects of its merits. Behind its mountain ramparts its horizons tend to be circumscribed, and, in general, neither its priests nor its Africans are *au fait* with vital movements beyond its borders; indeed, of these the African sisters (who, increasingly, will teach the next generation) know hardly anything at all.

Such insularity is fatal, however, to a university college. Roma suffered from it until a few years ago, when the position began to improve as the percentage of lay staff inevitably increased. In common with almost universal practice the great majority of its priest staff had gone from school to seminary, from seminary to priesthood, and from ordination to university teaching, with little knowlege of life in their own country and none of life in Africa. It was but natural that they should arrive at premature judgements; that they should be ignorant of the life and problems for which their students were being prepared; that, similarly, they should know nothing of South African university standards or procedure, and very little of the traditions and code of British administration. This was, admittedly, a handicap not of their own making.

It was natural, too, that with limited experience to draw upon they should tend to treat mature African university students, many of whom were married, as high-school boys and girls, expecting them to conform to the discipline and standards of piety expected of seminarians. Avoidable tensions were thereby created.

However, with the adaptability of the Rector, contacts with other universities, the development of cordial relations with the Basutoland Administration, and the recruitment of a preponderantly lay staff, the position has greatly improved for the benefit of all concerned, and the undoubted enhancement of College status in academic circles.

In Catholic high schools and teacher-training centres in Basutoland as elsewhere in Southern Africa, there appears to be more reluctance to approve appointments of African graduates to principalships or other posts of seniority than in State or Protestant schools. The natural result is a feeling of frustration on the part of loyal, well-qualified Africans; their avenues of promotion are thereby limited, and a strain placed on their loyalty. I have also known of staff meetings where experienced African graduates have not participated, presumably because they were not regarded as full professional colleagues, but as junior staff. Comment is unnecessary.

The seminaries, run on Continental lines, are closed institutions, so that throughout a very long training there are no home contacts, and the links with social and national developments are broken. With deference I would submit that this must add to the later difficulty of integrating Church and nation.

Until fairly recently, when the Rector wisely altered procedure and attitudes, Pius XII University College tended to regard Her Majesty's Administration as essentially secular and thereby suspect. Customary courtesies were ignored, and in the isolation that resulted, each side suffered from the lack of awareness of the good work and good will of the other. Happily, this has radically changed for the better to the advantage of both.

One is mindful, too, of the urgent need to improve the educational standards of the sisters, African in particular, but European also. Although the position is slowly improving in Basutoland, where the response to vocations is most encouraging, there are still many European sisters with inadequate academic or professional qualifications, or with none, and many convents where the African sisters cannot converse in English. To rationalize about it by saying, "They make wonderful religous", is rightly to emphasize their dedication, but wrongly to postpone the need for consecrated efficiency.

One cannot conclude this lengthy section without paying unreserved tribute to the superlative work of three laywomen, who for years, amid incredible difficulties, have sacrificed themselves unreservedly as medical missionaries in the mountain fastnesses. This has entailed running three hospitals without any qualified medical assistants, with but a few European nurses, only some of them trained, with the help of a few completely untrained African ward assistants. It has meant lengthy horseback rides in all weathers over the roughest of country, major operations with the minimum of equipment, the running of related clinics and dispensaries, fighting epidemics and visiting remote outpatients.

Their work has no cash equivalent; they work for a pittance; they save souls as well as bodies. May God love them.

A word may now be said about Southern Rhodesia.

In 1879 the first contingent of Jesuit Fathers, leaving South Africa by ox-waggon and travelling through Kimberley along the western borders of the Transvaal, went north to become the pioneer apostles of the Faith in Mashonaland, the original Zambesi Mission having been entrusted to the Society of Jesus that year. "It was thus", one reads, "that the Jesuit Mission, abandoned since 1759, but which had been honoured by the blood of Fr. Silveira, known as the Proto-Martyr of South Africa, came to life again. The area was 750,000 square miles." Father Brady tells us that "the Dominican Sisters of King Williamstown . . . joined the Pioneer Column in 1890, and by their devotion to duty and care of the sick, earned for themselves a name in the annals of the land beyond the Limpopo." This is an understatement, and today their name stands higher than ever it did, and most deservedly so, and Mother Patrick, O.P., who rode and marched with that historic column, is held in the highest esteem by Rhodesians of all denominations, or of none. The spiritual, educational and medical work of the Dominican sisters, their orphanages and the rest, are firmly established and intertwined with the history and development of a young Dominion which reveres its past and all who so honourably contributed to it.

That Archbishop Chichester, S.J., one-time Head of Beaumont, and now most actively retired within the Federation, was *persona gratissima* with the Territorial and Federal Prime Ministers and their Cabinet, is not without significance. Southern Rhodesia is rightly proud of its Catholic leaders, and they loyally reciprocate. Hence their integration with the national life, as it merges into the inter-territorial but more precarious life of the Central African Federation, has so far been comparatively smooth and richly productive. It is a soul-stirring sight to observe and participate in a Corpus Christi procession through the heart of Salisbury.

Whatever her limitations in African political and academic development, this senior territory of the three has contributed more peacefully and constructively towards federal amity than have her two northern neighbours.

The University College of Rhodesia and Nyasaland, with its conscientious and effective Catholic chaplain, has supplied the inter-racial milieu in which the African products of Catholic schools flourish naturally: the African sisterhoods have more than justified their foundation many years ago; the Campion Society of graduates and professional Catholics is as devoted as it is competent; the hospitals, orphanages and other social agencies have a well-deserved reputation; the European Catholic schools, boys' and girls', challenge comparison with the best English public schools; the African school and college system is of accredited standard, and, in general, the vigour and happy buoyancy of the Church in this rapidly evolving country is a source of justifiable encouragement to those who believe in her mandate.

Of roughly 200 priests in the diocese, many more should be African. Hence the emphasis so wisely placed upon the unceasing development of the Seminary, and upon the vocations which give it meaning.

Since it is pre-eminently in South Africa that Christianity is on its trial in the matter of race relations, and since we cannot expect others to be impressed by our claims unless our faith is seen to spur us on to redress injustice, discrimination, the exploitation of human personality, the lack of social charity and civic friendship, inevitably we must devote more attention to it in this chapter. "Today", writes Dr. De Kiewiet, "the course of history has brought all Africa to the end of a period of quietude. Events within and without Africa have made its political and racial problems into major factors in world politics." Granted this incontrovertible fact, what judgement will be formed of the Catholic Church in the Union by the prosecution? How valid and convincing will be its defence? How extenuating the circumstances? Does it carry out the terms of its own manifesto? Does it plead Guilty or Not Guilty? If based upon the fullest evidence, sympathetically reviewed by the final Judge, which way will the verdict go?

I believe there would be an honourable acquittal, but a soul-cleansing searching of hearts.

In the meantime it is but human to seek self-justification in the record of the main offender, concerning whose disastrous policy many books have been written, to be followed by many more.

The Dutch Reformed Church has been described by Philip Mason, the Director of Studies on Race Relations at Chatham House, London, as the only religious institution of which he knows today which defends racial separation and its attendant evils on spiritual grounds. Against this, Professor Keet of their Theological College, Stellenbosch, shows that there is a division on this issue. He claims that "the only *apartheid* known to Scripture is separation from sin, and neither differences in colour nor in social standing can be adduced as an adequate reason for organizing Churches on a basis of separation." His recent more forcibly expressed views have received wide publicity, and a small minority within his Church would agree with him.

It must be conceded, too, that among the proponents of *apartheid* are many of sincerity, spiritual conviction and personal worthiness.

In 1858, just over a century ago, in the Constitution of the Transvaal Grondwet, one finds the following declaration:

> The Volk desires to permit of no equality between coloured and white inhabitants in Church or State.

The same document referred to "the true burger-like freedom, equality and fraternity", thus completing the clear-cut racial divisions in a country which still believes that the voice of the people (the *Volkwil*) is the voice of God. How easy it seems to be to forget that it was the *Volkwil* that crucified our Lord and released Barabbas.

A hundred years later, Senator De Klerk, Minister of Labour, speaking of the deliberate packing of the Senate to obtain the two-thirds majority, constitutionally required in a joint sitting of both Houses, for amending franchise legislation, said in May 1955:

> We are taking this step because we are Calvinists who believe that God is sovereign and transfers that sovereignty to the legal rulers of the country.

It would almost seem that God the Unchanging changes his mind with each legislative amendment, provided that he is so persuaded by Christians of the right denomination.

Dr. D. F. Malan is quoted in *This Man Malan* as saying:

> The history of the Afrikaner reveals a determination and a definiteness of purpose which makes one feel that Afrikanerdom is not the work of man but a creation of God. We have a divine right to be Afrikaners. Our history is the highest work of art of the architect of the centuries.

In South Africa, the same stern and partial Diety, having led his chosen people to the promised land, naturally expects the elect to exercise authoritarian sway over lesser breeds without the law, a mandate they still find it convenient to obey. After all, they could hardly grant any hope of freedom to the Africans which God himself had denied them.

It must be remembered, too, that since political forces are so strong, and since their churches have helped to awaken the spirit of nationalism and become an integral part of it, even the more enlightened of Afrikaner ministers would find it extremely difficult to go against the current which gathers more and more strength and steadily grows more turbulent. The logical outcome of their unfortunate ideology is the spate of discriminatory legislation and harsh administration, which adds to the flood waters which threaten devastation.

The statements of the Catholic Church in support of racial unity are most impressive in volume, authenticity, scholarship and Christian ethics. Magnificently true of Southern Africa, this is particularly so of the last ten years.

Forthright, logically argued, factually correct, well presented, they have been received with hostile respect in Government quarters, and have heartened the underprivileged. Given publicity on platforms, from pulpits, and in the local and overseas Press, they have borne Christian witness at a time when it was invaluable.

No citations are made here, nor is it necessary, for the Church has always stood unflinchingly for the racial unity advocated and manifested by our divine Lord at the first Pentecost, throughout the centuries and across the world.

Philip Mason made no new discovery when he said in *Christianity and Race*, "This emphasis on the value of the individual and on his power to love other people, and respond to the world about him with generosity, with great-heartedness, takes on a new meaning with the Cross."

Dr. Edgar Brookes, for many years a Union Senator as Native Representative for Natal and Zululand, and a one-time President of the South African Institute of Race Relations, looking back as a devout Anglican on a life spent in trying to promote racial unity, wrote in his last book :

> Having spent ourselves without stint in an effort to put things right by purely human means, we in South Africa are faced with the bankruptcy of secularism.

How obvious this is to Catholics, but how good to find it endorsed by so influential, so dedicated and so experienced an ex-senator.

In South Africa's tragic circumstances, where warped values, which for centuries have been its guide, are now legally entrenched through State absolutism in education, and where administration is regarded increasingly as the machinery of control, the prospects facing Catholic education could not be more parlous.

At the time of writing, out of 662 mission schools, 500 are most uncertain of their future; of the aggregate the Government has registered but 150, all subject to restrictions and withdrawals; State subsidies have been withdrawn from the vast majority; in the near future only two of the Church's six teacher-training colleges will be allowed to function, and the qualifications of their products, never previously questioned, will no longer be recognized by the Government. Nor does this complete the rape of mission schools.

To a very great number of people of all races, probably the best known and the most revered mission in South Africa is that of Mariannhill, about twelve miles from Durban, a venue visited weekly by hundreds of tourists on organized and unorganized parties. As in the case of the Victoria Falls, they never leave disappointed.

Of Mariannhill, Prior Franz Pfanner of the Reformed Cistercians took possession in 1882, three years after the Zulu War. Living up to its motto of *Ora et Labora*, the monks steadily brought into being what closely resembled a Benedictine monastery, as was but natural. At one time forty trades were taught to the Africans; the rolling hill country of the Natal Coast belt was put under the plough and made productive. Orchards and vineyards were established; animal husbandry throve under competent direction; a seminary rose in the precincts of the monastery, and on other sites the pro-cathedral, chapel, a convent, schools, colleges, a most impressive hospital, the St. Francis' Teacher Training college, a sanatorium, workshops, farm buildings and the rest.

Land was bought extensively to be sold in freehold to African owners, assisted by their own co-operative society a wise and far-seeing provision. Thus was stabilized a Catholic community with security, and all within sound of mission bells.

Just before his death the Abbot, with refreshing understatement, said: "I believe that one day Mariannhill will be something great." It did not require more than one hundred outstations, which it established, to substantiate that, for its fame deservedly spread far and wide.

Many of its alumni have been men and women of real distinction, deserving well of Church and State, leaders well in the vanguard of emergent Africans. One such was the late Dr. Benedict Vilakazi, M.A., D.Litt., who was Senior Language Assistant in Nguni Languages at the University of the Witwatersrand, and a pioneer Zulu poet. He published two books of poems, three novels and two theses widely accredited, and in collaboration with Professor Doke, wrote the standard Zulu-English dictionary. Moreover he was President of the Catholic African Teachers' Federation, and editor of their review. I mention him to illustrate the eminence attained by some of the Mariannhill graduates, but it would take a volume the size of this to do justice to this all-important aspect of their work.

One therefore holds in homage the zealous missionary priests and brothers, the Congregation of the Sisters of the Precious Blood founded by Abbot Franz, and the loyal teachers and other lay helpers, who combined to realize the cherished aims of the great Abbot, adding lustre to the consecrated efficiency devoted to all branches of its mission work, supreme in which was its differentiated education. This may place in some perspective what follows.

Towards the end of 1956, an official letter was received by the Mariannhill Fathers from the Secretary for Native Affairs, above his own signature, serving notice of the early closure by the Government of their Teacher Training College, their early High School and their Technical College, and informing them blandly that £100,000 *per annum* in recurrent grants for teachers' salaries in their primary system was to be withdrawn.

This decision had not been discussed with the Regional Director of Bantu Education for Natal and Zululand, a non-Catholic of mission sympathies who had consistently befriended and supported their work, which he knew to be admirable.

Their teacher-training was the only post-secondary-training for Africans in the Union, the first year of its course being in degree subjects examined by the University, the second, examined by the Department of Education, being professional. The only mission approved by the Natal Department for this important work, its standard had received the highest appreciation.

Because of the need for extensions in teacher-training, high-school work and technical training, which their success had demonstrated, and encouraged by the Department, the Mission must have spent considerable sums of money—possibly £150,000—on the buildings and equipment now being put out of business, and had recruited an excellent staff.

When the Bantu Education Act was promulgated in 1953, with all its sinister implications, the government in power, believing in an enduringly separate socio-economic system for the Africans, had framed and legalized an inferior educational system to subserve it. Here was unworthy and inflammable material, spiritual values in education being threatened or denied, for they were to be replaced by State indoctrination.

Having fought it vigorously in every constitutional way, and having made appeal after appeal at Cabinet level, the Hierarchy then issued its financial drive and asked the faithful for a million pounds to enable Catholic schools to be maintained.

The response was magnificent, and the sum raised. But how totally inadequate; for, invested, it could but yield half the annual sum required for the primary schools alone, in one diocese alone—that of Mariannhill. The sequel? The Hierarchy admitted the inadequacy;

said that they must make the money go as far as it could, and later trust in God. And today? The Government has made it crystal clear that this is not merely a financial problem, since Government can outlaw and make subject to heavy penalties schools which it does not agree to register—the course it is now pursuing. It is as easy as that.

One could multiply instances, and deal also with the medical and other charitable works seriously endangered. No wonder that with regard to Mariannhill an Anglican Member of Parliament volunteered his conviction that this was but part of the first round of the attack on the Catholic Church. The bell will soon ring for the next round.

Educated African Catholics are aliens in a dying tribal society. In spite of all contrary evidence, the Government claims that only tribalism suits the African, citing in support spurious "authorities", remote alike from tribalism and from the urban, industrialized concentrations in which millions of Africans in the Union are compelled to live their uprooted, disenfranchised lives to meet European labour requirements.

The more moderate grow weary of their failure in seeking solutions in compromise and co-operation. Excellent men and loyal as so many of them are, they lose leadership to the less moderate, less spiritual, more militant products of Government policy. A few of the more fortunate and more highly qualified find their way to extra-Union territories; others, failing to do so, become dispirited and depressed, and see nothing but the darkness of clouds gathering over the horizon.

The Fifth Column grows as things of the spirit are sabotaged—something so much worse than any material damage.

In 1957, Father Colin Collins, one of the secretaries at the Delegation Offices, Pretoria, affirmed that:

> Today, White Catholics still form the same percentage of over-all population as they did fifty years back.
>
> Except perhaps very recently, there has been little sign of local vocations increasing rapidly, and giving to the Church its rooted qualities . . . The Church amongst the whites has remained inhibited; its contact system has hardly touched any block other than the English-speaking original groups in whom it strove to keep the Faith . . . It is an unadapted Church, one which has not found any local self-expression.

As against this criticism, I might quote the following words of Archbishop McCann :

> The work of the Church among the European section of the community has been directed by a recognition of conditions prevailing.
>
> Genuine charity towards those opposed to her doctrine has ever characterized her actions.
>
> She has shown sympathy with the language aspirations and cultural claims of the Afrikaans-speaking people, though her work lay mainly among the English-speaking section, because most of her adherents belonged to that group.
>
> As early as 1850, however, sermons in Nederlands were preached regularly at St. Mary's Cathedral, Cape Town, and where Afrikaans has predominated, that language has been used in her nonliturgical services and sermons.
>
> The priests who came to the Eastern Province in the second half of the last century included Flemings whose language was akin to that of the Afrikaner.

The opening paragraph of this excerpt suggests a realistic approach, but might possibly also mean maintaining the *status quo ante* after its justification has disappeared or is beginning to disappear. It may be relevant, therefore, that in the Orange Free State, where there is complete Nationalist political homogeneity (not a single opposition member in parliament, in the Senate, in the Provincial Council or the Municipal Council of Bloemfontein), Bishop Van Velsen, O.P., with his Dutch Dominicans, should regard his diocese as offering an Afrikaner apostolate, publish a thought-provoking magazine of high standard, in Afrikaans, called *Daybreak*, and in spite of natural opposition, build attractive churches, schools and convents. There is nothing here of the *status quo ante*.

When considering local vocations, Fr. Colin Collins is undoubtedly right when he describes them as the touchstone of success. He therefore decides that the Church is not yet deeply rooted, since the proportion between local and foreign personnel is still very unsatisfactory, for only one-eighth of the priests represent local recruitment, the figures of the brothers being comparable, but that of the sisters better. He shows an arresting fact, that whereas the whites have one priest per 500 Catholics, the Africans have but one per 1,500. It seems a grave reflection, too, that almost the entire body of about 240 teaching brothers are employed in white schools, and that of 2,400 teaching sisters in the Union only 300 are employed in African schools, the majority of the others serving the white population.

In this respect, whatever the historical reasons, must the Church continue to keep step with prevailing attitudes and racial values?

I think he claims too much when he holds that "very little of a specific Catholic life has been evolved in this country", but he may approach nearer to the truth when he avers that "Catholic action is not geared to meet the vast social changes that are taking place in a country that is already among the most urbanized in the world". In this context he speaks of the slow tempo of parish life among all races, and in connection with Catholic action and its insistent challenge it must be admitted that there is as wide a gap between its theory and practice as there is between encyclical teachings on the lay apostolate and their recognition and application by the average priest.

That there is not a single Catholic school catering for Afrikaans-speaking white pupils can hardly be justified, certainly not on historical grounds, or on present obligations and opportunity. What is needed in this and similar instances is not an explanation but remedial action.

With increasing State absolutism, the African Catholic must surely feel himself more and more a part of the Church from which he is displaced by no *apartheid*. At this time of crisis, with the need to mobilize the whole Church, it is clear that leadership-formation should be the keynote of every parish. Only then will Catholic action in its universality be given concrete direction; only then will it become dynamic, constructive, forward-looking and unashamedly Catholic. Here is an almost unlimited field to occupy. With the tacit surrender, under *force majeure*, of the educational field, herein lies the alternative challenge which should not unobtrusively replace educational topics on conference agenda papers, but do so with the fullest authority, with precise directives, without finesse.

Bruce Marshall once said that "it is in the United States of America that the clergy produce the most alert laity, both custom-made and off the shelf". Having met them over there and seen their dynamic and proud Catholicism, I am inclined to agree, for I have the fullest admiration for their attitude and achievement.

But I have had the privilege, also, of close association with the laity of all races in Southern Africa, and greatly respect the fervour, the constancy and the efficiency of their apostolate upheld amid the greatest of difficulties. I think with profound respect of the regular meetings and related work at many centres, of the Dominican and Franciscan Tertiaries, of the activities of the Legionaries; of the superb organization behind the monthly or periodic meetings, and the annual Summer School, of the Kolbe Association of university graduates and professional people; and know of no comparable groups of higher intellectual and spiritual standards anywhere.

I think, too, of those wonderful Grail women, of the National Seminary at Pretoria, the focal point for many hopes and prayers, of the scholasticate of the Oblate Fathers at Cedara, Natal, the Dominican novitiate and house of studies at Stellenbosch, the Oblate novitiate at Germiston, of St. Mary's at Ixopo and St. Peter's, Pevensey, and of others. They receive little publicity; they constantly operate against State obstruction, but remain the most strategic and deserving of financial, moral and prayerful support, being the sign and assurance of our heritage and continuity. One is mindful, too, of the Catholic societies and chaplains in the South African universities. Here, under recent legislation which enforces academic *apartheid,* which attacks a university's traditional freedom to decide its own policy in these matters, and which concurrently attacks the academic integrity of the lecturing and professorial staffs, now required to uphold Government policy, the legal fiction is publicized that separate ethnic universities will provide "separate but equal" facilities, a slogan decisively disproved in the United States. However restricted, Catholic influence will continue in this tragic environment; one derives encouragement from the continued presence on the senior tutorial staff of such accredited intellectuals as Dr. M. Versfeld, Senior Lecturer in Ethics at Cape Town University, Dr. Gardner, Professor of English at the University of the Free State, and Father G. Fortune, S.J., Senior Lecturer in African Languages (and potential Head of the Department of African Studies), at Cape Town University. All three are distinguished authors, acknowledged experts in their several fields, and much in demand as public lecturers. These and others in university posts will fight a valiant rearguard action until the signal for the advance is again given.

One comes to the conclusion that although one can never be complacent before the Cross, which will always dominate the Southern African scene, there is not much radically wrong with the Church there, but much in which to take reasonable pride, and much for which to give generously of confidence, gratitude and support.

In concluding this chapter, it may be fitting to quote an eminent Catholic ruler on what Africans seek from the Church, an article in *World Crisis and the Catholic,* being papers read at the Second World Congress for the Lay Apostolate in Rome, 1957.

The speaker was the late Mutara III, Charles Léon Pierre Rudahigwa, King of Ruanda. Ruanda does not belong to Southern Africa, but is a Trust Territory under mandate to Belgium. Nevertheless his views have validity throughout the whole of Africa, whether in the recently emancipated self-governing countries, those advancing with varying degrees of confidence to that status, or those in the South African Dominion devoted to white supremacy, racial discrimination and the denial of human rights.

Mutara III was the thirtieth of an unbroken line of rulers dating back for many centuries. In 1946 he solemnly consecrated his country to Christ the King, the following year being made a Commander of St. Gregory the Great.

Here then, are some of the convictions of this enlightened Catholic ruler in Central Africa. Brilliantly expressed, they reveal the spiritual insight of an African of ancient dynasty, to whom the gift of faith has meant everything.

> The African soul looks to the Church for all the moral values, the justice and the charity of her Christian civilization; for everything that is religious and not specifically Western.
>
> In a word, the African soul looks to the Church for the doctrine of Christ in all its integrity. The missionary, moreover, cannot present Christ's doctrine in any other way without betraying his mandate.
>
> The African soul looks to the Church for a definite dogma which will give him certitude in his belief. This amounts to saying that the ancient faiths left the African soul in a kind of vacuum.

In other words, throughout the whole of Africa, as in every other country, Christ's doctrine "in all its integrity" must be fully and unswervingly presented, whatever the political, social and economic milieu, to fill "the vacuum of uncertainty" left by past paganism and the ruthless application of present State determinism.

Recalling traditional African belief in the immortality of the soul Mutara III stressed its need to be purified and elevated by Catholic teaching; and he urged that the Church should purify the moral order, while reminding us that the twin pillars in the best of Africa's past were justice and charity—both sadly lacking today.

Pertinent to the Zulu and Xhosa in the Union, to the Basuto, Bechuana and Swazi of the High Commission Territories, to the Mashona, the Mandebele and Vakaranga of Southern Rhodesia, to the Herero and other tribes of South-West Africa—all of whom are within the Delegation of Southern Africa; his words both dispose of the facile but outmoded claims of the pseudo-anthropologist that the moral code of the noble savage should be left inviolate and that his phobias and superstitions should be conveniently overlooked, and underline the exacting moral demands thus made upon Catholics.

Speaking of the outstanding leadership so essential in the hierarchical order, in Church government, Mutara III—himself outstanding in tribal leadership—urged that the Church should share in the strength of the nation with which it should be integrated; that it should lower the barriers of tribe, caste, colour, social standing and race; that as it builds up its distinctive and national nature, it should retain its international character, and that its government should be "at once strong and gentle, centralized and personal, national and international".